Dec
2015
Enjoy The
Book
Merry Christmas
Jeff
Love
Peu & Helen

Hockey Towns

Hockey Towns

UNTOLD STORIES FROM THE HEART OF CANADA

RON MacLEAN
with KIRSTIE McLELLAN DAY

HARPERCOLLINS PUBLISHERS LTD

Published by HarperCollins Publishers Ltd

First edition

Population data collected from Statistics Canada 2011 census.

Grateful acknowledgement is made to the following for permission to reproduce:

Excerpted from *Stranger Music* by Leonard Cohen. Copyright © 1993 Leonard Cohen.
Reprinted by permission of McClelland & Stewart, a division of
Random House of Canada Limited, a Penguin Random House Company

RISE ABOVE THIS
Music and Lyrics by SHAUN MORGAN, DALE STEWART and JOHN HUMPHREY
© 2007 RESERVOIR MEDIA MANAGEMENT, INC. and SEETHER PUBLISHING (BMI)
All Rights Administered by RESERVOIR MEDIA MANAGEMENT, INC. RESERVOIR MEDIA
MUSIC (ASCAP) Administered by ALFRED MUSIC. All Rights Reserved.

HarperCollins books may be purchased for educational, business,
or sales promotional use through our Special Markets Department.

HarperCollins Publishers Ltd
2 Bloor Street East, 20th Floor
Toronto, Ontario, Canada, M4W 1A8

www.harpercollins.ca

Library and Archives Canada Cataloguing in Publication
information is available upon request

ISBN 978-1-44343-690-8

Chapter openers by Evan Adlington and Kaitlyn Kanygin of Pyramid Productions Inc.

Printed and bound in the United States of America
RRD 9 8 7 6 5 4 3 2

For my parents, Lila and Ron.

Throughout my nomadic childhood spent in several towns, the compass my parents used reflected two norths, one true, one magnetic. That leads me to a thought about fixed positions. Mom and Dad placed very little emphasis on agreement. With their blessing, I was free to inquire, to be wrong and to be sorry. The thought of them is thought itself.

Contents

Hockey Towns

Prologue

The first man to ever successfully put into words exactly what a big hockey game really means was Phil Esposito at the September 1972 Summit Series between Canada and the USSR. Fresh off the ice in Vancouver after losing 5–3 in Game Four, taking the series to 2–1 for the Soviets, Esposito, his curly black hair stuck to his head thanks to the gallons of sweat he poured into the game, sent an important message home to all of us.

To the people across Canada, we tried, we gave it our best, and to the people that boo us, all of us guys are really disheartened and we're disillusioned, and we're disappointed at . . . some of the Canadian fans—I'm not saying all of them . . . We're trying, but hell, I mean . . . they got a good team, and let's face facts. But it doesn't mean that we're not giving it our 150 per cent, because we certainly are . . . Every one of us guys, thirty-five guys that came out and played for Team Canada, we did it because we love our country, and not for any other reason, no other reason . . . They can throw anything they want out the window. We came because we love Canada. And even though we play in the United States, and we earn money in the United States, Canada is still our home, and that's the only reason we come. And I don't think it's fair that we should be booed.

After that little pep talk, and thanks to Paul Henderson, Canada came out and won the series. They held their flank on the Russian front. And then, thirty years later in Salt Lake City, Utah, Canada was off to another slow start—hammered by Sweden, they barely beat Germany and then tied the Czechs, their record 1–1–1. When Theo Fleury was levelled in front of the net by Czech player Roman Hamrlík, it was the last straw for the Great One, and he did something he rarely does. He went public.

"You talk about we're not a skating team, we can't move the puck, we have no finesse. That's crazy. We outskated them into the ground, third period. There should have been four or five penalties, blatant penalties. And [there] should have been two or three suspensions. Am I hot? Yes, I'm hot, 'cause I'm tired of people taking shots at Canadian hockey. When we do it, we're hooligans. When Europeans do it, it's okay because they're not tough or they're not dirty. That's a crock of crap."

The team would end up with a gold medal for the first time in fifty years. And at those same Olympics, the Canadian women's team won gold for the first time ever. As she came off the ice after the win, Hayley Wickenheiser, the undisputed face of Canadian hockey, was more than a little fired up. "You know what? The Americans had our flag on the floor of their dressing room, and now I want to know if they want us to sign it! I am so happy!"

It's usually hard to put these feelings into words, but Esposito, Gretzky, and Wickenheiser are the best of the best. They embody the Canadian spirit—play fair, play to win and don't mess with our hockey.

Lethbridge

ALBERTA

POPULATION:
83,517

It's God Calling, He Wants Us to Win Tonight

Mike Babcock had just been fired by the Moose Jaw Warriors. Although still in his twenties, he had been general manager and head coach of the struggling Western Hockey League team. It was tough to coach in Moose Jaw because the team was community-owned, and many of the owners wanted to have a say. In 1993, Babcock was all but drummed out of hockey and had lined up a job as an accountant in Strasbourg, Saskatchewan. And then he got a call from Peter Anholt, coach of the Red Deer Rebels (he's now the GM and head coach of the Lethbridge Hurricanes). Anholt told him the University of Lethbridge was looking for a head coach.

Mike tells a story in his book, Leave No Doubt, about some advice that John Chomay, one of his professors at McGill, gave him. At the end of Mike's teaching practicum, Chomay told Mike he was going to give him the highest mark he'd ever given one of his Faculty of Education students, but it came with "an obligation to live up to my potential."

In my view, the grade Mike got at McGill along with Chomay's comment stuck with him. He knew he could be in a better place than where he was in his career at that point. He could not leave all the hard work he had done behind. He could not quit hockey. He had to give it one more shot.

*M*ike Babcock came in to coach the University of Lethbridge Pronghorns on August 10, 1993. He interviewed all the assistant coaches, including young Trevor Keeper, who is now the coach of the Red Deer College Kings. In his meeting with Trevor, Mike grilled him about the players on the team. He wanted a sense of where the team would finish in the upcoming season. Former coach Dave Adolph had set the table. He started the program just four years earlier, and the Pronghorns were improving. They'd gone from 1–25–2 in 1989–90 to 9–16–1 in 1992–93.

Mike was determined to turn the team around. It was his last shot. He'd put in all that effort at McGill, and then as a player coach in the UK. And then he'd coached in Red Deer with the Rebels and after that, Moose Jaw. There was just too much to lose. Of course, nobody could have predicted what was about to happen that year.

Later that summer, Mike called Parry Shockey, a guy he'd met at a coaching clinic in Calgary. He said, "Hey, Shocks, I don't know if you know this, but I just got in to Lethbridge and I need an assistant coach. I don't have a bunch of money, but I need somebody that I trust. Will you come and do it?" Parry agreed, but when he got to Lethbridge, he discovered it was a little crowded—Mike had kept the three assistant coaches from the previous year.

At the end of every period of a Lethbridge game, Mike would ask each of the assistant coaches to tell him one positive and one negative thing the team had done. There was no time for hesitation. It was, "What didn't you like? Okay, good. Next guy? What did you like? What didn't you like? Good. Okay, get out of the way. Next guy?" Mike doesn't live in a world of black and white—he lives in a world of plus/minus. But his system is not goals for and against, which is the convention. Mike's plus/minus philosophy is to ask, when you move the puck—the minute you pass it, shoot it, dump it, whatever—what happens next? If something good happens next, you get a plus. If something bad happens next, you get a minus. Anywhere on the ice, any situation. That's his system.

After talking to the coaches and looking over the talent, Mike realized the Pronghorns had a pretty good team, but they had a record of losing close games. Two years earlier, the Pronghorns had lost fifteen games by only one goal. Mike was going to have to figure out how to stop that.

The Pronghorns played in the Canada West conference of the Canadian Intercollegiate Athletics Union (now the CIS—Canadian Interuniversity Sport). It's a highly respected level of hockey, but playing in the National Hockey League isn't the goal for most of the players. A few of the Pronghorns' best players were not interested in playing Mike's way, and so they left, which thinned out the ranks. Mike told Quentin Taylor, a reporter for the U of L's *Meliorist*, "After the first practice, I almost went home and cried."

He couldn't come up with twenty-six players, but he had twenty-two character guys. The Horns didn't have the depth of a school like the University of Calgary, but they did have some key players. Jarret Zukiwsky had played for Mike when he coached the Moose Jaw Warriors, and so he understood how important it was to be part of the team. Jarret was a big, strong kid from the Pincher Creek area. A fiery competitor, he had enough talent to play pro and would go on to win the Canada West rookie of the year award. Parry Shockey saw that in some ways, Jarret was like Mike. "They both had an edge and walked a fine line between arrogance and confidence."

When Jarret played for Mike in Moose Jaw, one day after a rookie party the guys kept messing up the drills. So Mike took the nets and pucks off the ice, lined the team up and blew the whistle. They were skating lines. After a minute or two, he yelled, "Okay, who had one beer last night? You can stop. Two beers? Okay, enough. Four beers . . . take a break." Guys were dropping off and standing at the boards, just watching. At six beers, there were only about four guys left, including Jarret. And then, all of a sudden, Mike said, "Okay, stop. You guys are fine—off the ice. The rest of you liars line up!"

Jarret went into the dressing room so tired he could barely unlace his skates. He had a long shower and then headed back to the ice to see what was going on. Mike had thrown a few buckets and garbage barrels out on the ice, and he had the guys who had dropped out early still doing lines. From that day forward, every time the team had a drill like that, nobody quit skating lines until *everybody* quit skating lines.

Some people make fun of ghost rosters—when a coach puts together a team before he knows his players. "We need this type of player and that type of player, playing with this type of guy or that type of guy." But Mike wanted four solid lines—two scoring lines and two checking lines. It makes for a versatile team, and there is less envy in the dressing room. Fewer guys will be jealous of ice time when they have set roles and responsibilities.

In Lethbridge, the veteran captain, Cregg Nicol, was rawboned and tough. In the two previous years, Cregg was on the first two lines as a scoring centreman, and he had just come back from the Detroit Red Wings' camp. Mike made him the centre on the Horns' third line. It was a checking, penalty-killing line—not the most glamorous position. Cregg, a team guy to the core, bought in immediately.

But most of the team had played together for four years, and so at the outset they weren't sure about all the changes. Every team has two leaders, a captain and a straw boss. Mike's straw boss was going to be someone he knew and trusted, and Jarret was that guy. But Jarret ruffled feathers right away when he questioned the players' work ethic. The first day of practice, one of the veterans was cheating on a drill. Jarret went up to him and said, "Why are you cheating? You're one of the fastest guys on the team."

Cregg intervened, calling over, "Hey! Just 'cause you played for Mike in Moose Jaw doesn't mean you get a say." Jarret looked at Cregg and said, "Look, you guys have won eff all. You've never even made the playoffs. We can't be taking shortcuts." Cregg registered the remark. He knew Jarret was right.

James Moller was a guy with NHL bloodlines, the younger brother of Randy, who played for the Florida Panthers, and Mike, who played with the Buffalo Sabres and the Edmonton Oilers. There was almost a ten-year difference between James and his brothers, but they always made sure to include him when they hung out at the house with their friends—the Sutter boys, future NHLers Kelly Kisio and Glen Wesley, and minor pros Doug Rigler and Graham Parsons.

Mike saw uncapped ability in James—raw talent that really hadn't been refined. Under Mike, it got developed. James was a forward, like his older brother Mike, who was a prolific goal scorer and point producer, so Babcock immediately took that pressure off. He put James on the third line with Cregg and told him, "You are going to block shots and kill penalties." He gave James a purpose on the team, and James excelled in the role.

Mike made a similar adjustment on the fly seventeen years later, early in the Vancouver Olympic Games. Canada was not doing well. They were set to play a key game against Russia in the quarter-finals, so Mike told Jonathan Toews, a big, tough number-one centre on every team he ever played for, a guy used to power-play time, that he was not going to be used on the power play or in offensive situations. Instead, Toews would centre the third line—a checking line. Mike put him with Rick Nash, a Rocket Richard–type goal-scoring leader. He told Nash he wanted him to use his size and speed to check Alexander Ovechkin, who was the key to a Russian victory. And then he filled out the line with Mike Richards, probably the smartest checking forward in the league. He created a matchup line out of three top-flight offensive superstars.

The Horns' twenty-four-year-old alternate captain, Trevor Ellerman, had played junior. He was a tremendous athlete and could golf like a pro. Under Dave Adolph, Trevor had played on the first line with his two buddies Greg Gatto and Dana McKechnie, but early in the year, Mike made Perry Neufeld, a skilled two-way centre, his first-line centre and put Ellerman on his left wing and Jarret across on the right.

Trevor had come back to the U of L for one more year just to play hockey and score a ton of points, and now Mike was messing with his plans. At the end of practice, Trevor confronted him. "What's the deal, Coach?" Mike told Trevor he had split the players up so the team would have two good lines. Trevor shook his head in disgust. He sure as hell didn't see it. Mike said, "Try it out." Their first game together, the new line got five points.

And then there were the goalies, Derek Babe and Trevor Kruger. Trevor had played goal for the Swift Current Broncos and won a Memorial Cup. He was an unorthodox, tremendously athletic goaltender with a Dominik Hašek style of play. But he was on the small side, so he was passed over. Trevor was a free spirit. Mike worked with him, giving him the boundaries he needed. Mike told him, "If you step outside those boundaries, then you don't play." Trevor lived within them. He knew when he could party, and he knew when he had to play. A year earlier, Derek Babe had alternated in net with Trevor, but when Mike made Derek the backup he didn't complain.

Mike took no prisoners. It didn't matter whether it was the captain or a walk-on, everyone was held accountable. It started in one of the first exhibition games. Trevor Ellerman was maybe the best scorer on the team, but he wasn't performing. However, Mike could smell that, deep down, Trevor was driven to win. So he went to Trevor and said, "You need to be accountable defensively. Let's focus on always being on the right side of the puck, and let's see some backchecking." Trevor blew him off—"Yeah, yeah, okay. Whatever." Later in the game, Mike had him serve a bench minor. When it was over, Mike told him to go back on. Trevor threw out a little attitude. He got up slowly, hit the ice and stretched, as if to say, "I'm cold from sitting out," so Mike threw him back on the bench and he didn't play another shift that game. Mike made it clear—"I'm going to coach this team,

11

and you are not, okay?" Mike had to make a statement early, and when he did, it was a turning point for the team.

The season opener was in Manitoba against the Bisons. Friday night, the student paper reported that the Horns "completely dominated, winning 5–1." Trevor Ellerman recalls that the next night they played well but then threw the game away.

Mike worked with each player, breaking down the opposition's plays and talking about their tendencies. And he had a knack for putting the guys in the right frame of mind. He'd look around and if he saw that someone was uptight or nervous, he'd give him a friendly jab. When the guys hit the ice, they were always amazed to find the game exactly as Mike had predicted.

Winning tight games is a strength Mike would become known for. It would define him as a coach. In the 2010 Vancouver Olympics, Canada beat Slovakia 3–2 in a semifinal nail-biter and went on to win the gold against the US in overtime 3–2. The same thing happened in 2014 in Sochi on the team's way to the gold medal game against Sweden. Canada won the quarter-final over Latvia 2–1 and beat the Americans in the semifinal 1–0 before defeating the Swedes. Over Mike's tenure as head coach in Detroit from 2005 to 2015, the Red Wings won an average of almost fifty games a year—475 wins over ten seasons. Everybody thinks these were 10–1 romps, but the truth is they were often one-goal games. And it all started in Lethbridge.

Two weeks later, Lethbridge was on the road again, in Brandon to play the Bobcats. The Bobcats' home record against the Horns was 12–3–1. But Saturday night the Horns swept, beating the Bobcats 6–5 in overtime. It was a huge, emotional win for the Pronghorns, knocking the one-goal-loss monkey off their backs. And they followed it up with a 9–6 victory on Sunday.

The whole team could see the chemistry between Ellerman and Zukiwsky. Over the season, they each averaged more than two points a game. Zukiwsky managed to lead the Canada West conference in goals despite being, as he put it, "the most benched player in the whole league." Mike wanted Jarret to play aggressively, but when he could see Zukiwsky getting to the point where he was ready to either get into a fight or take a dumb penalty, Mike would slap him on the bench to rein him in.

The Horns swept the UBC Thunderbirds and then the University of Alberta Golden Bears at home. They'd never beaten the Bears like that. The Horns moved into first place, and the team started to believe.

At the end of November, they faced the University of Saskatchewan Huskies and their old coach, Dave Adolph. Mike and Dave had played hockey together at the U of S, so they were friendly competitors. The Horns won two overtime games and were ranked number one in the country. They had finally found a way to win the close ones.

Lethbridge ended the season with a record of 19–7–2. They were not easy wins—tons of bullets were dodged. In the conference semifinals, they faced the Regina Cougars. Regina was the only team that had beat them twice in a row all year. Canada West was a much tougher league than those in the east, so the Horns felt if they made it out alive they'd have a chance at the championship.

They lost right out of the gate, 5–4, a one-goal defeat. Having never been in the playoffs, they weren't ready for the intensity level and the speed. The loss brought doubt. Would the Horns be haunted forever by a losing mentality?

The next night Regina scored early, and the Cougars kept the 1–0 lead all the way into the third period until Jarret shot one in under the crossbar. It hit the mesh and bounced out, but the goal light came on. The play continued for a few seconds until the linesman blew his whistle. Regina objected, but the officials ruled it a goal. The Horns scored on a power play in the second overtime, and the series was tied at 1–1.

Emotions ran high. Cougars head coach Bill Liskowich, still upset about the tying goal, stepped out onto the ice and was suspended for the final game of the series the next night.

The third game between Lethbridge and Regina was tied at three after regulation. In the dressing room between the first and second overtime periods, Mike could see that the guys were just vibrating with nerves. He came in to talk to the boys about pressure. He spoke about all the hard work they'd put in all year and how they had earned the right to feel confident about their preparation. There was no room for . . . the phone rang.

The landline was in the trainers' room at the other end of the dressing room. The team had two trainers, Don Matern and Dwayne (Dewy) Monteith. Dewy was a roofer by day. He'd been around forever, and he was all things—stick boy, trainer, skate sharpener, you name it. He ran to answer the phone. Mike took a breath, but he was steamed. He yelled out, "Who the eff is calling here right now?" Dewy, who had picked up the phone, yelled back, "It's God calling. He wants us to win tonight!" The tension broke and the team relaxed. When they went back out, Perry Neufeld tapped in a centring pass from Jarret Zukiwsky, and they took the series.

Up next were the University of Calgary Dinosaurs, a very tough team. The Horns took the first game in a squeaker, 2–1 in overtime. U of C came back and won the next game 3–2. In his pregame speech before the tiebreaker, Mike continued to focus on matchups and pairings. He looked James Moller square in the eye and gave him a mission—shut down the Dinos' best line, Greg Suchan, Sean Krakiwsky and Tracey Katelnikoff. Make sure to pressure those guys—no time and space . . . and then the phone rang. The guys all laughed and cheered, "It's God calling, he wants us to win tonight!" Just ahead of his speech, Mike had given Trevor Keeper a quarter for the pay phone down the hall.

The score was 1–1 late into the third, and then with six minutes left, Ellerman picked up a rebound and flipped it off his backhand. The Horns were on their way to the University Cup.

The papers said the Acadia Axemen had an unbeatable squad. Head coach Tom Coolen was quoted as saying, "I think that if we play our game, we'll be all right." The *Lethbridge Herald* reported that they were "licking their chops," they were "fearsome" and they had "clobbered Dalhousie." Ellerman said the Horns read all the hype. If the Axemen were overconfident, that was a good thing. Later, he told the *Meliorist*, "We played up the role. But deep down we knew we were there for a reason."

In their single-game, sudden-death semifinal, the Horns got swarmed in the first ten minutes. The Axemen scored a pair of fluky goals and built a quick 3–1 lead. Ellerman's line went out on the ice seven minutes in. Ellerman knew the big stage was making the team feel that they were in over their heads. From the bench, Mike shot him a look that said, "Should I call a timeout?" Trevor shook his head no. That would show weakness. Instead, he turned to his line and said, "Let's win this shift." By the end of the first period, the score was 4–3—for the Horns.

At the start of the third, Lethbridge was up 7–5, but Acadia kept up the pressure, outshooting them 18–8. Thanks to Kruger, the Horns were still in it, but as Babcock told the *Lethbridge Herald*, "Holy mackerel, there were a few fire drills out there."

The game ended 9–6 for the Horns, with Ellerman scoring three goals and adding three assists. The Pronghorns were through to the final against the Guelph Gryphons, scheduled for two nights later. During the season, Trevor Kruger and Trevor Ellerman would head out for a couple of beers after practice on the night before a game. Mike didn't acknowledge the activity, but he seemed okay with it. After practice on the off-day between the semifinal and the final against Guelph, Mike pulled Trevor Kruger aside, handed him a twenty-dollar bill and told him to go out for a couple of beers.

Before the final, Mike warned the boys to stay disciplined. All year, Mike had focused on their specialty teams, and the Horns had the top power play in the league. Perry Neufeld and solid defenseman Travis Kelln each scored early goals with the man advantage, and Guelph never got back into it. The Horns won 5–2.

As he held the trophy high, big D Johnny Curran yelled out, "This is for all the fans in Lethbridge who took a boot-lickin' all those years supporting the Pronghorns!"

Today, when Trevor Ellerman watches Mike being interviewed after games, he hears him say things like "We gotta be on our toes. We gotta keep the motor running." He gets a kick out of knowing that Mike has said the same things to NHLers like future Hall of Famer Pavel Datsyuk that he once told the Horns.

Ellerman is forever grateful. "Once, he was our coach and helped us climb to the greatest heights. He said it was his most amazing feat ever, to take this group who had never made the playoffs and win the championship, and he did it in ten months." But Mike told the *Toronto Chronicle Herald* what he told everyone else. "I didn't do it. I set out a standard, and the players lived up to it."

Winnipeg

MANITOBA

POPULATION:
663,617

Me Blue, You Blue

From 1980 to 1984, Gerry James was the coach of the Yorkton Terriers, the midget team that a young Trevor Keeper played for in Saskatchewan. Gerry tried to talk Trevor's teammate, defenceman Wendel Clark, into staying, but they lost him to Notre Dame.

In his youth, Gerry had been a pretty tough stay-at-home defenceman for the Toronto Maple Leafs in the winter and an all-star running back for the Winnipeg Blue Bombers in the summer and fall. At that time, the kids had no clue about his CFL background. Trevor didn't find out until Gerry missed a couple of practices to attend his Canadian Football Hall of Fame induction.

Gerry didn't talk a lot, but he had presence. After training camp that fall, Trevor was nervous when he walked into the coach's office for a one-on-one. Gerry asked him how big he was. Trevor was about 162 pounds, but he answered, "About 175."

Gerry laughed. "Is that with rocks in your pockets?

Gerry's eighty years old now. A couple of years ago, he was watching television when he saw a story about the research into sports concussions being conducted at London Health Sciences Centre at Western University in southern Ontario. In the 1950s and '60s, there were only two tests for concussions—"What's the score?" and "How many fingers am I holding up?"

Gerry never wore a helmet at any point in his hockey career, and he played football with only rudimentary head protection. Gerry phoned the centre and not only agreed to donate his brain after death to the institute, but offered to be part of the testing. The doctors were ecstatic.

Gerry flew down to Western, and for two full days they did all kinds of tests—an MRI, puzzles, psychological testing. The MRI showed evidence of numerous concussions, but there are no obvious effects so far. His wife, Marg, and he have been married sixty years, and she says he came through with flying colours, above average for his age. Mind you, she says if she asks him to take out the garbage, he forgets immediately.

---

*G*erry's dad was Dynamite Eddie James, a star running back in the '30s. But Gerry never got to know Eddie very well. It's a tragic story.

Eddie James received training in Winnipeg with the Princess Patricia's Canadian Light Infantry and then went to Europe to fight in World War II in 1939. He was a dispatch rider, a motorcycle messenger. The infantry units used couriers to take urgent messages back and forth. It was a dangerous job.

Gerry didn't see his dad during his formative years, ages five to eleven, so when Eddie returned in 1945, he was a stranger. Eddie drank a lot before he went overseas, and back at home it got worse. He couldn't keep a regular job. Gerry felt upset and ashamed of the way people treated Eddie. He wasn't a bum—he was a war hero and a football great.

When Eddie got deep into the bottle, he'd get so worked up he'd come at Gerry's mother, Moira, with his fists, and Gerry remembers jumping on his dad's back to hold him off.

Moira's life was misery, and so when Gerry was fourteen she finally left Eddie and filed for divorce. No one in the neighbourhood got divorced back then. Gerry rarely saw Eddie after that. One Christmas, when Gerry was twenty-three, the family invited him over for dinner, but a week before, Eddie checked into Notre Dame Hospital for surgery. Gerry wanted to go visit him but didn't. He was afraid, although he wasn't sure of what. And then Eddie died suddenly, on Boxing Day, 1958.

Eddie had never thrown a ball with Gerry or shown any interest in helping him in sports, but sports came easily to the boy. In fact, it's all Gerry wanted to do. He loved listening to Foster Hewitt on *Hockey Night in Canada* and he loved the Bomber broadcasts. Gerry rarely saw his dad and missed him terribly, so he'd constantly pore over Eddie's scrapbooks. He memorized his dad's stats and knew all the players he played with. He wanted to impress Eddie, get his attention, so he decided he was going to be a Winnipeg Blue Bomber *and* a Toronto Maple Leaf someday.

Gerry's brother Donald was four years older and not a lot of fun to be around. Gerry took a lot of beatings when he was little. When he was in grade school, Gerry would escape on an old bike he'd been given. It was basically a frame, a chain and two wheels, no fenders, but to Gerry it was a treasure. It gave him freedom. Every morning, he got up at five o'clock, hopped on his bike and delivered the *Winnipeg Citizen* even through January blizzards that buried houses and cars. Riding a bike through icy, rutted streets in Winnipeg helped him develop really good legs and upper-body muscles. In the summer, Winnipeg's forty-degree heat made it difficult to breathe if you were standing still, so Gerry rode fast to catch the breeze and get away from the mosquitos.

Moira worked in the garment industry as a secretary. She allowed Gerry to keep the money from his paper route. He needed it—he was always famished. The cheapest meat in those days was liver. And he hated liver. He'd try to get it down, but it would come right back up. Some days, he'd sit at the table for two hours, until Moira wasn't looking, and then his dogs, Oscar and Skipper, got fed.

Moira was a great cook. She used to make the best cinnamon buns anyone ever tasted, and she would sell them in the neighbourhood. While they were cooling, she'd tell Gerry, "Don't you touch those cinnamon buns." They were tough to resist, but he never did. Using his paper money, he'd fill up on sweets—chocolate bars, turnovers and licorice—from the local confectionery.

The boys were a handful and Moira had to work, so the summer that Eddie left, Gerry stayed with Moira's brother, Uncle Pat, in Grenfell, Saskatchewan, where he had a John Deere service centre. Gerry loved hanging with his uncle and learning how to fix engines. Grenfell is just fifteen miles south of Crooked Lake Provincial Park, near the Qu'Appelle Valley, where Moira's family had a cottage. Donald came to visit, and the minute they laid eyes on each other, the boys started to argue. Uncle Pat told them to take it outside. They thrashed around in the gravel and stubble. Gerry had grown a few inches that year and so he managed to hold Donald down and land a few good punches. It was their last fistfight.

Gerry had grown into a terrific athlete with incredible hand-eye coordination. When he bowled for the first time, he threw strike after strike. Kelvin High picked him to represent them in a city speedskating competition. All the athletes showed up in tights and skates. Gerry wore a plaid shirt, jeans and a pair of hockey skates. They started him on the inside lane, and he wasn't sure of the rules, but thanks to a couple of good body checks, no one passed him. He took home the gold medal that day. Gerry liked baseball too and played for the Sir John Franklin community team. He was the league's best pitcher. One of the headlines in the local newspaper during the season that year reads, GERRY JAMES SENSATIONAL. The story began, "Gerry James entered local baseball's Hall of Fame Friday night with a brilliant no-hit, no-run game as Sir John Franklin racked up its 11th victory in Bantam leagues competition." The next year, Gerry joined the Kelvin High football team, and that's when he found the sport he loved best.

Gerry and his buddy Jack Robertson couldn't afford tickets to the Bomber games, so they'd climb the forty-foot wall under the scoreboard at Osborne Stadium and sit on top to watch the games. Security would order them down, but Gerry and Jack would stay put, because they knew none of the guards wanted to climb up to get them.

When Gerry was fourteen years old and playing his last year of bantam hockey, he was spotted by a Toronto Maple Leaf scout named Squib Walker. It was around Christmastime. After the game, Squib patted him on the back and said, "That was a good game there, Gerry. Buy your mother a Christmas present." They shook hands, and Squib walked away, leaving Gerry to discover a twenty-dollar bill in his palm.

As a midget, Gerry showed remarkable endurance and often played a full sixty minutes on defence. He was so tough, his buddies started calling him Jesse James. In 1950–51, with

Moira negotiating for him, Gerry signed a C form, which gave the Toronto Maple Leafs control over his professional rights. He was paid one hundred dollars, and so he was disqualified from college teams. It didn't matter—Gerry wasn't much of a scholar.

That spring, the Winnipeg Monarchs, a Leaf-sponsored Junior A team, was on its way to the Memorial Cup final against the Eastern Canadian champions, the Barrie Flyers, and they called Gerry up as a spare defenceman. Barrie had a strong team that included future NHLers Jim Morrison, Leo Labine, Réal Chevrefils, Jerry Toppazzini and Doug Mohns. They swept the series 4–0, but the Leafs were impressed by Gerry's play so they asked him to come to Toronto.

With Moira's support, Gerry enrolled at Runnymede Collegiate Institute in Toronto and moved into a mansion in the Mount Pleasant neighbourhood with Toronto Marlboro manager Stafford Smythe's mother-in-law. It was like living in Downton Abbey. The family met in the parlour and dressed for dinner. Gerry was lost when they sat down to eat—he didn't know which fork to pick up. The family was kind, but they were gentry, and the food portions left him starving, so he moved out and billeted.

At sixteen, Gerry was almost six feet tall and 185 pounds. He became a football star at Runnymede, averaging twelve points a game. The coach, Hal Brown, told a reporter, "For years, I haven't had a boy any better than James and I doubt you'll see many better in high school. They call us a one-man team." In one game, with less than two minutes left, Gerry took a York Memorial kickoff behind his own goal line and ran it out 125 yards to score the winning touchdown.

The Winnipeg Blue Bombers sent him a letter inviting him to spring camp in 1952. He was thrilled but didn't want to quit school, so instead he attended the team's main camp that summer. He was fully expecting to get cut, but they kept him, offering him fifty dollars a week to play. He couldn't believe his luck. The money was good, but it was even better to play with his heroes, players like Tom Casey, Indian Jack Jacobs, Bud Tinsley and Dick Huffman. As far as Gerry was concerned, Huffman was one of the best defensive/offensive tackles in the history of the team.

Gerry moved back to Winnipeg that July, and every day he jumped on his trusty old bike to make it to practice.

Gerry had just turned nineteen, his second year of pro, when the Bombers won the western championship and met up with the Hamilton Tiger-Cats at Toronto's Varsity Stadium, before a crowd of twenty-seven thousand, in the 1953 Grey Cup game. The Bombers had flown him back from Toronto to sub in for fullback Lorne Benson, who was injured. Gerry scored the only Winnipeg touchdown in a 12–6 defeat. He also rushed for 167 yards in the game, more than any other player.

Gerry had long admired Indian Jack Jacobs, who he says doesn't get enough credit for the Bombers' success in the 1950s. Indian Jack was miserable to the rookies, but Gerry didn't care— Indian Jack was a competitor, just a fantastic athlete. He won the Manitoba amateur golf championship one year, and in football he could do everything—punt, play defence (he was a cornerback) and quarterback the team's offence. But Indian Jack had very small hands, so he couldn't throw a wet football. He had to palm the ball, and it was raining during the 1953 Grey Cup game.

Back in Toronto as a forward with the 1953–54 Marlies, Gerry played a tough game while putting up some points. They went all the way to the Ontario Hockey Association Junior A finals against the St. Catharines TeePees and were down 3–0 in the series when Gerry helped turn the tide. The Marlboros fought their way back to a seventh game, which they lost 5–3.

Hap Day, the Leafs' assistant general manager, offered Gerry a pro contract, but Gerry wanted to play for the Bombers again that summer and he wanted to win the Memorial Cup, so he turned down the offer. Gerry had another stellar season as a Blue Bomber in 1954, winning the first-ever Schenley Award for the most outstanding Canadian player, but Edmonton was the western team that went to the Grey Cup.

Meanwhile, Gerry and his high school sweetheart, Marg, got married. They had a small, quiet wedding in the chapel of a Winnipeg church. She was seventeen and Gerry was nineteen.

Turk Broda took over as Marlies coach midway through the 1954–55 season. He and Gerry had a pretty good relationship because Turk was easy-going. Gerry says Turk more or less took direction from his superiors, so he was able to be friendly with the players. Fifty years ago, practices were basically just shinny, with no drills. He remembers that for power plays, the coach just put the best players on the ice and said, "Go ahead, play."

In January, Gerry took a puck high on his cheekbone. He watched the end of the game and then was rushed to the hospital. The doctors wanted to save his eye, so he was confined to bed and ordered not to move for ten days. His face was so swollen that his new wife looked in and then walked right past his hospital room—she didn't recognize him. Gerry was back on the ice less than a month later. He'd lost part of his sight in his right eye, but he says it didn't affect his hockey at all because he was a right winger, so the play was usually on the left, the side of his good eye.

That year, the Marlboros beat St. Catharines and went on to defeat the Quebec Frontenacs to reach the Memorial Cup final against Regina. The Pats won the first game, so the Marlies got more physical. Regina changed its style of play to match, and that was the team's downfall. The Marlies took the next four games and brought home the Memorial Cup.

The next year, Gerry moved up to the NHL, and for the next couple of years he played for both the Leafs and the Blue Bombers. While Toronto struggled, Winnipeg won Grey Cups in 1958, '59, '61 and '62. Gerry was on all four of those teams. In 1959–60, under coach Punch Imlach, the Leafs wound up in the Stanley Cup final. Gerry liked playing for Punch—he said what he wanted to say, and he didn't sugarcoat it. Gerry says the team lost a few guys because a lot of players couldn't handle the truth and left.

Gerry also really liked Tim Horton. Tim had a terrible problem with his eyesight as well. Tim's vision was so bad, he couldn't see his toes. He wore contact lenses—big ones that covered the whites of the eyes as well as the corneas. Gerry says that's why, whenever Tim got into a fight, instead of standing back and trading punches, he would grab the guy in a bear hug and choke him out. Tim Horton was incredibly strong. He had washboard abs and never worked out a day in his life. Gerry so admired Tim that, when he sustained a shoulder injury and went in for therapy and the trainer asked him, "What do you want to develop?"

Gerry said, "I want a build like Tim Horton's." The trainer said, "Forget it."

In the 1960 Stanley Cup semifinals against Detroit, Gerry and Horton collided at full speed. They fell over each other and the Red Wings scored. In football, Gerry had been taught to meet force with force, and so rather than trying to get out of Tim's way, he had checked him. The next day in practice, they were both wearing blue jerseys. Tim skated over and said, "Me blue, you blue—we're on the same team," meaning, "For God's sake, don't hit me again." Bert Olmstead was on the left wing, playing on a line with Bob Pulford that was assigned to check Gordie Howe's line. At the end of his pregame speech, Punch said, "Pulford's line will start, and if Olmstead comes off, James, you go out and take his place, but if you hit anybody, try and hit somebody on the other team."

The Leafs went on to win over Detroit in six games but lost to Montreal in the final. Gerry is one of only two players in history to play in both the Stanley Cup final and the Grey Cup.

Dick Huffman died in 1992, but Gerry met up with him in 1987 at Dick's Canadian Football Hall of Fame induction. Dick asked Gerry if he remembered Shea's Brewery next to Osborne Stadium. He told Gerry that his dad, Eddie, as a former football superstar, was always welcome in the courtesy room up front where they served free beer. Eddie and Dick would drink together there after practice on occasion. Dick said that, one day, Eddie asked him a favour. "My kid is trying out with the Bombers. If he makes it, do you want to kind of keep an eye on him? He's kind of a brash kid and might get into some trouble with the vets."

Dick said, "Sure."

Gerry reflected back on the times when he might have been shooting his mouth off, like in the dressing room after a game when he'd had a few too many pops. It was true—Dick was always around, leaning against a doorway or somewhere in the background, arms crossed, watching, listening. Now he knew why.

He realized he hadn't gone to see Eddie in the hospital because there was just too much hurt there, and it had always been one of his life's great regrets, but knowing that Eddie gave a damn took some of the sting out of the bite.

Grand Centre
and
Cold Lake

ALBERTA

POPULATION:
13,714
AND
13,839

Great Sadness

Great sadness makes us understand the world.

After three seasons in Detroit with the Red Wings, Mike Babcock's assistant coach Brad McCrimmon decided to strike out on his own and take a head-coaching position with the Kontinental Hockey League team Lokomotiv in western Russia.

The team boarded a 120-seat Yak-42 on September 6, 2011, a clear, sunny Wednesday, near the city of Yaroslavl, which is northeast of Moscow. The plane crashed into a riverbank shortly after takeoff.

Before going behind the bench, Brad was a rugged defenceman who played in more than 1,200 NHL games with six teams. He partnered with five Hall of Fame defencemen in their early years. Ray Bourque, Mark Howe, Al MacInnis, Chris Pronger and Nicklas Lidström all learned the ropes from Brad. A Stanley Cup champion as a player in Calgary, Brad left his wife, Maureen, children Carlin and Liam, and a worldwide hockey family behind.

Like a caring uncle, father, or brother, Brad wrote letters—missives of support and perspective. In a November 2014 episode of our Hometown Hockey television series for Rogers, author Stephen Brunt talked about a letter Brad wrote to Todd Bertuzzi. Today, Bertuzzi keeps the letter tucked up in the sun visor of his truck. It gives him strength.

In March of 2004, Bertuzzi was a power forward and a fan favourite in Vancouver when he hit Steve Moore from behind, driving him to the ice. Bertuzzi was retaliating for a hard check Moore *had thrown three weeks earlier against Bertuzzi's captain, Markus Näslund. Moore suffered three fractured vertebrae, and his career was over. Bertuzzi served a fifteen-month suspension from hockey, and he pleaded guilty to criminal assault causing bodily harm. He was sentenced to one year of probation and eighty hours of community service.*

It's entirely understandable that one would say, "C'mon, Ron, what about Steve Moore?" Here's my take. Brad knew that Todd Bertuzzi was the perpetrator, but that hockey was an accomplice. In the end, we are shaped by the way in which we respond. In a path rarely taken, Brad decided to be part of a new narrative for Bertuzzi. He had the authority to reshape a life he understood.

Bertuzzi did what at least a thousand have done. Like the 1987 shove by Troy Edwards of the Moose Jaw Warriors that sent talented Regina Pats centre Brad Hornung into the boards, damaging his third cervical vertebra and spinal cord. It's the riptide of competition, nothing more. Neighbours of mine have been felled by such events. In the spring of 2015, James Hinchcliffe of Oakville, where I make my home, nearly died when he crashed into the wall as he was preparing for the Indy 500. A piece of the car's broken suspension sliced through his upper thigh, severing an artery. Skier Deidra Dionne from Red Deer, who is now vice-chair of the Canadian Olympic Committee's Athletes' Commission, was an Olympic bronze medallist in aerials. In 2005, on her final jump at the end of a training session at Mount Buller in Australia, she crashed and broke her neck. Thankfully, surgeons repaired the break with a titanium plate and a bone graft from her hip, and three months later she was training for the Torino Olympics. Duane Daines of Innisfail broke his neck and lost all use of his legs in a September 1995 bronc-riding accident. I could list countless injuries suffered through actions caused by riptides, a horse spooked, a car part failing, a moment.

As John Ralston Saul writes in his new book The Comeback, *we view our own reality through the details of the day. We see it as personalities, rivalries, divisions, failures. We perceive our job as determining whether Caesar ought to go to the Forum. We are on the lookout for suffering. "We are troubled by suffering," Saul writes. Not a bad thing. But the emotional drama can get in the way of ensuring that the issue is dealt with.*

That is why I don't like the psychoanalysis in some of the tough-guy stories—they are too predictable. Everyone presumes there is freedom in the convenience of not having to confront fears. I don't buy it. Suffering—Texas folksinger Townes Van Zandt wrote about it in haunting ballads that reflected his own life. His first serious song, "Waiting Around to Die," talks about a childhood of domestic abuse, followed by booze and self-destruction. Self-destruction is a path so many hard-boiled players in hockey take today. History is full of treacherous riptides. Todd Bertuzzi was caught in one, and so was tough guy Brantt Myhres.

---

*B*rantt Myhres was four years old in 1978. His family lived in Swan Hills, Alberta, north of Edmonton and south of Grande Prairie. Swan Hills was once home to a huge population of magnificent grizzlies, and then the oil and timber companies came in in the late '50s, and now there's just a handful left.

It was minus-30 out and Brantt had hockey practice, so he grabbed his bag and walked. He would have walked through fire if that was what it took—anything to get away from Jack (not his real name), his stepdad, an abusive drunk. As Brantt forced his legs through the hip-deep snow, he tried to shake off the image of Jack grabbing his mom by the hair, throwing her to the floor and stomping on her face with his big oil-rigger boots. When Jack was really drunk, he'd go after Brantt and his sister, Cher, too. So when a fight started, they'd jump into their bunk beds and hide under their Snoopy quilts.

One night during a big brouhaha in the living room, Brantt lay in bed, shivering with fear. He could feel his heart thumping in his ears, and his chest was so tight he could only take little, sharp breaths. Suddenly, he felt a hand on his shoulder. It was his mom, Barb. "Get up and get dressed," she whispered. "We're going to Grandma and Grandpa's."

Five hours later, totally exhausted, they pulled into Grand Centre, a frontier town ten minutes south of Cold Lake. According to the *Cold Lake Sun* that year, the town had a problem with the consumption of Lysol. "[It] can cause paralysis, convulsions and death, [and has] reached epidemic proportions on area Indian reserves." And just a year earlier, the paper reported, "Mayor Doug Wold said it's not safe for children to walk in town because they may be attacked by packs of wild dogs."

Five thousand people lived in Grand Centre, where Barb's parents, Jo and Robert Brady, owned a do-it-yourself hardware and housewares franchise called Macleod's. A lot of small towns had one. Roland Macleod started a mail-order business in 1917 in Watrous, Saskatchewan, and grew it into a major chain across Western Canada.

Grandma and Grandpa were hard workers, well respected in the community. Barb and the kids stayed with them until they got their own place on top of a hill in an area called Brady Heights, named for Brantt's family. Today, houses there go for more than $350,000—at the time, you'd be lucky to get $50,000. It was a great location for Brantt because there were so many kids who loved to play road hockey. After school, there was always a big game at the community tennis courts nearby.

Grandpa Robert preached honesty, character and hard work. He took Brantt to his practices and games. He'd pull up in his new Ford F-150 and tell the kid to hop in. Grandpa made sure Brantt always had new equipment, good sticks and skates that fit. But what meant even more to Brantt was that someone he cared about was watching him. Grandpa Robert had never picked up a stick in his life, so he was there for Brantt, and Brantt only—not as a hockey fan. Life was really good for the next four years. And then Barb let Jack back into their lives.

Nothing had changed. In fact, it got worse. One night, while Brantt was lying in bed, he could hear the happy squeals of his sister, Cher, and her friend outside playing. Jack was swearing and shouting from the living room—"Shut up!" Brantt squeezed his eyes shut. Cher had better be quiet, he thought, or she's going to get it! Suddenly, he heard the crack of his wooden bedroom door being punched open. The covers were pulled down and his stepdad had him by his hair, swinging him up over the floor. He threw Brantt against a TV stand. Brantt's eye hit the sharp corner, and then he bounced back onto the floor. Brantt started pleading, "Please! Please stop! I didn't do anything! I was sleeping!"

He looked into his stepdad's angry green eyes. They were slits of fury. "I told you to shut the eff up!" Jack roared. With one of his big, strong, hairy hands, Jack grabbed Brantt around the neck, cutting off his windpipe, and then tossed him onto the bed like you would a piece of garbage out a car window. And then he slammed out of the room.

Terrified, Brantt curled up under the covers. He didn't dare move or even breathe loudly, but he made plans. Barb was staying overnight at a friend's, and he was going to call her as soon as Jack left for work in the morning. She would be so mad! She'd come storming home and kick Jack out for good.

The next morning, as soon as he heard Jack's truck turn over, he was up like a shot and on the phone in the kitchen. He dialled Barb's friend and, swallowing his sobs, got his story out. "Mom! Jack beat me up and punched me in the face and choked me and—" She cut him off. "Cry me another river, Brantt," she said.

The day after the beating, on December 27, 1984, it was minus-40. Brantt's eye hurt and there were marks on his neck. He grabbed the new stick Grandpa Robert had given him for Christmas and asked Barb if she'd drive him down the hill to the rink.

It was a weird afternoon—very still, under heavy orange skies. When they got to the rink, it was later in the afternoon, about 3 p.m., but no one else was around. Brantt shivered a little. He made Barb promise to pick him up in an hour. The sun would set by then, and all he had on were his parka and jeans, hockey gloves and a toque. There was no little shack to warm up in, and as it got darker, it got colder.

Barb lit a smoke and rolled her eyes. "Yes, Brantt, I'll be back soon." He hopped out of the car and skated around. He was always Gretzky, picking up pass after pass from Mark Messier or Jari Kurri or Mario Lemieux, who sometimes magically appeared on the line. Brantt was working hard and staying warm when he looked up and saw that he was now skating by the light of the moon. He figured he'd been out there for at least three hours. His mom wasn't going to come. Something inside him told him he'd better walk the two kilometres downtown to his grandma's store or he would die out there. He hadn't brought his boots, so he hoofed it down the paved road on his skate blades.

Brantt had trouble turning the knob on the big door to the store—his hockey gloves were too bulky. He shook off the right one and found that his fingers were frozen solid. Finally, he managed to get the door open and saw his grandma sitting at her desk at the right of the till. Her smile quickly faded as she took inventory. His face was an ice cube, making the black eye Jack had given him stand out even more. Her hands flew to her mouth. "Oh my God, sweetheart! What happened to you?" He didn't answer. Jack had warned him not to tell anyone about the beatings, and his mother's words from the day before—"Cry me another river, Brantt"—still echoed in his head. But he was exhausted. He bowed his head, summoned up all his courage and mumbled, "Jack beat me up last night, and Mom forgot to pick me up at the rink."

His grandma came over and put her arms around him and started rubbing his back to increase his circulation. "You will not spend another night at that house. You're living with me and your grandpa from now on." He threw his arms around her waist. Those words warmed him up faster than a hot bath.

When Brantt was fifteen, he was invited to the main camp of the Portland Winterhawks of the WHL in Edmonton. He planned on turning heads with his fast skating, hard shot and sharp passing. And he did score a couple goals during the game, but every time he skated past the other team's bench, their backup goalie would yell, "Ahh, Myhres, you effing hot dog, you puss, you suck. Nice white gloves, you homo!" So when the game ended, Brantt skated by their bench and said, "Go eff yourself, dickhead." Then, for the first time in his hockey career, he heard two words he'd hear over and over again for the next eighteen years. "Wanna go?"

They skated to centre ice to square off. By this time, Brantt was tall—six foot three, on a 190-pound frame—so he had an incredible reach. He grabbed the goalie with his right hand by the front of his jersey, and with his left he pummelled the guy's face with a series of rabbit punches. The goalie's nose was pouring blood, which ended things quickly. Brantt skated off, passing a guy on the ice, who he thought was a fan there, to congratulate him for a good fight. He was wrong—it was the goalie's brother. He suckered Brantt and landed right on top of him, still punching. As Brantt struggled to get rid of the guy, he thought, "Holy crap, this is what the WHL is all about? I'm in big trouble."

The next year, Brantt made the Hawks' lineup, but his fate was sealed. He was a tough guy, fighting almost every night. The year ended with him setting a record for the most penalty minutes ever by a seventeen-year-old—381 minutes in fifty-three games. He was rated by *The Hockey News* as the toughest junior player in North America.

By nineteen, Brantt was playing for the Lethbridge Hurricanes and attending Tampa's training camp. His first exhibition game was against the St. Louis Blues. At the faceoff, he found himself next to Tony Twist, who leaned in and said, "Hey, kid, wanna go?" Tony hit him so hard he couldn't say hello for two weeks.

Brantt got the tap from Tampa in midseason. He'd made the Show. He'd reconnected with his biological dad, so that was the first call he made. He asked him, "Hey, Dad, any advice for me before I play my first game tomorrow?" His dad replied, "Yes, son. Keep throwing."

The day of his first game in the NHL, Brantt woke up and couldn't eat. His gut was churning. He didn't want to fight anyone on the Hartford Whalers that night—he wanted to play. But he knew that wasn't going to happen, so he made a decision. He looked over Hartford's lineup and zeroed in on a tough guy about his size, Mark Janssens.

Brantt pulled his number 27 jersey over his head, went into the bathroom and slathered his face with Vaseline. The game started and he was just bouncing on the bench, nervous as hell. Three minutes later, his coach, Terry Crisp, tapped his shoulder. "Myhres, you're up next." Brantt jumped onto the ice and into the play. He was in his own end, along the boards, when the puck came to him. Janssens checked him hard. Brantt looked at him and said, "Wanna go?"

The gloves were off and they traded punches. Janssens landed one that made Brantt take a knee, but he got up fast and threw a hard left that caught Janssens on the chin. He watched Janssens' eyes roll back as he fell to the ice like a tree that had just been felled by the last swing of an axe. Brantt skated to the penalty box filled with wonder. He'd just cold-cocked a guy who played in the NHL!

Three years later, in 1997, Wayne Cashman, the former assistant coach in Tampa, was head coach in Philly. Tampa had traded Brantt to Edmonton for Vladimír Vûjtek, and a few months later Cashman traded big winger Jason Bowen to the Oilers for Brantt. Brantt's new teammates were Eric Lindros, Paul Coffey, Ron Hextall, Rod Brind'Amour and Joel Otto, guys he really looked up to.

As he was getting dressed for his first game, he was sick to his stomach. He'd checked Colorado's roster and found six-foot, seven-inch, 240-pound François Leroux. Leroux was the biggest guy in the league and Edmonton's first-round draft pick in 1988. But Brantt knew he needed to make an impression or he'd be gone.

He skated out with the team to the deafening cheers of 20,000 Flyer fans. He'd never heard anything like it. Cashman sent him out and he went right over to Leroux and said, "Come on, you big bitch, wanna go?" Gloves were off and Brantt summoned all the dread and outrage from all those nights he heard Jack beating on his mother, all those nights hiding under the covers, all those nights dreaming he was going to kill his stepfather, and threw as hard and as fast as he could. Less than a minute later, Leroux was done. He covered his face and skated away, but Brantt wasn't finished. He chased his opponent down and threw one more, falling on top, and the fight was over. Brantt got up, his whole body still surging with testosterone. The crowd went nuts as he skated to the penalty box.

Fighting gave him quick relief, but drinking and cocaine gave him an entire night off, and so he started self-medicating—big time. Finally, in Tampa, Brantt and some of the boys went out for a few pops and ended up in Paul Coffey's room. Eric Lindros was there as well. The Big E was good to Brantt. He'd even taken him along to the David Letterman show. But that night in Tampa, Brantt was totally out of it. Words were exchanged, and suddenly he had Eric by the throat. The anger didn't last—they were hugging like brothers thirty seconds later—but the next day Brantt felt bad. He couldn't trust himself. What if he had hurt his buddy?

That summer, he was twenty-four years old when he entered the NHL's substance abuse program for the first of five times. He joined the San Jose Sharks that fall. He'd been sober all summer and worked his butt off, losing twenty pounds and gaining a ton of muscle. He looked like a different guy and he showed up ready to play. During exhibition games, he was flying and did well in a couple of scraps. But two weeks in, he ordered an orange juice with two shots of vodka and proceeded to get obliterated, so it was back to rehab.

Sharks coach Darryl Sutter cut him a lot of breaks. He'd pull Brantt in and talk to him, mostly about drinking. Brantt felt Big D cared about him as a human being, not just as a player. Brantt wanted to give Darryl his best on every shift. Big D was like a father, a really tough father.

And the players were like brothers. London's Joe Murphy, a crazy talented winger, was the rebellious son. Darryl and he had a history together. Darryl coached him four years in Chicago, from 1992 to 1996. Trouble was, if Joe didn't feel like playing, he'd just go through the motions. Those occasions didn't sit well with the team's tough guy, Ronnie Stern. Brantt saw that Sternie was a warrior. He wore an A on his jersey. He was one of the leaders on the team.

With about thirty seconds to go in the second period of a home game, Ron stood up on the bench and yelled down at Joe to get going. Murph yelled back, "Go eff yourself, Ronnie! Don't you ever tell me what to do!" And then he popped up and they were both standing up on the bench, trading comments. With ten seconds left in the period, they headed for the dressing room so that they could finish the conversation in private.

The team walked in about a minute later and saw Ron on top of Murph, throwing punches. A couple of the guys tried pulling him off, but Big D walked by and said, "Don't break it up, boys. Let 'em go," then walked into his office. He believed guys should settle their differences and move on. He didn't like things to fester.

Brantt stayed clean for Darryl until near the end of the season, and then he blew it and it was off the team and back into rehab. After that, he shuttled between the International, American and National Hockey Leagues, spending time with Nashville, Washington and Boston.

But Brantt was Darryl Sutter's kind of meat-and-potatoes player. He was coaching in Calgary, so he asked Brantt to join the Flames. At the end of that season, Brantt went back to Cold Lake to see his grandparents. He was at a house party when he saw a guy sitting in a chair, smoking crack. Brantt grabbed the pipe, put a lighter to it and pulled back a hit. As soon as he exhaled, he was on the floor, his heart trying to explode through his chest. An ambulance was called and he was rushed to the hospital.

Brantt wrote his third letter to Gary Bettman asking for one last reinstatement. "Mr. Bettman, I know there is no stage five, this would be my last chance. I will not let the NHL or myself down.

I will make everyone involved glad they stood by my side during this journey. Please consider reinstatement so I can play again."

Bettman relented. Brantt was in the 2004–05 Calgary lineup.

At Cowboys, during the Calgary Stampede, Brantt met one of his new teammates—a big, good-looking kid named Steve Montador. Monty had had an amazing playoff run in 2004—the Flames had gone to the Stanley Cup finals and he had scored an overtime winner in one of the series. They got to talking, but Steve seemed a little bit reserved and quiet. A few minutes later, Steve told him he'd just come out of treatment, but Brantt had already figured that out. He knew what happened when guys were newly sober—they really didn't know how to react in social situations, especially a bar. Brantt noticed he and Steve were probably the only two guys at the whole bar not drinking.

Brant always gravitated towards the more physical players, so he and Monty would hang out. Brantt was two years sober, so they talked about the program and about playing as an enforcer when you were stone-cold sober versus playing with an edge. Brantt wasn't really keen on playing exhibition games because that's when teams dress their tough guys to test them out. He was intimidated by that because he was a paid gunslinger, whereas Monty would take that role if he had to, but he was on a regular shift because he could play.

Chris Simon and Darren McCarty were both on the Flames that year. Brantt called it a "Darryl Sutter lineup." Brantt and Monty talked about a tough guy that Calgary had let go, Krzysztof Oliwa. Oliwa wasn't a heavyweight, but he would fight whomever he had to for his team. Brantt thought Monty was a "gamer." He had a ton of respect for Monty because, at around six feet and

210 pounds, he was fighting out of his weight class most of the time. This made hits to the head even more dangerous. But they never got into what could happen. Talking about it was bad luck.

On September 23, 2005, before a preseason game against the Edmonton Oilers, Big D walked into the dressing room and sat down next to Brantt. He said, "Congrats, Myze, they cleared you to play. Real proud of you. I hope you're ready, 'cause you are on the roster for tonight."

That meant he'd likely face Georges Laraque—six foot four, 270 pounds, with Thor's hammer for a left hand. Brantt skipped his pregame meal and went back to his hotel room, falling into bed and rolling up in the covers. He was nine years old again and filled with dread. It was as if Jack was standing over him, yelling, making him feel powerless, inadequate. "Laraque is going to kill you tonight! You are such an embarrassment! But maybe the world will get lucky and you'll hit your head on the ice and die!" Brantt started shaking so hard the bed was shimmying off the floor.

His teeth were still chattering during warm-ups and on the bench. And then the game started and everything slowed down. "Myyyzzze, youuu'rrre uuuppp." He jumped on the ice and Georges was right there. "Hey, Brantt, let's go."

They squared off, Georges turned sideways, and the last picture Brantt took was of his opponent's big fist—cocked. Then everything went black. When he came to, he was down on the ice and could hear the linesman saying, "It's over, Georges. Let go."

Brantt's left eye felt like it was hanging down his cheek. His ears were ringing and he had a terrible headache. He was helped into the dressing room. Jarome Iginla was right there with him.

"Hey, Myze, are you going to be okay? Man, you've got some balls!" Jarome was the captain and a standup guy.

The doctors stitched him up and arranged an X-ray for the next day. His orbital bone was crushed—in other words, there was no floor left in the eye socket for the eye to rest on—so Brantt was rushed to surgery to have a mesh plate inserted.

As he left the hospital, he knew it was over. Seventeen years of looking over his shoulder, worrying about someone tapping him on the shin pads, wanting to fight. Seventeen years of channelling rage, making himself into a mean son of a bitch. Seventeen years of acting like someone he wasn't. He took a big gulp of air and stepped into the sunlight.

St. Catharines
and
Niagara-on-the-Lake

ONTARIO

POPULATION:

131,400

AND

15,400

Cheesy

Pals of mine, Murray Scott and Todd Anderson, drive up from St. Catharines every Wednesday to play a 10 p.m. pickup game. It's an hour each way, so they rarely drop in for a postgame pop. But recently Murray did, so we chatted about St. Catharines. Murray explained that beyond the hockey, the place is renowned for world-class rowing and lacrosse. He's coached the St. Catharines rowing club and at the school level for years.

This got me thinking about a St. Catharines connection—a guy that I know of, but haven't met, Jason Dorland. Jason was an Olympian in 1988 in Seoul, Korea. His men's eight rowing team had a disappointing sixth-place result, but it started Jason on a wonderful journey that he details in his book, Chariots and Horses.

The former Ridley College student has gone on to a career in coaching and public speaking. After that sixth-place finish in Seoul, Jason's crew was eviscerated in the media. He was devastated and it took years to overcome. One thing he knew was that it was not for a lack of effort.

His team was well conditioned, driven and good to go. But there was a snag on the day of their final in Korea. Just as they lined up for the start, one of the other boats had a technical glitch, so the crew asked for the start of the race to be delayed fifteen minutes. The other competitors agreed. The Canadians, however, were profoundly rocked by that delay. Their boat became "unplugged"—it was flat. It happens.

Naturally, the team that had requested the timeout won the gold. It was another reason to be furious. Jason used hate as a prime motivator. After losses, he despised the winner. Before races he would scan the other boats, look at the athletes sitting in his position, the three-seat, and conjure anger.

But Jason soon realized that all the hate he had been using to psych himself was not easily mustered twice in one sitting. In the years since, he has learned that hate and revenge are terrible reasons to chase victory. He now teaches to stop reaching for wins and fearing losses, and to make fun the foundation of the experience.

He says, "When we feel safe to fail, when we have that freedom, we fail less often." The only guarantee of a great effort each and every time is when love is at the heart.

---

*S*t. Catharines is still the same as it was when he grew up in the 1940s, as far as Gerry Cheevers is concerned. In the winter, he played hockey. In the summer, lacrosse and baseball. Just like the kids do now. The first public rink he ever played on was the St. Catharines Arena. But his first ice was across the street from his house on Geneva Street. It was an open field that the fathers in the neighbourhood took turns flooding. There was shinny all the time because every other house on the block had a rink too.

Gerry's dad, Joe Cheevers, was a competitive guy, an Ontario Hall of Famer in lacrosse. Joe was a Damon Runyonesque character, right out of *Guys and Dolls*. He was a scoundrel, slick and persuasive, and had real charm. Joe was one of the top car salesmen in the country, but he never sold a car from the lot. Instead, he'd make his deals at the Legion or the local gin mill. He brought a guy named Haggis MacIntosh home with him one night, and Haggis stayed for seven years. Gerry's mom, Betty, who was initially tolerant, finally put her foot down and said, "Joe, it's Haggis or me," and so Haggis moved out.

Gerry first played hockey for the St. Denis Shamrocks, a team linked with a new parish in the local Catholic Youth Organization. There were at least four or five teams in the league. The Shamrocks got beat 18–0 in their first game. And when their little goalie didn't return for the next game, Joe put Gerry in. At least he'd be sure to have a goalie who showed up. Joe was pretty hard on Gerry when he didn't perform. The only nickname Joe ever gave his son was "Red Light." It was his way of grinding the kid, trying to get him going.

He didn't have to grind too hard. Gerry inherited his dad's eye of the tiger and his nickname, Cheesy. Joe and his buddy, Hall Judd, founded a St. Catharines league—the Little NHL—and signed Gerry up. Gerry remembers putting on the big, thick chest protector and the old mask. Each year, he'd play for a different team—the Blackhawks, the Canadiens or the Bruins.

When Gerry was twelve years old, he wanted to leave the Little NHL and move to a city team, but Joe didn't want to lose his best goalie. They went back and forth on it, but Gerry eventually won out and joined the St. Catharines Bantams. It was a team full of future NHLers—Stan Mikita, Ray Cullen, Dougie Robinson, Ed Hoekstra and Jack Martin. The Bantams were coached unofficially by a volunteer named Vic "Skeeter" Teal, who played one game in the NHL for the 1973 Islanders. Gerry says if you look up Vic Teal, you'll find he was one of the most successful minor coaches in the history of Canada. Sadly, Stan Mikita, who now suffers from Lewy body dementia, is not doing very well, but he always said that any guy from St. Catharines who made it in the hockey world should thank Vic. Simple as that. Vic put the St. Catharines Bantams through their drills three mornings a week at 6 a.m.

In the days before butterfly goalies, Vic never wanted Gerry to go down in a game. When he did, it meant a lot of skating drills next practice. Vic was always shouting at him, "Stand up! Stand up and out!" Vic also wanted his goalies skating as much as the forwards and defencemen. He'd tell Gerry, "You better skate as good as these guys if you want to even think of playing hockey." He made Gerry stay late, practice after practice.

Gerry didn't know a lot about equipment, but he says that back then the most important thing was a catching mitt. It was part of his identity. Today it's the mask. Gerry wore a Rawlings first-baseman's glove with a blue felt cuff on it that covered the back of his hand—handmade. He'd go on to play goal for more than fifty years, but rarely changed up his glove. He used only three different catchers his entire pro career. Vic taught him the main function of his glove wasn't to catch the puck, it was to stickhandle.

The team won the All-Ontario bantam title two years in a row, beating the Toronto Marlies both years in the final. When you beat the Marlies, you've accomplished something. Toronto drew its players from a population of one and a half million, while the St. Catharines teams came from a pool of 25,000.

In the final game against the Marlies, the St. Catharines Arena was packed—3,200 screaming fans. Gerry led the way onto the ice. He shot their only warm-up puck into his own net, just missing the head of his team's best player, Jack Martin, by inches. To this day, Gerry still puts the puck in the net when he skates on.

After the Bantams' second championship, Joe became a scout for the Maple Leafs. He recruited Gerry in 1959 to play on a scholarship at St. Michael's College School. The school had a Leaf-sponsored Junior A team, the St. Michael's Majors of the OHA. In the Leaf system, the Catholic boys played for St. Mike's, while the Protestants played for the Marlies. But it turned out that Gerry was Joe's only recruit, so the Leafs let Joe go.

Father David Bauer was the Majors' coach. He was slender and not very tall, but a tremendous athlete from a great hockey family. His older brother was Bobby Bauer, who played on the famous Kraut Line with teammates Milt Schmidt and Woody Dumart in Boston. Gerry admired how, in baseball, Father Bauer could pitch with either hand. Like Vic Teal, Father Bauer believed a goalie had to be a skater. He drilled that point home by making Gerry skate in the forward's drills. In fact, in Gerry's last year, Bauer put him on a line for twelve games.

Gerry couldn't be contained at St. Mike's. At first, his dorm room was on the third floor, so he couldn't sneak out, but the last two years he was there, he was moved to the first floor. When the lights went out, Gerry would climb out his window and down the little wooden fire ladder, and then run down to the community dry cleaners and play Hearts with the owner, his wife and their nephew until the wee hours of the morning. Then he'd sneak back in and be up and on his knees at mass by 7 a.m.

In 1958, Gerry's third year, he'd duck out to the Greenwood Raceway with one of the priests, Father Flanagan, who was a real racetracker. Father would venture out under a big pair of sunglasses and a ballcap. He'd find Gerry and whisper to him to meet at the car.

That year, everyone was talking about the Kentucky Derby and the handsome dark bay colt, Tim Tam, that was favoured to win. Gerry and a pal, John Chasczewski, decided to take some action on the race, but instead of going with track odds at about 6–1, they cut the odds in half, to 3–1. That way, they couldn't lose. The boys got a little nervous when their handle got up to about five hundred dollars. That's equivalent to more than four thousand today.

On the Friday night before the race, Gerry got called in to see the principal, Father Reagan. Gerry's heart sank to the bottom of his feet. He figured somebody had blown the whistle on him and he was going to get kicked out of school. Father Reagan was a rigid disciplinarian. Very tough.

He walked into the big office in a sweat, and Father Reagan threw him a stern look. "Gerry, sit down."

Gerry felt like throwing up. "Aw nuts," he thought. "How am I going to explain this to my mother?"

Father Reagan straightened the papers on his desk and said, "Listen, Gerry, what are the odds on Tim Tam?"

Gerry blinked. "Three to one, Father, but I'll give you four to one."

Father Reagan nodded. "Put ten dollars on him for me." Tim Tam won, Father Reagan was forty dollars richer, and that was the end of it.

In the meantime, the hockey team under Father Bauer was winning like crazy. He would go on to become a big fish in Hockey Canada with the development of the Olympic team program, and he became one of the most influential persons in Gerry's life. The Majors made it all the way to the Memorial Cup for the first time in fourteen years. Father Bauer was ahead of his time in the way he coached a psychological game. In fact, he taught psychology at St. Mike's. During the playoffs, they lost a very physical game to Hamilton. Father Bauer publicly objected to how rough things got on the ice and threatened to pull his team if Hamilton didn't dial it back. Meanwhile, in the dressing room, he sang another tune. "C'mon, boys! Let's go beat the hell out of them." It was part of the way he kept the opposition off balance.

St. Mike's had such a good team. It was the kind of team Father Bauer created, full of speedy checkers. Terry O'Malley was the team captain and a very good defenceman. He went on to become president of Père Athol Murray's school in Wilcox, Saskatchewan. Barry MacKenzie was on that team too. He's the coach who brought along players like Russ Courtnall and Wendel Clark at Notre Dame, and he preceded Terry as president. There were the Draper twins, Bruce and Dave. Bruce was probably the best player on the St. Mike's team. He and Larry Keenan would go on to play with Gerry in Rochester of the American League, and Bruce would help the Hershey Bears reach the Calder Cup final in 1964–65. Sadly, Bruce was diagnosed with leukemia and died three years later at twenty-seven years of age. Then there was Arnie Brown, who has been ranked ninety-third on the all-time list of New York Rangers. Billy MacMillan, who made the NHL at age twenty-seven and ended up assisting Al Arbour when he coached the New York Islanders. Terry Clancy, who could skate like the wind and was the son of longtime NHLer King Clancy. And Gerry Cheevers.

Half that team wound up in the NHL. The first three games of the Memorial Cup finals were held at Edmonton Gardens, and not many of the boys had ever flown, including Gerry. It was a great back-and-forth series, but St. Mike's persevered, winning in Edmonton's rink, thanks in large part to Gerry's performance. Afterward, Gerry said it helped that whenever he walked into the old rink, he'd smell the onions they fried for their burgers. That's what got him going.

A lot of college scouts were in attendance. Murray Armstrong, the head coach of the University of Denver in Colorado, was so impressed by Gerry's goaltending, he offered him a scholarship. But when word got back to the Leafs, the deal fell apart. Back then, the Leafs paid amateur goalies to be standby netminders in case of an injury. In his last two years of high school, the Leafs had paid Gerry ten dollars a game for this service, and NCAA rules don't allow players to receive money from professional teams.

In those days, when it came to negotiating with the NHL, it was their way or the highway. But Father Bauer was mad that Gerry wasn't going to be able to attend college, so he went in to see the Leafs with Gerry and did all the talking. He got the best contract possible for the kid—$5,000 his first season, $5,500 in year two and a $3,000 signing bonus. Gerry drove home to St. Catharines that night, feeling like he had just won the lottery. But he didn't have the bonus money long—the next day, Joe sold him a car for $2,700.

Gerry went on to play goal with Bobby Orr and the Boston Bruins, winning two Stanley Cups, in 1970 and 1972. He was inducted into the Hockey Hall of Fame in 1985. In his opening remarks on live television he said, "They haven't given me long here. And so on the two most important times of my life, tonight and my honeymoon, both are all over in ninety seconds."

Little Zee

Wednesdays during the winter, I play hockey with a group of guys who've been skating together for more than twenty years. Three of our stalwarts are the Piercey brothers, Doug, Darren and Ronnie. Tough as steel—all with good hands.

Doug, a Peel Regional police officer in Toronto, has a good friend named Zenon Konopka. They're birds of a feather. Zenon was an NHL policeman on the ice and although not the fastest skater, he too had good hands.

You might have heard that Zenon had to sit twenty games while playing with the Sabres in 2014 for using a performance-enhancing substance during off-season training. Turns out it was an over-the-counter supplement that did not pass muster. The time missed cost him. His NHL career was over. A tough smear on the resume of a man held in the greatest regard by teammates and friends.

Zee deserves to be remembered another way. He had an impressive career with 346 games in the NHL, and he skated for the 1999 Memorial Cup champions, the Ottawa 67's, under Hall of Fame coach Brian Kilrea.

My favourite memory of Zenon is the time I ran into him at an NHL playoff game in Calgary. He and former 67's teammate Lance Galbraith were playing in Idaho for the ECHL Steelheads. Just visiting, they came over to meet Don Cherry and told us about their recent victory at the Kelly Cup. During the team's first sea-

son, they'd won the league title at home in Boise. Zenon shared some Kilrea stories with Grapes and then mentioned their goalie, Saskatoon's Dan Ellis, who was the Kelly Cup MVP. (That performance launched Dan's career, big time. Fourteen years in the NHL and counting.) I had refereed Dan in the OHA when he was with the Junior B Orangeville Crushers. He, like Zenon, was a bit of a long shot to make the NHL.

Zenon shared great stories of that run in Boise and never mentioned himself or his contribution—leaving out the fact he led the team in goals and points. Zenon shares my mother's birth date, January 2. His humility and his wonderful storytelling reminded me of Mom. Doug Piercey and I feel you should know a very special man.

Martin Konopka worked extremely hard to have a good life in Poland. In 1939, he and his wife Katarzyna (Katherine) and four children lived close to the Russian border, in Lwów, now Lviv, which is now part of Ukraine.

Elżbieta (Elizabeth) was seven, Jadwiga (Jennette) six, Zenon—the only boy—was four years old and Waleria (Valerie) was three. All were well taken care of. They had a nice house on a big acreage, they had a maid and they owned some good horses. And then, twenty-five years after the start of World War I, Germany invaded Poland on September 1, 1939, triggering World War II.

On September 17, Soviet Russia attacked Poland unexpectedly from the east thanks to a secret protocol attached to the Molotov–Ribbentrop Pact—a treaty of non-aggression signed by Germany and Russia just a month earlier. The two countries split Poland in two and pledged to remain neutral if a third party attacked either nation.

For about six months, Russian tanks overwhelmed the country and deportations of the intelligentsia began as Josef Stalin got rid of professors, scientists, doctors and artists. Next, the Soviets began nationalizing businesses, so shop owners and the middle class were arrested too. All in all, 1.7 million inhabitants of eastern Poland were classified as Soviet citizens of the second category and sent into the bowels of Russia.

At about three thirty on the morning of February 10, 1940, there was a loud and terrible pounding on the Konopkas' front door. The family's two big blond Labradors, Rex and Lord, scrambled for purchase across the hardwood foyer. Both were barking furiously. The maid hurried down the hallway, quickly tying her housecoat about her waist. She opened the door and screamed as two Russian soldiers holding machine guns burst in. Katarzyna joined them, clutching her dressing gown tight to her chest. The soldiers ordered her to get herself and the children dressed and to pack up just what they could carry.

Katarzyna pleaded with them to wait for her husband, who was away on business. He was supposed to return the next day. But they told her there was no time. The Germans were preparing to attack, they lied. They bullied her—where exactly was Martin? She insisted she didn't know, and they let her go. Katarzyna ran to get her children ready. She was in tears as she shook them awake, telling them to get up and to dress in several layers of clothing, as many as they could. Meanwhile, the maid frantically stuffed as many of her mistress's good clothes and jewels as she could into a large suitcase.

Four-year-old Zenon was waiting in the hall, rubbing his sleepy eyes, when in came a Russian captain dressed in his army-green tunic and jodhpurs with big black boots. He spotted Katarzyna running around and smiled at her reassuringly. He told her not to panic and to stop crying, that she and her family would be taken good care of. He told her she would be travelling far by train and that she and the children would need warm clothing and to take some dishes and food because they were not going to be fed for some time. He patted Zenon on the head and said, "Of course, you have small children, so bring milk."

Zenon ran into the kitchen, where the maid was filling another suitcase full of dishes and cooked food, everything they had in the house. Zenon pulled up a stool to reach the cupboards and packed his pockets full of pierogies, pastries and cookies.

The family was taken to the nearest train station. That day, 175,000 others in the country were ordered to board cattle cars already full of people. Katarzyna hesitated. There was no room in the wagon! But she and the children were pushed forward into fifty voices full of shouts and questions. Little Elżbieta looked around in the dimness. There was only one small window near the top of the wall, and the car was freezing. Early February meant the days were short and cloudy, with almost always a little snow or rain, and the cast-iron stove in the middle of the car had no fuel. She spotted a hole in the floor, and when her mother explained that it was to be used as the toilet, she blushed. How could she be expected to do her business in public?

The doors were slammed and bolted, thrusting them into near pitch darkness. At one end of the car there was a little platform in the corner, and Katarzyna was invited to use part of it for her and her children. Many of the people in the car worked for her father, who was a fair and generous man, and so they were kindly disposed toward her.

The soldiers met Martin on his way home the following day. They refused to let him into his house. Instead, they took him straight to the station. Martin pulled up in front of the cattle cars in his huge sleigh drawn by four horses, and several train car doors were opened as he searched for his family. Finding them gave him a mixture of relief and sorrow. Thankfully, he had a wagon full of food and supplies. Most of it was pushed into the car with him.

The train didn't move for two weeks. Some of the people cried quietly and most prayed, but there was little commotion. Even the children stayed still. The car doors were rarely opened because the guards feared their passengers would escape. Conditions continued to deteriorate. The smell in the car was sickening. Every breath filled their noses and throats with a musty and bloody burn from the stench of human feces and vomit. Most had brought very little food, so Katarzyna shared what she could, but nobody ate much anyway. One day, little Zenon surprised the family with the pierogies and cookies he had stored in his pockets.

The biggest problem was getting water. Each car was given a small jug to share every few days. Everyone was dirty and dehydrated, especially the children. Polish people in the area brought food, water and milk and stood outside the train cars, begging the Russian soldiers to open the door just a little.

At the beginning of the third week, the train started to move. By then, everyone had heard they were headed to Siberia. As the trains pulled out of the station, the people in every car came together in one tearful voice, singing, "We will not abandon our land."

Occasionally they would stop along the route and the door would open. A Russian soldier would poke his head in and ask, "Is anybody dead?" Bodies were thrown out into the snowy ditches along the tracks. People were allowed out to melt snow for water and to relieve themselves. The soldiers knew they wouldn't escape. Where to?

Finally, they arrived near the large city of Sverdlovsk, now called Yekaterinburg. It's the fourth-largest city in Russia, located at the foot of the Ural Mountains, right on the border between Europe and Asia. The people were told to unload and then were forced to walk for hours until they reached their new home—a set of poorly constructed barracks. Each family was assigned to one room, but many of the parents were forced into hard labour. Six days a week, Martin and Katarzyna were sent deep into the forest to cut trees and send them down the river to other prisoners who were building a railroad track, which would never be completed. The Konopkas worked in the wet snow from 5 a.m. until well after dark. And then, on Sundays, because there was only one travel permit per family, either Martin or Katarzyna would make the twenty-kilometre walk back to the barracks to check on the children. Weekdays, Elżbieta, who was now eight years old, was in charge of the children, who were always hungry. There was so little food—no breakfast, soup for lunch and only a small ration of bread for supper. Fortunately, Katarzyna had packed some beautiful clothes and jewellery that she was able to sell to the commandant's wife for a cup of milk here and there.

Katarzyna had also brought along her greatest treasure, a blue crystal statue of Jesus. Martin's mother had given it to her when Elżbieta was a toddler and very ill. Katarzyna was told that if she prayed to Jesus, her child would live. The statue was sacred to the family.

Under Stalin's orders, Russians were not allowed any religious icons. Communism dictated that there was no God. One day, the camp commander came through the door for inspection, machine gun at his side. He picked up the statue and turned it over, examining it, then held it up, intending to smash it on the floor. Little Zenon ran over to him and raised his hands in protest. "Don't touch it!" he yelled. "That's God! We pray to Him. Put it down."

The commander looked at Zenon and then placed the statue gently back on the table. "You are a brave little boy," he said.

A little while later, the men in the forest camp were gathered to hear a speaker talk about the glories of Russia and about how lucky and proud they should all feel now that they were part of such a great country under a great leader like Stalin. After the meeting, Martin walked out with a friend. He told the man, "I wish lightning would strike the great Stalin dead." Someone overheard him, and Martin was arrested. Several people had already been shot for treasonous remarks. As his family wept and waited for news of his fate, Martin held firm in insisting he said no such thing. Finally, the same camp commander intervened and Martin was released.

On June 22, 1941, Hitler organized a surprise attack on the Soviet Union. General Wladyslaw Sikorski, head of occupied Poland's government-in-exile, had taken refuge in England. He signed a treaty with the Soviets leading to the pardon of the captured Poles, and a Polish army was organized in Russia to fight against Hitler.

Martin immediately signed up so that his family would be allowed to leave Siberia for Uzbekistan. From there, the family went to Persia—modern-day Iran. When they crossed the border, they were met by members of the Polish army, who had organized hot showers for the family. Their heads were shaved, their filthy clothes were discarded and they were given a warm meal and new, clean clothes.

Katarzyna and the children lived in Tehran for six months. They were housed in tents, with no ground sheets or any kind of floor, but in comparison to Russia, it was heaven. The Persians were exceptionally kind to the Poles, bringing them boiled eggs and pickles. They were given all they could eat, but hundreds were dying due to typhus, dysentery and the effect of the new abundance of food on their starving stomachs.

Persia couldn't possibly accommodate all the people who were flooding in for refuge, so they were dispersed to several countries. Some went to Lebanon and other parts of North Africa, and some to Mexico. The Konopkas were sent to East Africa, but they first stopped in Karachi, India, which is now in Pakistan.

India was incredibly hot. The children had to be very careful because of all the snakes in the area, and there was something in the air, so they all had sore and watery eyes.

While Martin fought in Montecito, Italy, his family settled just outside of Arusha in Tanzania, seventy miles from Nairobi. They were on the first transport to arrive. The children loved it there. They went to school from eight o'clock in the morning until two in the afternoon and played soccer in the big fields nearby. Zenon especially loved all of the sports, and he became fluent in the local language. There was a high wire fence around the camp to protect them, but it was normal to see lions, giraffes, baboons, African buffalo and gazelles. The mosquitoes were very bad, and everybody got sick with malaria, but the quinine tablets they took daily did seem to help.

When the Polish soldiers joined the Allies, both England and the United States promised they would be able to return home after the war. But that became impossible. Poland was under communist rule, and the few Polish soldiers on the first transport home from Italy were arrested once they arrived and were taken back to Russia as enemies. Martin and many others felt Poland had been betrayed by England and the United States at the Yalta Conference, a wartime summit meeting between US president Franklin Roosevelt, British prime minister Winston Chuvrchill and Stalin in 1945.

Stalin wanted Poland. He said it was not only a matter of honour but also "a question of security." He said Poland was a corridor for Russia's enemies. Roosevelt wanted Russia to participate in the United Nations and to join the Allies in the Pacific War, so he acquiesced. It wasn't until three weeks before Roosevelt's death that he understood he had made a deal with the devil. He told his advisors, "We can't do business with Stalin. He has broken every one of the promises he made at Yalta."

The war ended, but the odyssey of the Konopka family continued. Katarzyna and the children stayed in Africa until 1947 before finally joining Martin in England. Martin had a choice of going to either Canada or the United States, but because he felt Roosevelt had betrayed his country, he chose Canada, where after the war Polish soldiers were contracted to work on farms. In exchange, they were offered citizenship, wages and accommodations for their families.

Martin's family arrived in St. Catharines, Ontario, in November 1948. Martin had a cousin there. When he completed his farm labour contract, he got a job at General Motors, where he worked until his retirement. He missed his country, but fortunately, there were a number of Polish veterans around St. Catharines, so Polish clubs sprung up throughout the community and people adjusted.

When Zenon arrived in Canada with his mother and sisters, he was nine years old. Zenon loved everything about his new country, especially hockey. He couldn't afford skates, but one day he found a discarded pair that someone had put out with the garbage. They were too small, but it didn't matter—he was just so excited to own a pair. He was really musical as well. He could sing and play all kinds of instruments, including the accordion and piano. He joined Polish clubs and the Polish Legion as an associate member and played trumpet with the orchestra.

Having lived through the toughest conditions possible didn't harden him or take away his joy in life. It made him resilient. He backed away from nothing. In the 1960s, it was common for a fight to break out at a community dance. Zenon wasn't a big man, but he was powerfully built and handsome, with Slavic blond hair and lashes. He also had the biggest hands you ever saw and a presence that warned others not to mess with him. If any of his friends were threatened, he would stick up for them with his fists.

Zenon was twenty-seven years old when he spotted Arlene at a Polish club dance in Buffalo, New York. He asked her to dance, and they talked a bit. Afterward, Arlene really didn't think much about it. She was only sixteen and was dreaming about her upcoming prom. All her girlfriends had boyfriends, but nobody had a car to get there. And then she remembered Zenon. He had a car. She knew he belonged to the Polish soccer club, so she wrote him a letter. She lied to her mother about his age, telling her he was only twenty-one. But at the prom, something unexpected happened—Arlene fell in love with him. They married when she turned eighteen.

After two beautiful daughters, Cynthia and Celeste, they had a boy. They called their baby son Zenon, after his father. Zenon's friends called him Big Zee, and so the kid became Little Zee. When he was born, Little Zee was all Zenon talked about at work. He was so proud and excited. He made a promise to himself—his son was going all the way to the NHL.

The youngest group of players in organized hockey in St. Catharines was seven years old, but Zenon signed his four-year-old son up anyway. Little Zee didn't touch the puck once the whole season. The next year, he scored a goal. At six, he scored a lot more, and then, when he was seven, the kid scored eighty goals.

Zenon figured that the more Little Zee played, the better he'd be. So by the time his son was seven, he belonged to five different teams. He played in St. Catharines in a house league and for a select team, for a team in Merritton (a community in St. Catharines) and on house league and select teams in Niagara-on-the-Lake. He had ice time nine times a week. Little Zee would finish a game at Niagara-on-the-Lake and his dad would simply pick him up off the ice, throw him over his shoulder, strap him in the car—still dressed in his equipment and skates—drive him to St. Catharines, carry him into the arena, where a new game was already in progress, and drop him right on the ice to play.

Hockey ruled their lives. Between games one day, Arlene and the girls were in one car and Zenon and Little Zee were in another. The road was slippery and Zenon's car slid into a ditch. So he grabbed Little Zee and traded vehicles with Arlene. He told her, "Wait here with the girls for CAA—we've got to get to the arena."

Before Little Zee was old enough to play novice, the family took a winter vacation in Florida every year. Then Big Zee decided that hockey was more important, so there were no more winter trips. Father and son were together every minute that Big Zee wasn't working. Every day was taken up with baseball, hockey and roller hockey.

In the car, they listened to music that Little Zee liked, unless it was between 7 and 8 p.m., when one of the local stations played an hour of Polish music. When Little Zee got older, it would drive him up the wall. He'd say, "Tata, why are we listening to this garbage?" And Big Zee would reply, "It's not garbage, it's where you came from!" And then he'd launch into the family history and how his son should be proud of his roots. If Little Zee continued to complain, Big Zee would weave down the road, singing loudly to songs like Frankie Yankovic's "Who Stole the Kishka?" just to make Little Zee laugh.

Zenon's son saw him as a loving but very intimidating person. There was never a shortage of hugs and kisses for his children, but he commanded a room. When he came home from work at three thirty, if the kids were watching TV, Arlene would yell a warning—"Dad's home!"—and the TV would be off. By the time he was through the door, books and homework were out on the table.

He wasn't extravagant, but he bought his son the very best skates and sticks. There was never debate about eating. Whether or not you liked Brussels sprouts or broccoli, you finished your food. The little boy who'd hidden pierogies in his pockets so his family wouldn't starve didn't spank, he just had to give a look.

Zenon worked his way up to manager of the tool grind at General Motors. He saved his money and managed to buy fifty-three acres of farmland plus another fifteen acres of fruit trees on the outskirts of Niagara-on-the-Lake, three minutes from St. Catharines. The Konopka family grew apples, grapes, pears and plums and had 2,800 apple trees. The region was part of the wine boom in the Niagara fruit belt. Now, instead of a nine or ten-hour day, Big Zee worked fourteen.

He worried that his son wouldn't be tall enough to play hockey. There weren't a lot of tall people in the family. Big Zee claimed he was five foot eleven and a half, but he was really five-ten or so. He heard that sleep would help a boy grow, so he wanted Little Zee to sleep an extra hour in the mornings. So every day, instead of taking the bus, the kids were driven to school by Arlene. Big Zee also heard that whole milk instead of two per cent would add height, so they bought only homogenized milk. Someone told him lentils make you strong, which meant Little Zee ate vats of lentil soup and drank shakes with brewer's yeast. Thanks to his diet, sleep and constant exercise from playing sports, when Little Zee was twelve he was getting noticeably bigger and stronger.

Father and son would never miss *Hockey Night in Canada*. During commercial breaks, they'd often wrestle around. When the game came back on, Big Zee would say, "Okay, enough." But one time, Little Zee said, "No!" and kept on wrestling. Big Zee said, "No, enough, you're done." But Little Zee ignored him. Suddenly, Big Zee grabbed him by the back of the neck and put his forearm up against the boy's throat. It got to a point some might consider a little bit over the line, but the message was received loud and clear. "Okay, I guess we're done."

Big Zee had been extremely tough on Little Zee when he was six, seven and eight years old. After a hockey game, he'd yell and scream at him about his performance. The team played in Welland one time and lost 3–2, with Little Zee scoring both of his team's goals. Big Zee was angry and ranting, and Little Zee was crying and defending himself. Big Zee shot back, "Well, you didn't win, did you?" When Little Zee turned nine, his father did an about-face. No one was sure why, but there was no more yelling, it was just, "You played well. You tried your best."

Big Zee wanted to sign his son up for boxing lessons. However, Arlene was dead set against it. She said, "I don't want him getting hit in the head." Big Zee told her not to worry. "They've got the helmet on and all this gear." But she put her foot down. So he took Little Zee to classes without her knowing. The kid was good at it. He had a knack. Big Zee thought knowing how to fight would come in handy in the schoolyard. Young Zenon had a bit of a temper and got into a lot of fights. One time at the rink, he was trading punches with a kid who scratched up his face. Big Zee demanded to speak with both of them. He stared at them sternly as they stood in front of him, and then he said, "Okay, now let's finish this fight. No scratching this time."

By 1993, Young Zenon was playing Peewee Minor AAA in Niagara Falls with the Niagara Falls Thunder. It was a good team, but they hadn't won the OMHA championship in twenty years. With a population of only 75,000, Niagara Falls was too small to compete against cities of 120,000, like Oakville, or 250,000, like Brampton. Normally, the Thunder would get to the provincial semifinals and just get hammered. Then, when Little Zee was twelve years old, a friend of Big Zee's, Al Boone, became their coach. Zenon was named captain, and the team went all the way, beating Barrie in the provincial finals. It was a Cinderella story. The Thunder headed back to Niagara Falls and celebrated at a pizza place until 5 a.m., playing pinball, eating pizza and wings and sneaking celebratory sips of beer from Big Zee. Little Zee couldn't stop smiling. Life just didn't get better than this.

Big Zee loved celebrating the Victoria Day weekend. Each year, they'd invite all the kids' friends and neighbours over to enjoy Polish food and fireworks. Their house on the farm was on a hill, with a basement walkout. It was a perfect place to set off a spectacular display. By Victoria Day weekend in 1994, Big Zee was a month retired from General Motors and he'd just bought another little farm. Young Zenon's class was going to Quebec City for a school trip that weekend, but Big Zee vetoed it. Arlene said, "What's the big deal?" And Big Zee replied, "One, a waste of money. Two, he should stick around here, maybe practise some sports."

On May 23, as Big Zee got ready for the party, he pulled Little Zee aside and gave him a top-of-the-line hardball bat, a black aluminum Louisville Slugger TPS. He said, "You're going to hit a lot of line shots with this."

It was a fun day and night. All the cousins and buddies were over, the fireworks were bigger and better than ever, and they built a huge bonfire. The celebration didn't end until the wee hours of the morning.

The next morning, Big Zee slept in, which was extremely rare. When he came into the kitchen, he was in a great mood. He hugged Arlene and danced her around a bit. They had a coffee together, and then he said, "I'm going to go to the barn for a bit." She smiled and tapped his cheek. "You know, I don't think anyone is married twenty-nine years and so in love as we are." Big Zee kissed her again and said, "That's true, Mama," and walked out.

Arlene was bustling around, cleaning up after the party, when she heard all the sirens. She looked out the back window and could see fire trucks whizzing by. She thought, "Wow, it must be something big happened."

A few minutes later, the doorbell rang and there stood a policeman. Thinking he was there for some kind of fundraiser, Arlene turned to grab her purse but stopped in her tracks when he said, "Mrs. Konopka, I'm sorry to tell you there was an accident and your husband was involved." Arlene said, "What? He just went to the barn about a half hour ago." She looked out into the yard. "No, that's impossible. You've made a mistake. My husband's van is here."

The policeman looked at her. "Oh my God," she said. "Was there a tractor involved in this accident?" Big Zee would sometimes take the tractor from the barn and go down the side road to the next farm to pick up manure for the field.

He said, "Yes, there was a tractor involved." Arlene held her hands over her face, "Oh my God."

The officer moved toward her. "Can I please come in and call someone for you?"

She grabbed his arm. "Is he okay?"

The officer shook his head. "I'm sorry to tell you that he passed."

Arlene said, "No. Maybe he's in the hospital. How do you know?"

He said, "I'm sorry, Mrs. Konopka. They called the air ambulance, but before it got there, he was gone."

Zenon's three sisters came quickly. Arlene fell into them, crying. "Zenon's gone. Zenon's gone." The girls were in shock—their big, strong brother gone? "What? No. It can't be."

Arlene would tell the story again and again over the next few days. Zenon knew that the richer your soil was, the better your fruit was going to be. About two kilometres down the road, there was a horse farm. Zenon had made a deal with his neighbour to trade apples in exchange for horse manure, which he used as fertilizer. That morning, Zenon was driving down the road on their big four-tonne tractor. He was turning left into the neighbour's farm when the car behind him decided to pass. The tractor was across the road, almost in the driveway, when the car hit the big back wheel. The tractor started to spin, so Zenon dove into the ditch. His arms were stuck in the mud up to his elbows, but he was alive. And then the tractor hit a tree and somersaulted backward, flying through the air. The spreader bar came down on the back of Big Zee's neck and broke it.

News of his death hit the airwaves fast. Arlene sent her in-laws to the school to pick up her girls before they heard about their dad from someone else.

Little Zee loved that he could sleep in, because when he was sleeping, it meant he wasn't picking apples or working on the farm. His bedroom was downstairs. The ringing of the doorbell woke him, but he pulled the covers over his head and went back to sleep. A little while later, something was happening upstairs. He could hear the commotion, but he closed his eyes and went to sleep again. Finally, he got up and walked past the bottom of the stairs on his way to the bathroom. He could hear his aunts crying. He thought, "What the hell is going on in my house?" and bounded up the stairs to investigate. When he entered the living room, his mom grabbed him and said, "There was an accident."

Everyone was crying. He looked around for Big Zee, but he wasn't there. He threw his arms around his mom and held her for a long time. By the time he'd let her go, his childhood was gone.

People say you're in shock the day you hear news like that. Young Zenon suspended it, for years. He didn't want to talk about it, didn't want to deal with it. The old-school European mentality held. Don't wear your emotions on your sleeve. Move on, get past it. He didn't want to hear anything about his dad, and he didn't like it when people talked about their dads, either. It hurt.

Hundreds and hundreds of people showed up for the funeral and crowded inside the forty-three-year-old local Polish church, Our Lady of Perpetual Help, a red-brick building with two impressive white spires and colourful stained-glass windows. As the family entered, Zenon saw all the kids from Denis Morris High School, which he and his sisters attended. They created a hallway of candles as they lined both sides of the tall stairway and all the way down the carpet on either side of the pews.

At the viewing, which took two and a half days, Young Zenon, now the man of the family, stepped up, shaking hands and accepting condolences. The other men in his family and his father's friends all came up to him and reminded him, "You have to be strong for your mother and sisters," and yet, when they said it, they were crying. Hundreds of men were openly weeping.

Arlene came into Young Zenon's room a few days after the funeral and noticed a little handmade sign he'd tacked up on his wall. It had three letters—NHL—coloured in with crayons. "Oh that's nice," she thought. "He has that dream."

But when hockey season came around, Little Zee just didn't seem to have the same heart for it. As soon as he'd get on the ice he'd feel upset, bitter and confused.

And politics in kids' hockey being what they are, after the Thunder won the championship a year earlier, the president of the local minor hockey association decided he was going to coach the team, so his dad's friend Al Boone was out. When that didn't work out, the president stepped down but gave the team to his nephew to coach, and the team still struggled. Finally, when Zenon was fifteen, the nephew quit and Boone was invited back, and Zenon started to get his mojo back.

The team was now called the Niagara Falls Canucks. Al coached with a professional attitude. He had four assistants, and they all wore suits. They kept stats, goals, assists, plus/minus, shots, checks and faceoffs. Al fostered Zenon's competitiveness. Unlike most coaches, Al was no bag skater. He worked on systems and encouraged his players to follow them. Under his guidance, the team won the OMHA minor bantam championship that year.

Zenon was drafted in the fifth round by the Ottawa 67's, one of the best teams in the country. They had twelve returning forwards, plus three guys in the draft ahead of him. They'd lost in the OHL finals two years in a row. Brian "Killer" Kilrea's team was full of top-line guys, guys like Mike Bell, Matt Zultek, Dan Tessier, Justin Davis. Knowing he didn't have a prayer of making it, Zenon headed for camp anyway.

Kilrea was looking for guys who were a little unconventional, maybe even a bit of trouble, but who got the job done. A lot of people thought Killer wanted tough guys, but what he wanted was guys who were tough-skinned. He'd yell and scream and swear, and he needed players who could take it. And when two forwards broke their hands at camp, miraculously, Zenon was in. His first year there, the 67's won the Memorial Cup. His third year, they won the OHL championship, and his final year, 2001–02, he led the league in assists.

Zenon went from the OHL to the American League, with the Wilkes-Barre/Scranton Penguins, and then the Wheeling Nailers of the ECHL, under coach John Brophy, and back to the AHL. But Zenon wasn't a great skater. He had to work hard to catch up to the speed of the game. He knew the only way he'd be able to stick around was to fight. That was fine—he was young and invincible.

He still refused to talk much about Big Zee and used his anger to scrap his way through. And then one day he got the tap. The Anaheim Mighty Ducks called him up. That's when it hit him that, if somebody had asked Big Zee, "Would you give your life for your son to play in the NHL?" he would've said, "Yeah, take it." In Zenon's head, he felt his dad had literally died so that he could have a great life and play in the NHL. He was going to take that gift and make his dad proud.

With the girls and Zenon moved out, Arlene decided to sell the farm. As she was packing up, she walked into Zenon's room and saw the little NHL sign he had made after the funeral. She smiled and pulled it off the wall. There was something written on the back. She turned it over and read, "I will make it to the NHL."

After a nine-year NHL career with the Mighty Ducks of Anaheim, Columbus Blue Jackets, Tampa Bay Lightning, New York Islanders, Ottawa Senators, Minnesota Wild and Buffalo Sabres, Zenon signed with a professional team in Poland—KH Sanok—in February 2015. The team competes in the country's top league, Polska Hokej Liga. Zenon's grandmother Katarzyna was born in Sanok. It's two and a half hours from Lviv, the home stolen from his family seventy-five years earlier, when the Russians showed up on a cold winter's night.

Castlegar

BRITISH COLUMBIA

POPULATION:
7,816

The Role Player

Marcel Dionne has strong ties to St. Catharines from his time on the St. Catharines Black Hawks. One night I was out to referee an OHA Junior C game in Glanbrook Township, and Marcel was in the lobby. He was helping coach Chippewa.

"Look at that guy, always smiling," he said, referring to me.

In one simple phrase, the Hall of Fame player lifted me to that place that a compliment takes a person. Marcel had that gift. In Los Angeles, he took rookies Luc Robitaille, Steve Duchesne and Jimmy Carson under his wing. He made Charlie Simmer and Dave Taylor stars.

Dionne was a spectacular player, a team player, wise and fun, and like Jason Dorland, known for helping others on the same boat including a young rookie named Steve Bozek.

The "Old Barn" in Castlegar in the 1960s and '70s was a half oval shared with the curling club. The roof wasn't really solid—kids would show up to play and get rained out. Sometimes they played anyway, but the rain made the ice lumpy, so the dads and the caretaker would be chopping away at it before the whistle.

You'd walk into the building and the smell would punch you in the nose—popcorn, hot dogs and hot chocolate, mixed with old wood, chest protectors, pants, gloves, shin guards and skates. It got more pungent as you neared the dressing rooms, which made your heart race with excitement.

There was no glass along the boards, just wire mesh behind the goals, and there was hardly any seating, so most of the dads stood and yelled from the sidelines.

Steve Bozek lived next door to his best friend, Brian Verigin. They met when they were five and they grew up together. Castlegar winters are too warm now, but back then the Verigins always had a rink in their backyard. When it snowed, Steve was the Tom Sawyer of the group. He'd watch out his window for Brian to finish shovelling, and then he'd head out. There was a whole group of five or six guys who were fairly good hockey players—Steve, Brian, Bruce Martin, Gordy Pace and Dave Kanigan. In most small towns, friends do what their friends do.

At seven fifteen every Sunday morning, they'd get up and head down to the Barn. They'd walk into the pitch black, and one of the parents would feel around for the power panel to turn the lights on. The ice would get brighter and brighter, and after about five minutes you could see the puck. It was so cold in the rink that after practice when the boys loosened their skates, their feet would burn so much they'd get tears in their eyes.

Steve's dad, Big John, was a pipe fitter at the Castlegar pulp mill. There were always things bursting, and he was the guy responsible for fixing them. He wasn't a big guy—five foot ten, 170 pounds—and he was a bit of a curmudgeon. He wasn't a smoker either, but in the locker room and behind the bench, he'd walk around with a rolled-up paper napkin and put it between his lips and puff away. Legendary habs GM Sam Pollock did that too. Big John didn't believe in the reward system. He was old school that way, strict and regimented. He worked a lot on fundamentals and conditioning and was ahead of his time in believing that skating made the difference. You had to be able to know how to stop and turn both ways. His philosophy was put yourself in good position and skate well, outlast the other team, and you will win. Basic hockey.

Big John coached Steve and his group of friends on the rep team all the way through from the time they were eight to when they were twelve. The rep team was made up of all the best players from house league. Like a lot of fathers, he figured if he was going to take his kid down to the rink, he might as well do something useful.

In the 1970s, the defencemen were the bigger, less mobile kind of athletes who hacked and whacked and cross-checked guys, and coaches would put the guy who couldn't skate in net. Being really agile and able to get in and out of the corners was Steve's ticket. He was wind on ice, but he didn't have size, so Big John cut steel, weighed it and welded a set of homemade weights together for him, and he shellacked Steve's skates to protect his toes.

By the time they got to Grade 12, both Steve and Brian had tried out for a couple of major junior teams, but neither wanted to take the path through the WHL. They both wanted to continue their education. So they wrote to all kinds of universities to try to get scholarships. Nobody replied—the University of Denver, Colorado College . . . nobody.

By this time, the town had a new rink, and Mark Pezzin had been recruited to start up a junior team, the Castlegar Rebels. He pulled the five boys up from midget onto his roster and they won the Kootenay International Junior League championship in their inaugural year and the next year as well.

Pezzin heard that Northern Michigan University in Marquette, Michigan, was starting up a Division I hockey program. He reached out to Rick Comley, the coach, and told him he had a couple of players who were really good, especially one of his defencemen, Brian Verigin. He told Comley these boys wanted to go to college but nobody had yet seen them. Comley, who didn't have a full-time assistant coach, had to make the most of his time and money. He'd had some luck recruiting five kids from a team in Bramalea, Ontario. In fact, Donny Waddell was his first recruit—he's now the president of the Carolina Hurricanes. Comley felt that finding pockets of kids would make it easier to get his program off the ground, so he decided to take a chance and sent a young graduate assistant named Rod Hooktwith to see the boys. Rod flew to Spokane and was supposed to make the three-hour drive straight north to Castlegar when Comley got a call. "Coach, I'm trying to get to Castlegar, but I have to go up through this mountain pass and they won't let me without tire chains. What should I do?" Comley said, "Well, get some chains on the damn tires, then."

Rod made it to the arena, and during the second period Comley got another call. "Coach, I like Verigin a lot, I think he's going to be a good player, but there's another kid here that I think is a can't-miss player." He was talking about Steve.

Comley made the drive during the playoffs to see for himself. Were Castlegar and this Bozek kid the little gold mine his junior assistant said they were?

By the end of the first game, he was convinced. Bozek was young and still growing and maturing, but his skating ability was something else. While everyone else on the ice worked to get from point A to point B, for Bozek there was no effort at all. He could change direction without changing speed, and his lateral movement was as fast as his straight-ahead skating. He was so shifty that you'd think you had him when all of a sudden he was gone at full speed in a different direction.

Comley saw Steve as a new wave of player with the dynamic of a Richard or a Lafleur. The game is just so much easier for players who have the luxury of that kind of talent. Steve and Brian jumped at the chance to play for the only school offering them a scholarship.

Steve was in great shape. In some ways, he frustrated the other players because he never got tired. They'd be gasping for air and he was ready to skate another hour. He could run, he could skate and he had brains. On the ice, he could see the opportunities shaping up. It seemed he was always in the right place at the right time.

The second year, Comley went back to Castlegar and recruited the other boys—Gordie Pace, Bruce Martin and Dave Kanigan—and the Castlegar boys became a strong nucleus of the Northern Michigan Wildcats. That year, they finished 34–6–1, taking the Central Collegiate Hockey Association regular-season championship and the CCHA playoff tournament champion-ship. They were on their way to the NCAA Frozen Four.

They played North Dakota in the championship game. Northern Michigan had beaten UND twice just after Christmas in Marquette, even though five players on North Dakota's roster would be taken in the NHL draft. But Comley had a big problem—his goalie, Steve Weeks, had pulled a hamstring the weekend before in Minnesota.

There was a game on Thursday, a game on Friday and then the championship game on Saturday. North Dakota played Thursday and won, so they rested until Saturday. The Wildcats played the top-seeded team, Cornell, on Friday. The game was very physical, but the Wildcats won, and so they met North Dakota on Saturday in what was one of the first major championships to be televised on the brand new ESPN network.

Weeks was hurt, but he gave it his all. The Wildcats fell behind and battled back, pulling ahead 4–2, but just couldn't pull it off in the end.

In 1980–81, Jeff Pyle, another tremendous college player, and Steve both had about ninety points, and Northern Michigan made it to the Frozen Four again, this time losing to Wisconsin in the semifinals.

But Bozek was drafted and Pyle had an offer to play pro. Sitting in a hotel room in Duluth, Minnesota, after getting beaten a second year in a row in the Frozen Four, Comley asked the boys what they were going to do. They insisted they were coming back. The fourth year was going to be the ticket. But the pros were dangling money in front of them. Steve was offered $65,000 to join the Los Angeles Kings, and in the end he took it.

At Steve's first training camp in 1981, Charlie Simmer broke his ankle, so Steve was put up on left wing with Dave Taylor and Marcel Dionne. He had twenty-seven goals in the first thirty-four games. His coach, Parker MacDonald, had him flying, but the team wasn't winning, and so MacDonald was fired in January.

Don Perry came in. He was a coach who insisted on positional play. Perry wanted Steve to just go up and down, up and down, up and down. He told Steve it would cost him a hundred dollars any time he ventured more than six lengths away from the left wing boards. This changed Steve's game completely, and he scored only six goals the rest of the year.

Dionne ended the season with 117 points, but that was the year Gretzky scored 92 goals and had 215 points. An average game between the Kings and Edmonton would result in a solid thrashing—Edmonton 8, Kings 3.

Steve was a rookie. Bernie Nicholls was a rookie. Daryl Evans was a rookie. Doug Smith was a rookie. But when they came up against Edmonton in the first round of the playoffs, they had somehow convinced themselves they were good enough to go up against Gretzky, Glenn Anderson, Paul Coffey, Mark Messier, Jari Kurri, Kevin Lowe, Dave Hunter, Lee Fogolin, Dave Semenko, Charlie Huddy, Randy Gregg, Grant Fuhr, Andy Moog and Ron Low.

That confidence carried the Kings into a win in Game One of the 1982 Stanley Cup preliminary round, 10–8, in Edmonton. They lost the second game and headed back home to the Forum, which was located on Manchester Boulevard in Inglewood. On April 10, in Game Three, Edmonton had a point to prove and started pounding on the Kings. The Oilers were up 5–0 going into the third period. The Forum was already half empty when the Kings just started picking away. A goal here, another there. And before you knew it, the team had momentum. They got some breaks and started scoring. With four seconds left, Steve was standing right in front of the net and a shot came in. It came back to him and he backhanded it in to tie the game, 5–5. And then Evans scored in overtime. The Kings' Miracle on Manchester is still talked about by the old purple-and-gold fans. It stands as the biggest comeback in NHL playoff history.

The fourth game was a squeaker, 3–2 for the Oilers.

The Los Angeles Kings had so little faith in the team that they never dreamed there would be a fifth game, so there was no flight booked. This meant they had to join the Oilers on their charter flight back to Edmonton. It was about 3 a.m. as they waited together at the airport. Like at a high school dance, the Oilers sat on one side of the lounge with the Kings on the other. The Kings boarded first, heading to the back of the plane, and the Oilers sat at the front. It was a very, very silent plane ride.

The Kings took that fifth and final game 7–4, eliminating the Oilers from the playoffs. Steve closed out his rookie season with fifty-six points. He was traded to the Calgary Flames two years later, where Bob Johnson was the coach. Bob coined the term "role player" while talking about Steve. If everybody was healthy, Steve sat out, but as soon as somebody got hurt—and there are always going to be injuries—Steve was in at centre, or left wing or right wing, and the team didn't lose a step.

And then Johnson realized that, because of Steve's skating ability, he'd be a great penalty killer. He could hound the puck and take away time. Bob Johnson was a great teacher, an Xs-and-Os guy.

When Terry Crisp took over the team in 1987, he had an advantage—everyone knew how to play, knew their positions and knew their role. Terry was more of a yeller, a screamer. It was his way of motivating. He grabbed the reins of a team where all the pieces had come together, a team that was playoff hardened, and he took them over the goal line. But Steve wasn't the kind of hard-nosed player that Terry seemed to like. Gary Roberts was Terry's kind of guy. One night in Edmonton, when Steve was sitting out, he watched Gary go toe to toe with Mark Messier and he knew right then and there that he would never see the ice again.

Meanwhile, his teammate Brett Hull had battled his entire life to overcome the shadow of his dad, Bobby. Brett had played in Penticton of the B.C. Junior Hockey League and got a scholarship, scored fifty goals at the University of Minnesota-Duluth, got signed by Calgary and turned pro in '86 during the finals against Montreal. Everybody recognized his talent, but he wasn't considered a team guy, and because the Flames had so many good veterans, the fit wasn't there.

So on March 7, 1988, Brett Hull and Steve Bozek went to St. Louis for Rob Ramage and Rick Wamsley. Steve played ten games, but Ron Caron wanted him to take a pay cut. Steve didn't really understand why. The team had a fairly good run in the playoffs, beating Chicago, and all he heard was, "We want you to be a part of our future." He was making $185,000 and Ron wanted him to take $170,000. Steve was three days from moving into a new house in St. Louis when all of a sudden he got a call from Flames general manager Cliff Fletcher, who had just traded him six months earlier. Cliff told him he had just traded tough guys Mike Bullard, Tim Corkery and Craig Coxe to St. Louis for Doug Gilmour and Mark Hunter, along with a big defensive prospect named Michael Dark. He said he wasn't sure what had happened down in St. Louis, but Ron Caron wanted Steve included in the trade. "I have to take you back," he said.

Steve said, "What does that mean? What are you going to do?" Fletcher said, "We're going to try to move you right away."

"Well, what if you can't move me?" Steve asked. Cliff said, "Well, then, you'll be coming to camp as a Calgary Flame."

Steve got off the phone and called the movers. He said, "Don't unload anything. Keep it on the truck. I don't know where it's going." An hour later, he heard from Pat Quinn, who told him he was now a Vancouver Canuck. Steve belonged to three teams in one hour.

After three years in Vancouver, he signed as a free agent with the expansion San Jose Sharks. It was a fun year, but the team won only seventeen games. It appeared that Sharks management had decided that if you were over thirty, you weren't in their future plans. So with the exception of Doug Wilson and Kelly Kisio, the rest of the veterans were gone.

It's the unglamorous part of professional sports. At 10:30 p.m. on July 31, 1992, after twelve years in the league, Steve got a call from the Sharks, who told him, "Thank you for your time. We're buying out your contract. Good luck."

Steve hung up the phone and thought, "Well, I guess that's it. Forget the gold watch. Now what am I going to do with the rest of my life?"

Very few players leave the game on their own terms. Only the absolute superstars have that ability. Lanny McDonald did. He went out in a beautiful way, capping a sixteen-year career with the Stanley Cup, but for the majority of the guys, the end comes via a phone call.

Steve went back to Northern Michigan University, finished his degree and looked for an MBA program. He settled on

Harvard because all the other MBA programs talked about team-work. He figured he'd been on a team for twenty-something years and knew all about teamwork. Instead, he wanted a program that would teach him to stand on his own.

Today he's senior vice-president with Simon Property Group, the largest real estate company in the world. He's back in Boston, running a half-billion-dollar high-rise residential project.

Big John passed away in 2005. He had a bad heart. His first heart attack happened while playing sponge hockey in Trail when he was only forty-four years old. It just so happened that a cardiologist was playing too. So Big John hung around for another thirty years and managed to see his boy succeed in both hockey and business, and for Steve, that meant more than a truckload of gold watches.

Victoria

BRITISH COLUMBIA

———

POPULATION:
80,017

The Curse of the Leafs

The very same Terry O'Malley who played defence with Gerry Cheevers at St. Mike's in the '50s went on to become president and coach of the Notre Dame Hounds. His former boss and friend, Martin Kenney (the father of Jason Kenney, Canada's minister of both National Defence and Multiculturalism), died in 2010, but he always insisted there was a curse from heaven on the Leafs.

During the 1986 Stanley Cup playoffs, Notre Dame alumni Russ Courtnall, Wendel Clark—who was a rookie that year—and Gary Leeman made a name for themselves as the Toronto Maple Leafs' Hound Line. Russ made a special connection with Harold Ballard, who was the Leafs' owner at the time. Russ called up Martin Kenney, who was always fundraising, and said, "I think Harold Ballard is prepared to donate some money to the school."

So with Russ's help, Martin Kenney, along with Barry MacKenzie—who was also on the team with Gerry and Terry at St. Mike's and who was the principal and head coach at Notre Dame at the time—made an appointment to see Mr. Ballard and flew from Wilcox, Saskatchewan, to Toronto.

When they walked into the Leafs' front office and said, "We're here to see Mr. Ballard," the secretary said, "Well, he's not here."

Martin said, "I've got an appointment. Where is he?"

She said, "You might have an appointment, sir, but you're not going to have a meeting with him here. If you want to see him, he's up in the blues and he'll be there with King Clancy and

Gerry McNamara [the general manager], watching the practice." So Martin and Barry walked into the rink behind the blue seats and spotted the three men. Martin called out, "Mr. Ballard! Mr. Ballard!"

Ballard looked up. "Who the hell are you?"

"I'm Martin Kenney! I have a meeting with you!"

Ballard said, "Why the hell would I want to have a meeting with you?"

Martin nodded toward the ice. "Well, because of that Hound Line out there."

Ballard said, "Oh yeah! Come down here!"

Martin thought to himself, "This is going to be a good ask." The two men sat down in front of Ballard, who said, "So what's this about?"

Looking back over his shoulder, Martin started talking. "Well, I'm from Athol Murray's College, Notre Dame, where those boys down there—"

Mr. Ballard interrupted, "Oh, Athol Murray! I saved his life one time." And he went on to tell a story about how Père Murray was at a Stanley Cup final in April of 1964 in Detroit, when Leafs defenceman Bobby Baun broke his ankle, carried on and scored the game-winning goal in overtime, forcing a seventh game. While they were celebrating up at the hotel, Murray came up to Mr. Ballard and said, "Harold! You've run out of scotch!"

Mr. Ballard replied, "Yeah, that's 'cause you drank it all! If you want anything more to drink, you have to go into the bathroom. There's some beer in the bathtub."

"All of a sudden," Mr. Ballard said, he heard this crash, boom, bang, and so he jumped up and ran into the bathroom. There was Murray, headfirst in the tub. Mr. Ballard pulled him up. Père Murray's hair was stuck to his face like a drowned rat's as he gasped for air. "And you know what he says to me after I saved his life? 'Harold, damn that water's cold!'"

Ballard told Kenney that story and then said, "Let's cut to the chase. What do you want?"

Martin gave him the best line ever. He said, "Well, if I ask for too little, you'll think I'm stupid. If I ask for too much, you'll think I'm greedy. I'd much rather you think I'm greedy than stupid. I want a million dollars."

King Clancy jumped up laughing and said, "He's got you there, Harold! You've got to come up with it now!" Both McNamara and Clancy were ribbing Ballard because he'd got caught in the web.

And Ballard said, "Okay, you got it." Everyone was surprised. And then he added, "But you're going to have to wait 'til I croak. I'll put it in my will."

The thing is, Ballard never got around to changing his will. So after he died, Terry O'Malley, who was president of the college at the time, wrote a letter to Ballard's son. But Bill Ballard had been estranged from his father, so he directed Terry to Ballard's foundation. Terry wrote to the foundation, but they turned him down, saying Notre Dame didn't fit the criteria. Today O'Malley swears that you've got Notre Dame Hounds supporters like Father David Bauer, Athol Murray, Wild Bill Hunter and now Martin Kenney up above, saying that until the Leafs come up with that money, Martin Kenney was right. They will be cursed.

———————

*P*ère Murray used to travel with his team as a recruitment tool to showcase how good they were. The Hounds came out to Victoria, British Columbia, when Russ Courtnall was just a little kid, and his dad, Archie, took him to see them play. Archie was really impressed, especially because he knew local players who'd played for Murray. A couple of the boys had a tough time in and out of school, but they had come back not only better players but better people.

On the ride home, Archie told Russ, "You're going to go to that school someday." He worried about Russ becoming too soft growing up in a place where flowers bloomed all year. Archie was tough as nails. He grew up in Winnipeg, where they had a real winter. Russ thought Notre Dame sounded like a great idea— snow looked like a lot of fun. Archie just smiled. "Someday, Russ."

Russ thought Archie looked like John Wayne. Over six feet tall and tanned from working outdoors, with thick, windswept hair and green/hazel eyes. He was one great-looking guy. Men wanted to be like him and women adored him. He had a very deep, loud voice. He worked in a lumber mill where it was really loud, so his vocal cords got a constant workout. And Archie coached a lot, so he was always yelling across the soccer fields, baseball diamonds and hockey rinks. The family lived about a block away from school, and when supper was ready, Archie would stick his head out the front door and yell, "Dinner!" His voice carried such resonance that when he called for the kids, the doorbell chime would ring.

He started as a log scraper at the local mill and worked his way up to become general foreman. Archie didn't have the white-picket-fence upbringing he'd given his four kids, Cheryl,

Geoff, Russ and Bruce. His mom died after giving birth to him, and when his dad started drinking, Archie moved in with his grandparents. He was sent to boarding school with his brother in Winnipeg at a very young age, but when he was fifteen or so, his aunt took custody of the boys. She moved to Victoria, and so that's how they ended up there.

Archie wanted life to be different for his sons. Geoff was three years older than Russ, and so they were always at it, like most brothers. Bruce, the youngest, would become the toughest because they both picked on him, but beyond stealing carrots and apples out of people's gardens, they were good boys.

The boys often played more than one sport at a time. Saturdays they'd get up, eat, get ready for soccer and run to the car, throwing hockey gear into the back seat. Mom Kathy worked the snack shack and Archie ran the park and coached. The Courtnalls volunteered at every level. At home, Archie was handy. He finished the basement, and when they needed a new roof, he shingled it himself. He was a fun, happy, incredibly great guy.

Archie and Kathy would rent a cabin every year, and the family would sit around a bonfire while Archie and his buddies told stories. Sometimes Russ didn't know what the hell the adults were talking about, but he loved listening to Archie talk about his grandparents and his uncle, who were from England and moved to Canada in the early 1920s.

And then when Russ was twelve years old, Archie was offered a promotion at the mill that involved a move to Vancouver. It was the sort of thing he'd worked his whole life to achieve, the money was great and it meant a move up in the company chain. But Kathy didn't want to go, and so after several arguments Archie turned the promotion down. Unfortunately, the mill had already replaced him in his original job, and the disappointment he felt in himself destroyed him.

The boys noticed a change in their dad. Something was going on. He just wasn't the same. He became somebody they didn't know, a different human being. He wasn't the same coach, he wasn't the same father, he wasn't the same husband, he wasn't the same friend. He wasn't the same anything.

He lost a bunch of weight, dropping from 215 to about 175. He didn't eat, and he slept a lot. He'd come home from work, lie down in bed and then wake up later and watch TV all night. He'd quit smoking cigars years earlier, but he took up the habit again. When the boys woke up, the house would be heavy with the smell.

He hadn't been much of a drinker—maybe the odd beer or Bacardi and Coke, a little bit of wine at dinner. But he started drinking more, self-medicating. When Kathy and the kids talked to him, he was somewhere else. He'd drift off, and when he did answer he zeroed in on some mistake he'd made in the past.

For an entire year, his family watched Archie fall apart. Geoff was sixteen and dealing with his own teenage life. Cheryl was eighteen, so she was doing her own thing. Bruce was a little younger, so he didn't quite understand. That left Russ. Conversations were always hard for Russ—he was a really shy kid—so he didn't say much. But he *heard* everything. Watching the person he loved and respected more than anyone falling apart was just devastating.

There were arguments and a lot of blame. Archie talked constantly about the promotion he'd turned down. Kathy begged him to get help, and he did see a doctor who wanted to admit him into a sanatorium, but there was no way he was going into an institution. The truth was, he needed full-on therapy, a professional to talk to instead of just sitting there, going through everything himself.

Kathy tried reasoning with him, but it was impossible. He still had a job at the mill. They shuffled him around a bit, but he was making himself sick over a decision that had simply cost him an opportunity. Nobody could understand how somebody so strong and wonderful and well respected could be so weak and vulnerable and sad. Lots of people would tell Archie, "Come on, man, just snap out of it!" But the chemistry in his brain had changed. It was not something he could change back without help, which just compounded his shame and guilt.

Archie attempted suicide twice that year, but when he came home with his wrists all bandaged, he told the boys he'd had an accident at the mill. Kathy was worried about the kids, and so Archie moved in with the aunt who had raised him. They told the boys he was living with her so she could help him get better.

That August, Geoff was working at the Keg and Cleaver. Cheryl was with her boyfriend, who was playing for the Victoria Cougars. Bruce was away in Penticton with friends, and Russ and Kathy joined Archie's closest friend, Gary Simpson, and his family at a cabin in Powell River. The Courtnall kids called him Uncle Gary. He and Archie had gone to school together. Kathy really needed the break—it had been an awful year.

Russ and the Simpson kids were playing around the pier when a big RCMP boat pulled up. They asked to speak to Mr. Simpson and Kathy, so the kids ran inside to get them.

Uncle Gary and Kathy joined the RCMP in the living room, and the kids were sent into another room so the adults could talk in private. One of the kids was listening under the door and he thought he heard someone say that Russ's younger brother Bruce had died in an accident, and so for about a half an hour, Russ was just vibrating with worry.

Suddenly, Gary came in and grabbed all the kids. He loaded them into his boat and sped over to a little island near the cabin. He unloaded everybody but Russ and then whisked him back to the cabin, where Kathy was waiting. She'd been crying. She asked Russ to sit down beside her and she put her arms around him. Uncle Gary leaned forward in his chair and delivered the terrible news. Archie was dead by suicide.

A year later, Russ had just turned fourteen when Kathy got a call from Martin Kenney, who had taken over as president of Notre Dame after Père Murray died in 1976. Martin asked if Russ would be interested in coming to Notre Dame to go to school and play hockey. An alumnus from Victoria had heard about Archie's suicide and called up Kenney—"You know, he's got these young lads and perhaps to ease the pain, Russ, the middle boy, would be a good candidate to come to Notre Dame."

Kathy told Martin, "No, he can't go. He's too young, he can't come now." Martin thanked her, and then a week or two later at lunch hour, when Kathy was at work and he could speak to the boy directly, he called back and got Russ.

Russ loved hockey. Archie had always been his coach, and now that he was no longer there, Russ felt a big hole. Playing for the Hounds was an exciting opportunity and a new challenge. Mr. Kenney told him, "Hey, we think you are a good hockey player. We want you to come. Affordability isn't a problem." He explained that as long as his mom could come up with five hundred dollars, an alumnus would take care of the rest. Russ had never wanted anything more in his life. He told Mr. Kenney he'd be there. When Kathy got home from work, Russ told her he was going. She didn't like it, but she wouldn't stand in his way.

Four days later, Russ was on a plane to Regina. It was fate. His dad had promised him he would go to Notre Dame, and one year after he died, he got the phone call.

Gerry Scheibel, a no-nonsense teacher with a heart of gold who would become his bantam coach, picked Russ up at the Regina airport. But they got off to a rough start when they were halfway to Notre Dame and Russ slapped his forehead and said, "Mr. Scheibel, I forgot my hockey bag."

Gerry told Russ he could call home on Sunday nights after six, because long-distance rates were cheaper. That night, after a big dinner, Russ called Kathy from the Scheibel home and told her he'd made it safe and sound.

But the first week was tough. He was so homesick that, most nights, Russ cried himself to sleep. He couldn't wait to call home on Sunday. At six o'clock he ran to the only phone in the dorm and dialled. When he heard his mom's voice, he started bawling his eyes out, sobbing so hard he could hardly get the words out. Poor Kathy was beside herself. She said, "I haven't any money to send you an air ticket. But I'll find it and we'll get you home. You call me next Sunday."

Some of the guys had seen him crying. There was another kid from Victoria there, an older boy. He invited Russ to go for a walk to settle him down, and they hung out for a couple of hours before bedtime. Meanwhile, Kathy fretted and worried all week. She hardly slept a wink. But she managed to scrape together enough for airfare and then waited for Russ to call.

The following Sunday night, Russ got on the phone and said, "Hi, Mom! Everything's fine." He told her how many friends he'd made and how great it was at Notre Dame. And then he said, "I've got to go now. I've got to run," leaving her staring at the receiver in her hand.

Like the other boys, Russ was assigned three roommates, and they became close friends, like brothers. It was good to know that when you came back to your room, there was always someone to talk to. The students helped one another get through tough times, and so did their house parent, Phil Ridley. He was a young English teacher, in his early twenties. Phil was Mr. Good Chips personified. He'd played football in the Canadian Football League and hockey at Notre Dame. Whenever Russ had downtime, he'd go and sit in Phil's office for a conversation. Russ didn't share the truth about Archie's death. He said his dad had a heart attack. Everyone felt for Russ because he'd lost his dad at such a young age.

The summer after his first year at Notre Dame, a really good midget team in Victoria contacted Russ. He got talked into coming back home to play, but he regretted it and returned to Notre Dame for Grade 11. The coach that year, Barry MacKenzie, was phenomenal. He had a presence. When he walked into a building, everybody would say, "There's Barry MacKenzie, the coach of the Notre Dame Midget AAA team." No one had been able to live up to Russ's expectations after he lost Archie, until he played for Barry. Barry was just like Archie in many different ways. He was a disciplinarian—but not too strict—he had high morals and good principles, and he made Russ a better player and a better person. Russ loved playing for him because of the similarities to his dad.

If Barry saw a weakness in a kid, he'd work on it, but mainly he taught the boys to play defensive hockey. They had to play hard, finish their checks and do the right thing for the team. He saw that Russ was a talented offensive player who had tremendous speed, but he told Russ that, as much as his offensive skills might dominate, he couldn't sit back and not be responsible defensively.

Barry wanted the boys to block shots. Russ had never blocked a shot in his life, but Barry taught him to go down on his knees or to slide along, depending on the angle. Blocking a shot was a sign of a player's commitment to team play and to doing everything possible to win. While he didn't become a prolific shot blocker, Russ learned the value of putting the team before himself and how important it was to work together as a unit on the ice. Barry was also about respect, the discipline of respecting your opponent, your team and yourself. Archie was like that. When "O Canada" played during *Hockey Night in Canada*, he'd have his kids stand, hands by their sides.

Russ shared with Barry his dream to be an NHL player, and Barry saw how committed the boy was to learning. Barry thought Russ was like a sponge.

One day, Barry had a talk with the team, pointing out that if you're going to be an NHL player, there are two ways to get there. One is major junior and the other is college. He finished his talk by saying, "And by the way, we'll be very lucky if there are even two of you here that will make it to the NHL." Russ looked around and thought, "I wonder who the other one is going to be."

As it turned out, it was one of the defencemen on his team—a kid a year younger than Russ. A kid named Wendel Clark.

London

ONTARIO

POPULATION:
366,151

Tea for Two

London lies on the forks of the beautiful Thames River, which was cut by water from melting glaciers more than 15,000 years ago. It's the largest city in southwestern Ontario, home to the London Knights of the OHL and to the University of Western Ontario. People call it the Forest City, but there was a time in the early nineteenth century when trees were not popular. Local writer and historian Pat Morden writes that, in 1793, "trees were the enemy, standing in the way of construction and commerce." Toward the later part of the 1800s, the trees were almost all gone. In fact, the city looked so bare that by 1871, "15,000 trees were purchased at 25 cents each and planted along city streets and in the newly created Victoria Park."

NHLers from Nazem Kadri to Rob Ramage, Rick Nash to Brendan Shanahan, Drew Doughty, Craig MacTavish and Eric Lindros have grown up shaded by those magnificent nineteenth-century maples. The city has shaped some of the game's top players—players who either started there or came to play junior.

Brad Marsh is from London, but he now lives in Ottawa. I have so many memories of Brad. In the third round of the 1987 Stanley Cup playoffs, we were in Philadelphia as Brad's Flyers hosted Montreal. Our studio for "Coach's Corner" was half of a dressing room we shared with the Canadiens! Only a heavy curtain separated me from the Habs' trainers' table, where the players would receive pregame treatments. Can you imagine?

In the first intermission, Brad was my guest. He sat down next to me and, before we went live, Don Cherry said, "Brad me boy, you look like you're eighteen again. I've never seen ya skate so great!" And from the other side of the curtain, the Canadiens' Chris Nilan hollered, "B.S., Grapes. He's a lumberjack! A plodder from day one."

You should have seen Brad's face. I don't think he said ten words in the interview, and none were any more than a whisper. Actually, Don was right about Marsh's skating, but as they were preparing the team for the new four-on-four rules, assistant coach Ted Sator worked with Brad for two years building his leg strength and agility. Suddenly Brad was winning all the icing races. His son Patrick became a competitive speed skater, so there was an added benefit to Brad's hard work.

Brad drank tea, not coffee or soda, before games, and that reminds me of a story the wonderful writer Roy MacGregor told. It was the tail end of Brad's career, and he was a member of the Ottawa Senators. One night on the road, it was time for Sylvan Lake, Alberta, native Darcy Loewen's rookie dinner. The team dined lavishly and the rookie footed the bill. At dinner's end, Brad ordered ten shots of hundred-year-old cognac. Loewen was terrified his credit card wouldn't be able to cover the bill. Turns out Brad had been scheming with the waiter. The shot glasses were filled with iced tea.

---

*B*rad Marsh's spirit was developed on a front-yard rink in London. It was a big rink and the entire neighbourhood came to play. There was a fire hydrant in the middle, so everyone kept their heads up.

A lot of NHLers talk about how they could hardly wait to get outside after school to play shinny, even when it was thirty below. When it's that cold, you feel it behind your eyes. Sniff, and your nostrils stick together. Shinny means no refs, so you're on the honour system. No equipment means you're faster and lighter. And no coaches telling you what to do made room for a lot of dangling and dipsy-doodling. Somebody always raised the puck, so you'd get whacked in the shins a few times. Without boards, guys were always flying into the snow. Skating backwards meant hitting a rut and landing hard. None of it mattered. Late evening on a backyard rink is the closest thing to heaven. The smell of wet spit on your scarf, the reflection of the moon bouncing off pockmarked ice, and no other sounds but a dog barking at a car in the distance and your blades scraping the ice. You wouldn't come in until it got so dark you couldn't see the puck anymore.

Back in the day, when Brad played, minor hockey was just an extension of the corner pond. There were no AAA teams, no AA teams, no big travel teams. Organized hockey meant dividing the kids who signed up onto teams. Friends played with friends. The only difference between the games and shinny was that they were played on an indoor rink and had referees.

Brad's dad would pick him up outdoors somewhere. The kid had already been on the ice for hours. He'd jump into the car and away he went to his game. When it was over, Brad didn't bother to take off his skates. He was dropped back off at the pond for a few more hours of fun.

Brad now makes an outdoor rink for his kids the way his dad did for him. He's as happy with a shovel in his hand as he is with a hockey stick. Brad is enthralled with the game, from first freeze to last thaw. He truly is a child of winter.

The 1968 Southwest London Bobcats were made up of guys born ten years earlier. Maybe there is something in the London water, but two of the team's players, Craig MacTavish and Brad Marsh, were the last guys not to wear helmets in the NHL.

The Bobcats won fifty-three games in a row that year and then lost in the provincial final against Riverside. There were games where MacTavish and his linemate, Doug Berk, got more than twenty goals each. Their goaltender, Robin Smith, had thirty-six shutouts.

MacTavish's nickname was Gabby. Robin says Craig was a hummingbird on speed, always going eight thousand miles an hour. He was like that on the ice too—an incredible talent.

The Bobcats' biggest game that year was at Treasure Island Gardens, the home of the London Knights. At the time, it was a fairly new arena—only three years old. The game was tied with only minutes left when MacTavish, with that big sheet of ice ahead of him, stickhandled through the entire opposition, deked out their goalie and . . . shot it wide. Behind the bench was a brick wall. Bobcats coach Bruce Stewart punched it in frustration and broke his hand.

When I interviewed Marsh one time on *Hockey Night in Canada*, I asked him to name the best coach he ever had. Brad had had some great and storied coaches in his career, including Pat Quinn, Mike Keenan and John Brophy, but his answer was Bruce Stewart, his minor-hockey coach. Brad says Stewart brought the best out in the guys. He understood the game, and

Babcock and the 1993–1994 University of Lethbridge Pronghorns, who were national champions. Mike told me that the most important thing is that the player leaves with more respect for the game than he had when he arrived.
COURTESY UNIVERSITY OF LETHBRIDGE ARCHIVES

Pronghorns players John Curran, Trevor Ellerman, Colin Baustad and Corey Hastman. Ellerman said that when the team first started winning, Babcock was happy, but he wasn't satisfied. COURTESY TREVOR ELLERMAN

Trevor Keeper, coach of the Red Deer College Kings, March 2014. When he was a young coach and high school teacher, Trevor met Mike Babcock to talk about assisting him with the Pronghorns, but he had no idea what he was getting into.
COURTESY TONY HANSEN

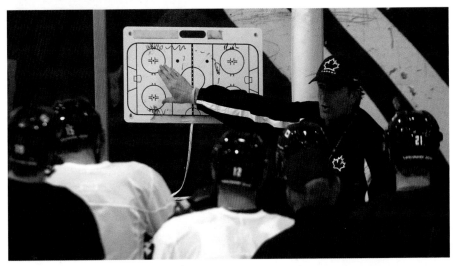

Regarding Sochi 2014, Babcock told me he likened going to Russia to sending your kids off to university. In surroundings where it was easy to get derailed, Babcock created an environment within the team of looking out for and protecting one another. This photo was taken at the 2010 Vancouver Olympics.
STEVE RUSSELL/GETTY IMAGES

Gerry James played for the Leafs and Blue Bombers simultaneously. When he was injured while playing hockey, his football teammates stopped passing him the ball and were surprised when he caught it.
HOCKEY HALL OF FAME

When Gerry was invited to try out for the Bombers, he couldn't believe it. He'd only played high school football. *WINNIPEG FREE PRESS*

With Lanny McDonald in Fort McMurray, Alberta. It takes Canada's finest moustache to cover the greatest smile. Lanny makes everyone and every event better. ROGERS MEDIA

Brantt Myhres and sister, Cher. Brantt said that as a ten-year-old boy watching *HNIC*, he admired Dave Brown, Tony Twist and Bob Probert, but until he landed in the WHL, he never fully understood what their jobs meant. COURTESY BRANTT MYHRES

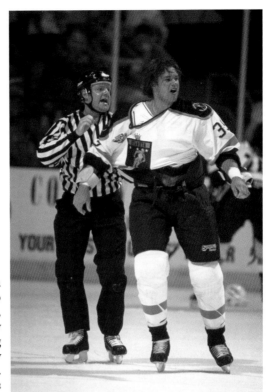

Brantt Myhres with the Atlanta Knights circa 1993. Brantt made it to the Show but struck out five times, leading to a lifetime ban. Today he's eight years sober and running Greater Strides Hockey Academy in Edmonton.
CUNNINGHAM/HOCKEY HALL OF FAME

With Chicago, Bobby Hull scores his 600th goal—on Gerry Cheevers. Mike Walton is shot blocking. Gerry and Mike "Shaky" Walton were roommates on the road in the early '70s. ASSOCIATED PRESS

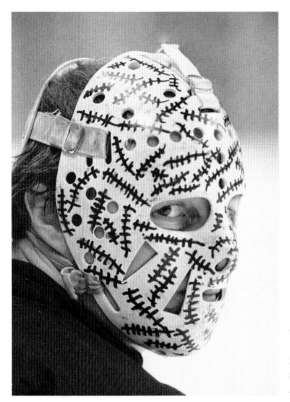

Gerry Cheevers, May 20, 1978. Gerry was known for his mask, but he says he was more attached to his glove.
ASSOCIATED PRESS

This game of shinny and a visit to Science North was a highlight. In Sudbury, kids are born wearing skates. ROGERS MEDIA

Big Zee and Little Zee circa 1989. Big Zee took his son everywhere—baseball, hockey, roller hockey. Whatever it was, he was by Little Zee's side.
COURTESY THE KONOPKA FAMILY

Big Zee, Arlene, Cynthia and Little Zee at Celeste's first communion. The family was really proud of their Polish heritage.
COURTESY THE KONOPKA FAMILY

Zenon using his childhood boxing lessons on Dale Weise.
ASSOCIATED PRESS

Steve Bozek with the Northern Michigan University Wildcats circa 1980.
COURTESY CENTRAL UPPER PENINSULA AND NORTHERN MICHIGAN UNIVERSITY ARCHIVES

The Castlegar boys were the nucleus of the Northern Michigan University Wildcats in 1979–80: Gordie Pace (*top row, third from left*), Bruce Martin (*top row, fifth from right*), David Kanigan (*top row, fourth from right*), Brian Verigin (*centre row, seventh from left*), Steve Bozek (*centre row, sixth from left*) and coach Rick Comely (*centre row, first from right*).
COURTESY CENTRAL UPPER PENINSULA AND NORTHERN MICHIGAN UNIVERSITY ARCHIVES

Coach Terry Crisp circa 1980, nine years before his Stanley Cup win.
COURTESY TERRY CRISP

The Hound Line. Gary Leeman, Russ Courtnall and Wendel Clark revived the Leafs in the mid-eighties. They were a joy to be around.
FRANK LENNON/GETTY IMAGES

Père Athol Murray at Duncan McNeill Arena in Wilcox, Saskatchewan, 1968.
COURTESY ATHOL MURRAY COLLEGE OF NOTRE DAME

This photo of Russ is very fitting. Anyone who saw him play knows he had an extra gear! FRANK LENNON/GETTY IMAGES

the boys respected him because he demanded 100 per cent. "I can't really sit here and say he taught me how to pass, or he taught me how to shoot, but he taught us the importance of hard work. He taught us the importance of winning and he taught us the importance of playing together as a team."

If a player didn't do his best every shift, he heard about it. Stewart's work ethic stayed with Brad and carried him through his formative years, because those were his traits throughout junior hockey and in the NHL. Stewart coached the boys five years straight, and every guy on the team feels the way Brad does.

Teams didn't travel much back then, so they'd play different London communities—Stony Brook, Oakridge, Sharon Heights and Byron. That February, the boys were invited to the Strathroy Olympics, which was a big tournament in the area. There was school the next day, so afterward they all made the one-hour drive back. Highway 402 wasn't complete yet, so they had to deke south through Mount Brydges. It was slow going because there was a snowstorm. Without the wind chill, it was minus-28, and the roads were murderously slippery. Brad and his brother were half asleep in the back seat of the family's big new Buick, and their dad was driving with their mom beside him. As the car approached a big, lazy curve, it collided with another car headed toward them. The Buick took a beating, but thankfully everyone in both cars was okay.

This was the era of the Broad Street boys—Bobby Clarke, Reggie Leach, Don Saleski, Bob Kelly and Dave "The Hammer" Schultz. Brad Marsh was never the most gifted player, but he understood the game and was a hard worker. He made the Junior B London Squires as a fourteen-year-old because he was such a big boy—six foot one, 195 pounds. His dad lied about his age, so Brad was playing with twenty-year-old men. He was on a really steep learning curve, but he always showed up with the Bruce Stewart attitude—you play to win.

When it came time for the rookies to be initiated, the veterans decided to start with the youngest player first, but they walked right past Brad in the dressing room. The guys never dreamed he was only in grade 9. When they finally found out, they nicknamed him Baby Huey. To this day, when Brad runs into guys he played with back then, it's "How're you doin', Baby Huey?"

In London, there were the Junior B Squires and the Junior A London Knights. The senior team was called the London Kings. They all wore the same jersey, because they were one big team for the city, and you could aspire to play all the way up. Brad was fifteen when he got called up to Junior A with the Knights.

His first road trip was to Sudbury and Sault Ste. Marie. It was so cold that the driver kept the bus running overnight. Big Betsy was parked right outside Brad's window, and so he woke up every hour thinking he was going to miss his ride because he could hear the engine.

Brad's Brick Street public school teacher in grades 5 and 7 was Donna Ramage. She had a son named Rob who played for Byron, the Bobcats' biggest rival. It was a hate-hate situation—there was no love involved. Eventually, Rob and Brad would play together on the Squires and Knights and become co-winners of the Max Kaminsky Trophy—given to the best defenceman in the OHL—in 1977–78.

At the start of the Knights' season, long before the Teenage Mutant Ninja Turtles, Rob Ramage and Brad Marsh were climbing up and down manholes. They'd grab some of the rookies, gear up with flashlights taped to their hockey helmets and a couple of cases of beer and lead them through the storm sewers of Byron, scaring away the rats with loud drunken choruses of songs like the Doobie Brothers' "Minute by Minute."

In his last year with the Knights, Brad came away with sixty-three points, but his offensive skills didn't compare to the Scott Stevenses of the world, and there were a lot of players his size. If he was going to make it in the NHL, he would have to adapt, find his niche. Brad knew if he tried to be offensive he wouldn't last, so he focused on his strength—looking after his own end.

Brad's NHL career began with the Atlanta Flames in 1978–79. He would become one of the best defensive players in the league. He wound up playing 1,086 games, and when he hit 1,000 he was only the sixteenth defenceman in the history of the NHL to do so. There's a whole other dimension certain players bring to the rink. A dimension that fans don't see because it happens in the dressing room. Brad wasn't the first around a pylon in practice and he would never be able to turn on a dime, but there was always a *C* or an *A* on the front of his sweater.

Rob Ramage was the first-overall pick in the 1979 NHL draft and played fifteen seasons in the Show. He was just a fantastic athlete. He played three years with the Knights, who retired both his and Brad's sweaters together on Sunday, January 6, 1991. His first NHL contract was with the Colorado Rockies to play for coach Don Cherry. Rob went on to play with eight NHL teams. He won two Stanley Cups and played in four NHL All-Star Games.

On December 15, 2003, Rob attended Keith McCreary's wake. Keith was a former NHL player and NHL Alumni president. He was extremely popular and was deeply mourned after losing his brave battle against cancer. Afterward, Rob took the wheel of a rented car, and his friend, former Chicago Blackhawks captain Keith Magnuson, hopped in the passenger seat.

Rob's car swerved into an oncoming SUV and Keith, who was fifty-six years old, was killed. In 2007, Rob was found guilty of impaired driving causing death and was sent to the Frontenac Institution.

Tuesday nights at 6 p.m., he'd brew a pot of tea in his cell and bring two cups out to the visitors' room, where he was greeted by the same face. Brad Marsh—his teammate, a guy who'd stood up for him hundreds of times—made the two-hour drive from Ottawa down to Kingston every week, come hell or high water. Brad put the word out and other guys showed up on Saturdays— Rob's brothers from the Knights, Doug Berk and Tim Whitehead. And other NHL alumni showed up too, guys who didn't even know Rob, like Boston's Rick Smith, and Fred Barrett, who played defence for Minnesota. Rob's goalie in St. Louis, Ed Staniowski, visited too. They'd sit and tell hockey stories and chuckle about the sewer tours and road trips, and talk about different coaches and the crap they used to pull on each other. Week after week, different guys would show up.

But for two hours each and every Tuesday night, Rob and Brad were ten-year-old kids, back in London again.

One Great Keeper in the Hands of Another

Ian Jenkins, a phenomenal fifteen-year-old midget goaltender, was drafted by the London Knights in May 2011. A good-looking kid, his picture could easily be shuffled in with photos of Zac Efron and a young Ben Affleck. Ian—or Big E, as they called him—was on skates by the time he was two years old. His home in Milan, Michigan, is a three-hour drive up through Sarnia to London.

His dad, Joel, wanted badly for the kid to play hockey, but Ian wasn't a natural. So Joel decided to let him progress without pushing him. At seven, Ian got his start in organized hockey Tim Hortons–style. No goalies, just go for the puck. Near the end of the season, they'd have about six little scrimmage games. Ian couldn't wait. He kept asking his coach, "When we play the real games, can I play goal? I really want to be the goalie." Coach would say, "Yeah, yeah, Ian, we'll rotate you in. Don't worry about it." Finally, in the very last game, he got his shot. And when he pulled on the goalie jersey—number 35—he found his place on the ice.

When Ian and his father got home after the big game, Joel said, "Hey, son, come with me." He opened up his old scrapbook and showed Ian a picture of himself between the pipes. He said, "That's me, your dad." But instead of saying, "Oh wow, how cool!" the first thing out of Ian's mouth was, "Oh my God, Dad, those are ugly old pads." Joel laughed, "That wasn't the reaction I was expecting out of you, buddy."

The Jenkins family had a fairly large home, so they set up a net in the basement. Joel and Ian practised daily. Joel, whose idol growing up was Vladislav Tretiak, told Ian, "It's very important to grab on to somebody so you can study him as part of your development."

Father and son would go to University of Michigan Sabres games where Ian would watch Ryan Miller, who had twenty-six shutouts during his time there. Ian was in awe of the Hobey

Baker Award winner. He couldn't believe it when a family friend had Miller send him a signed jersey. He treasured it along with a signed Nikolai Khabibulin jersey that Joel's buddy, the marketing director for the Tampa Bay Lightning, sent him. Both sweaters hung in the basement near Ian's net, which was where he spent most of his time.

Like something right out of a scene from *Star Wars*, Joel would rent ice and sometimes throw a puck bag over Ian's head. He wanted Ian to know and feel the crease without looking at it. Ian was gifted, very athletic, but Joel didn't want him to turn into a Dominik Hašek, relying only on his athletic ability. He wanted Ian to be more. So even if Ian had a good game, Joel would point out mistakes and together they'd work on fixing them. "Yeah, you got a shutout, but you did this or that and this wrong, so let's make sure you don't do that again." Ian didn't argue. Getting better was what mattered.

Hockey wasn't the only thing Ian had going for him. He was an A-plus student and a gifted musician. He started playing the guitar when he was four years old thanks to his mom, Gloria. She wanted to make sure he was well rounded. He was into a lot of classic rock and alternative music. He played some pretty hardcore guitar and was part of the rock band at the Ann Arbor Music Center. They'd perform at the University of Michigan Starbucks and at art festivals. His favourite band was Rise Against. Before big games, Ian would plug in his earbuds and stretch and warm up to his favourite songs, like "Behind Closed Doors," and then he'd sit and focus.

Ian was really tight with his family. He'd always shared a room with his younger brother, Garrett, and yet they never once had a fight. They might as well have been twins, they were so close. His little sister, Cassidy, was a few years younger and he treated her like gold. Cassidy and Garrett were a huge part of his life. Joel and Gloria divorced in 2005, but it wasn't a bitter split— they remained friends.

Joel married Debbie in 2008. Debbie didn't try to mother Ian, but she was always there for him. Her son, Lester, was the same age and the boys became best friends. They played with and against each other growing up. His coaches would always tell Lester's team that Ian's glove was so strong they should try to get in on the stick side if possible, but that was tough too because he was just so quick to move over.

As Ian got older, there was pressure to get somebody else as a goalie coach, so Joel bowed out. Ian had been taking lessons at Bandits Goalie School and liked the owner, former pro Stan Matwijiw. When Stan jumped on board, Joel still helped out for the first couple of years. It was great for Ian and his goalie partner because when Stan wasn't there, Joel reinforced his teachings and helped out.

Stan taught Ian a philosophy called "Have a Purpose (HAP)." He told Ian, "Every opportunity you have on the ice is an opportunity to improve—reach higher, get better." Stan told the kids he coached to start keeping a journal and to stash it in their stalls. He wanted them to record two things they wanted to improve each time they stepped on the ice. "If you get better at two things each practice, imagine how much better you will be in a year," he said. Every once in a while Stan would ask his players, "What'd you write down in your book today?" He wanted to see who was following through. Ian was religious about it. Ian really bought into the philosophy and started writing HAP on the inside wrist of his gloves. When Joel asked him why, he said, "It's the last thing I see when I go out on the ice."

By the time Ian was fifteen and in his sixth season playing AAA, HoneyBaked Hockey, the website *The Scouting News* reported that "The most effective 1995 goalie playing in the USA Hockey system could very well be Ian Jenkins." But Ian found that year incredibly stressful. He was torn between college offers and the OHL.

His folks really wanted him to go the college route. Numerous schools, at least eight of them, flew him in, trying to get him to verbally commit. He was also invited to try out for the US National Development Team, a forty-man camp held in Ann Arbor. He went to the camp with all the top kids and played unbelievably. After his second game, he had yet to be scored on. Two Toronto Maple Leafs scouts came up to introduce themselves. They were chatting when one of them said, "Our GM, Brian Burke, favours goalies six foot three or taller. That's where the game's headed, but you're getting there, Ian." Ian was five foot eleven, weighed 185 pounds. He hadn't said much up to that point, but any time you talked about height, it pissed him off. Tim Thomas would win the Conn Smythe Trophy that year and he was five-eleven too. Ian always thought it was total horse crap that they all wanted these huge goalies. What counted was keeping the puck out of the net.

Suddenly, Ian interrupted the scouts. He was confident but not cocky when he said, "What's size got to do with it?" And then he thanked them and turned away.

Ian continued to hash out the pros and cons with both his dad and Stan. Should he go with the US Development Team and then move on to college? Or go with the development team and go on to major junior? Or just go on to junior? In the end, he decided his best way to the NHL was through the OHL. He was so serious about hockey he broke it off with his first and only girlfriend. Love was just too distracting. It messes up your head. He flat out told her, "I need to focus on hockey. I just can't do this."

The week of the 2011 OHL draft, it was all he could think about. During camp, he could barely sleep. There are twenty clubs in the OHL, which means there's only room for forty goalies, and they are almost always older. Ian had a game so he was on the ice while the draft was happening. His head kept swivelling up to the stands where Joel was monitoring it on his phone. Round One, one goalie, Spencer Martin, 1995, big kid, six-three, 204 pounds—he went to the Mississauga Steelheads. Ian wanted to play for the London Knights. His number one concern was clicking with the coaches, and he thought Dale and Mark Hunter were really good guys and knew what they were doing. He'd also fallen in love with the city. The Knights had the ninth pick. They took a forward, Bo Horvat. Joel was getting texts telling him the Windsor Spitfires were trying to trade up to get Ian. It was really dicey and there were a lot of head games being played between the teams and Ian's agent, Jason Woolley, a former NHL defenceman who worked at The Players Group Hockey. London's turn came around again and Ian's name popped up. Joel met Ian's eye and put both his thumbs up in the air. Ian couldn't contain himself. He started circling his net, pumping his fist. Joel watched his boy with an apple in his throat. All their hard work was paying off. All their dreams were coming true.

At the first whistle, Ian skated over to Joel at the boards. He said, "What's up, Dad?" Joel grinned. "You went to the London

Knights, second round, twenty-ninth overall." The bench started high-fiving him and pounding his back. Everyone had the same feeling—Ian was headed for the Show someday.

May 19, 2011, was a beautiful day. Seventy-something degrees and the sun was shining. It was one of those days when you wake up and the lights look brighter. A big wet sandbag had been lifted off Ian's back, he was going to London the next day, and Joel was taking the kids out for dinner because it was Cassidy's tenth birthday.

Ian and Garrett ran track for their high school, so they had practice after school, but Ian was so pumped about leaving for London, his track coach told him to skip practice and get ready for his trip.

Perfect! It gave Ian time to hang out with his two best buddies near his mom's place in Milan to say goodbye. Joel was going to swing by and grab Cassidy from school, and so he made plans to pick up Ian too. Ian left Joel a cell phone message. "Hey, Dad, I'll wait for you at the corner around four o'clock. Just pick me up there. Love you." Ian always ended his messages with a "love you." He was thoughtful that way.

Cassidy and Joel stopped by the ice cream store to pick up some chocolate for Ian, his favourite. And then when they were about five minutes from the corner, a fire truck whizzed by with a couple of police cars and an ambulance in its draft. Joel pulled over. The sirens were so loud it made their ears squeal. Suddenly, Joel's phone was ringing. It was Gloria. She was breathing hard. "There's been an awful accident. Will you hurry down the street to Ian?"

Joel raced to where he was supposed to meet Ian and slammed the car into park so hard it almost rocked off its wheels.

He jumped out, yelling at Cassidy not to move. She was crying because she'd never seen her dad so scared. Ian was lying in the road, foaming at the mouth, and his limbs were contorting. Joel had some medical training and so he knew this implied a disconnect between the spinal cord and the brain. In acceleration/deceleration types of injuries, the axons—or fibres that transmit information to the muscles—can tear, cutting the connection and causing the arms to curl up. Joel knelt down and started rubbing Ian's shoulder, trying to reassure him. He was talking softly. "Hang in there, Big E, you're going to be okay. Help is here. They're taking care of you. I love you, buddy." Joel searched his son's eyes, but he couldn't find him.

The paramedics moved quickly, and Joel jumped up to follow. But as a female paramedic was closing the door to the ambulance, she turned and gave Joel a look that sent his heart rocketing to the bottom of his gut.

Ian was rushed into the trauma unit, and Joel got on the phone to Debbie, who was a flight attendant. She was in New York, and she started making arrangements to get home. While the family waited for news about Ian, the story of what happened began to unfold. Ian had hopped into the back of his friend's pickup for a ride to the corner, and when his buddy took off, Ian wasn't prepared and fell, whacking the back of his head on the trailer hitch.

One of Ian's early hockey coaches was the ER physician. He came out and said, "Ian is getting a CT scan right now, but in my opinion I think it looks good." In that moment, Joel allowed himself to take a full breath for the first time since he heard about the accident. The family celebrated, hugging each other through tears. "Wow!" "Amazing!" "Trust Ian to pull through this." "Thank God it's not as bad as we thought."

But it turned out Ian's CT scan was horrible. The medical team reported to the family that his brain was swelling. They would have to perform surgery immediately. The blood vessels inside and on top of the brain were broken and causing clots. Because there is only so much room inside the intracranial sac, the pressure of the clots was squeezing the brain, pushing it downward toward the stem, so the surgeon was going to drill a hole in Ian's head to suck out the extra blood and alleviate the pressure.

Ian got out of surgery just before midnight. By that time, there were more than twenty people at the hospital waiting for news. Looking at him lying there with tubes and wires running in and out of him was really scary and sad. The surgeon sat with the family and told them he'd never seen anybody survive an injury like Ian had. He told them that all vital functions go through the brain, so when the damage is as great as what Ian had suffered, the drive to breathe stops and the body goes into cardiac arrest. Ian was going to die.

Just a couple of weeks earlier, in the car on the way to camp, Ian had told Joel it wasn't lost on him that he couldn't have made it to the Knights without all the support he got at home. He thanked Joel for all he'd done, and for his new pads and his custom-painted mask with "Big E" painted on the chin. He said he felt bad for all the kids who couldn't afford to play hockey. That conversation stuck with Joel. And so the family made the decision Ian would have made. They agreed to allow the hospital to harvest Ian's organs, whatever was still viable.

Twenty-four-year-old Kevin Folster was at a service in a church close to where the accident happened. It was the same church Ian Jenkins and his family attended. He'd never met Ian, but when he heard about a local teenager fighting to survive, he prayed for him. Kevin had severe health problems and desperately needed a kidney donor. His phone rang. There was a kidney available. And that kidney, Ian's kidney, would save Kevin's life.

One of the first things Joel did after Ian's funeral was reach out to Ian's buddy, the sixteen-year-old kid who'd been behind the wheel of the truck. Joel told him, "Accidents happen. You've got to be strong." But nothing made life easier for Joel—he's got a hole in his heart that will never heal. How could it? He will always be missing a piece of his own HAP.

The family started the Big E Foundation. It supports amateur sports through equipment donations, grants and events, and it talks about organ donation. Lester started a charity golf event in Ian's name that is held every August, and he plays a big role in the Big E Foundation through Athletes With a Purpose. It's how he copes. He talks about Ian and thinks about him all the time. The pain and sadness still reach out and bite, but there are a lot of laughs when talking about Ian too. Like the time he cut the cheese so bad that Garrett, who had a broken leg, rolled back his wheelchair to escape the fumes and fell right out to the floor. Or the time they were in a snowball fight and Ian moved behind a tree to write his name in the snow, and then stepped out and mooned a couple of cars. Sometimes they smile and shake their heads and talk about how, despite Ian's athleticism and school smarts, he wasn't very street smart and so he walked around with his head in the clouds.

Stan Matwijiw took Ian's death hard. Ian had called him about a goalie session before heading off to sign with London. Stan had an opening on the day—and at the time—of the accident, but Ian asked for a spot a day earlier. Stan said he couldn't. He was booked up. They went back and forth until finally Stan relented and moved things around. He's haunted by the thought that, if he had just put his foot down and insisted on the May 19 lesson, Ian would have been with him instead of falling off the truck. It eats him alive.

But it may be toughest for Garrett. He's had a lot of struggles and is just now starting to be able to talk about Ian. He thinks about his big brother every day. He's proud of him.

All any of them can do is hang on to the words of one of Ian's favourite songs, "Rise Above This" by Seether. *I'm fallin' down, fallin' down, but I'll rise above this, rise above this, rise above this.*

The Big Red Turtleneck

Eric Lindros was a two-time World Junior champion, an Olympic champion and a winner of the 1991 Canada Cup, as well as a 1995 Hart Trophy winner and a seven-time All-Star. He's the fifth fastest to reach five hundred points in the NHL (352 games) behind Wayne Gretzky (273), Mario Lemieux (323), Peter Šťastný (394) and Mike Bossy (349). Since NHL players began taking part in the Olympics in 1998, the team has been captained by five players—Sidney Crosby, Scott Niedermayer, Joe Sakic, Mario Lemieux and Eric. Three are in the Hall of Fame, and Crosby is sure to be inducted one day.

I like that in the 1997 playoffs, in order to get Philadelphia to the Stanley Cup final against the Rangers, he was the key to a win over the Wayne Gretzky–Mark Messier tandem. His goals were big. He scored the winner in Game Four and the first goal of Game Five.

But more than all that, he championed player rights. Eric was chosen first overall in the 1991 NHL Entry Draft by the Quebec Nordiques but refused to play for them and was eventually traded to the Flyers in June 1992. In his 1994 memoir, *My Life in Hockey*, Jean Béliveau praises Eric's abilities and says, "I watched each episode of this [Lindros] soap opera as it unfolded over two years with more than passing interest and more than a little sympathy . . . Unfortunately Eric's situation became fraught with emotional and political baggage which pitted the Lindros camp and the Toronto media against the Nordiques and the Quebec media . . . But in my view, the situation was cut and dried: Lindros was within his rights." Maurice Richard described Eric best. He called him "a mean Jean Béliveau." Injuries finally got Eric, the way they got Bobby Orr.

Eric Lindros was one of those kids who refused to come in off the ice as long as it was light out. He just loved being out there. He says, "You just kept going. You just kept playing. It was just you, your stick and a couple of pucks. Time just flew." He didn't pretend he was Bobby Orr. He wasn't a kid who fantasized about being in the NHL. It was just what he liked to do.

Eric's dad, Carl, and his mom, Bonnie, started him out on bob skates when he was two. They'd bundle him up and take him down to the big rink in London's Victoria Park. Carl says it wasn't really skating, it was more like walking on blades.

London is situated in the snowbelt. The first snowfall usually comes in November, but a white October is not unusual. In 1975, Eric was almost three years old when Carl built their first backyard rink. It was smooth as glass, much better than the rinks at the local arena. Eric says Carl had a white thumb. He'd been building rinks since he was a kid in Chatham, but they had never lasted more than two weeks because the weather there is much milder.

Carl had two secrets—hot water and rink snow. Early in the winter, there wasn't enough snow to pack down the base and the banks, and so to get the crust going Carl would drive his Volvo station wagon over to the Argyle rink and fill up garbage pails with Zamboni-dumped snow. By the middle of winter the snow would get built up around the sides well over the kids' heads and they would make caves and forts.

Carl's philosophy was not to use hot water within the first two weeks of building a rink. Instead, use it as a finisher to smooth things out. He doesn't remember Eric and his brother, Brett, doing the flooding, but they'd help with the shovelling. Sometimes they'd wake up to a foot and a half of snow. Carl would get home at seven or seven thirty at night, wolf down something to eat and head out to flood the rink. The wind would die down and it was unbelievably peaceful. Carl found it a good way to unwind and collect his thoughts.

Eric's bedroom was right above the rink. The year he was in Grade 1 was the year Ontario had some of the lowest temperatures on record. It was minus-31 in December in Toronto with wind gusts up to twenty-five kilometres an hour. He would hear the hose in the backyard and he'd look out at his dad, standing in the freezing cold, wearing his big red turtleneck with layers stretched over it. Carl had the hose hooked up to the kitchen sink, and as he moved it back and forth across the ice, the steam rose two storeys high.

"A lot of times, a bunch of kids would show up and there'd be snowball fights and chasing around and tag. Sometimes they'd play with a puck and sometimes they'd play with a tennis ball, and everybody would take a turn playing in net. So that's why we did a lot of extra skating in the backyard rink, but it sure as heck had nothing to do with being a hockey player."

Carl's office building, a five-minute drive from home, over-looked the rink where Eric played hockey. Carl would take Eric over an hour before the school bell rang. They'd bring a shovel and clear the ice together. Early mornings were the only time you could use sticks, so Eric would shoot and skate around. Carl says he liked being outside and skating and being active. However, he wasn't all that thrilled about hockey. "But at that time hockey meant the Philadelphia Flyers and the tough guys, and Eric loved it. So what are you gonna do?"

Organized hockey began for Eric at Argyle Arena in the Red Circle League. But Carl says he's not sure how organized it was. They played cross-rink and used upside-down benches for nets. "There used to be partitions on either blue line, and there was six teams playing at once. Three pucks. I don't think we even had referees. We had a couple of coaches on the bench just pointing people in the right direction of the 'nets,' and then there was an automatic change and the next group went out. We always had a good time."

Eric was a good little player, so he was invited to join a rep "travel team," which was non-competitive. At the end of that first year Eric asked his dad, "Can you sign me up to play with London minor hockey?"

Carl and Eric spent a lot of time working on skills and stuff. Even though hockey wasn't Carl's thing, his philosophy was if you're going to do it, do it well.

On their way home in the car after a game, in the spirit of helping Eric get better, Carl was critical and commented on Eric's play. Later, Bonnie took Carl aside and set him straight. "You shouldn't be doing that. You should just talk about how fun it was or mention the good stuff that happened. Don't get into picking on things he could have done differently. He'll end up hating the game and he'll resent you for it." Carl took what she said to heart.

Whether Eric's team killed or got killed, after every game Eric would come home and plug in the family's radio/cassette player outside and load up an AC/DC cassette tape his uncle Mark had given him. While it blasted through the yard, he'd skate onto the ice and replay the whole game, shot by shot. He'd circle and shoot, picking up phantom passes and pouncing on rebounds over and over again. He didn't know it then, but as he carved up the ice to "It's a Long Way to the Top (If You Wanna Rock 'n' Roll)," he was starting his own climb up the mountain.

Swift Current

SASKATCHEWAN

POPULATION:
15,503

Reckless Abandon

When Eric Lindros retired from hockey, he donated five million dollars for concussion research to the London Health Sciences Centre at Western University. In August 2014, I joined him there as honorary chair of the second annual education, awareness and fundraising event for See the Line—a collaborative effort between world-class health care and research partners, including the Sports Legacy Institute in the US and Canada, who are taking a leadership approach in the field of concussion prevention and finding ways to improve diagnosis and treatment.

Former Canadian Football League player Tim Fleiszer, who was the first-ever freshman to start a game for Harvard in football, breaking a 121-year precedent, is the executive director of the Sports Legacy Institute Canada.

Trent McCleary grew up in Swift Current, Saskatchewan. He is one of those rare kids who played hockey all the way from tyke to junior in his hometown. Swift Current is a great little city, and hockey is a big part of its culture. It's the smallest market in the Canadian Hockey League by far, and yet 20 per cent of its residents come to the Broncos' games. As Trent says, "Name any other city that holds an event where 20 per cent of the population attends on a regular basis. You can't."

Trent was in a near-death accident in 2000, while blocking a shot in a game between the Montreal Canadiens and the Philadelphia

Flyers, and because Tim's father, Dr. David Fleiszer, was at that game, Trent is still alive today.

A similar accident happened to Mark Goodkey, a University of Alberta Golden Bears defenceman who died blocking a shot in a pickup game at Clare Drake Arena in March 1996. Mark was from Sangudo, Alberta, a hamlet near Stettler, ninety-nine kilometres northwest of Edmonton. He was a selfless player trying to get in front of a slapshot, and the puck struck him in the back of the head. Don Cherry broke down while telling that story on "Coach's Corner" at the time. It's a vivid and profound memory that will likely stay with me forever.

---

*T*rent McCleary's most vivid memory of hockey is of being nine years old and wanting more than anything to get out onto the ice to try out for a select atom team, but feeling so sick with the flu he could barely stand up. His dad brought him into the bathroom and said, "Yeah, son, put your finger down your throat and puke. You'll feel a lot better." Trent did as he was told—and made the team, so obviously it helped.

His dad, Ken, played a bit of junior back in the day—in Estevan with Ernie "Punch" McLean, an old, old hockey guy. Ken didn't really want to coach Trent and his brother Scott's teams— he didn't have time. He worked in the oil patch so he was on call a lot. But no one else in Swift Current stepped up for Tom Thumb, so he volunteered.

Every Sunday morning, he'd have the guys doing drills and running the gamut. He wanted his boys to be able to play old-timer hockey when they grew up, because everybody ends up in old-timer's.

Ken knew what every other guy who puts on a sweater knows—that there's nothing better than a hockey dressing room. And it doesn't matter whether you're sixty-five or fifteen, it's the happiest place on earth. Everybody had a nickname—today they are a bit of a thing of the past. Almost every great player had one— Mr. Hockey (Gordie Howe), the Great One (Wayne Gretzky), *Le Gros Bill* (Jean Béliveau), the Rocket (Maurice Richard), the Golden Jet (Bobby Hull), the Stratford Streak (Howie Morenz), Super Mario (Lemieux), the Flower (Guy Lafleur). The only great without a nickname is Bobby Orr.

One of my favourites is Todd "One Touch" Warriner. Pat Burns was mad at Todd for trying a Dougie Gilmour–style one-touch pass, so he walked into the Leafs room to give him hell, saying, "Where the eff is 'One Touch'?!"

Others are based on the way you look. Mark Hunter played with the Flames for three years—1988–89, '89–90, '90–91—and that's where they started calling him "Heifer Head." God help you if you come in puffed up, because you will leave with your ego in check. The guys love that. A good putdown can make you chuckle for days. But most of what happens in the dressing room doesn't translate outside.

Ken could see that Trent had talent. He was a good skater and good on his edges. He had the ability to keep his ankles stiff and distribute his weight evenly. More weight on an edge slows you down. It's physics. Trent could take two or three hard strides, glide, and not lose speed. Going that fast helped force turnovers and caught guys off guard. But what set him apart was his energy.

He was a spark plug. He'd go full speed and stop only when he connected with an opposing player.

Trent was a hometown boy who played his entire amateur career in the same town—three years with the peewee Kings, who were division champs, and then in bantam, where they won the Western Canada bantam championship. In midget, his team made it all the way to the provincial final and lost against the Regina Pat Canadians. Next, he played for the Rotary Raiders and then the Swift Current Legionnaires.

The Swift Current Broncos came back to town in 1986, when Trent was fourteen and a right winger for the Legionnaires. The Broncos team was started in Swift Current in 1967 and then moved to Lethbridge in 1974. Management decided to bring in some of the higher-end locals, which was a popular move in the community. No one was kidding themselves about Trent, except Trent. A guy his size with a lack of spectacular talent would never make it to the NHL. He was considered one of the best of Swift Current's young players, and so they listed him, but c'mon. Trent knew otherwise. On every team he'd played on, he'd had to prove himself. He'd do it again.

Back then they didn't have a draft. If you were fourteen or fifteen you took up two spots. If you were between sixteen and twenty, only one spot. So Trent was a two-spot practice player on the Broncos for one year.

Walking into that dressing room the first time and seeing Sheldon Kennedy and Joe Sakic and all the guys was unbelievable. Sakic was quiet. He got a lot of well-deserved attention from the media, but it's not like he drank it up. Sheldon Kennedy was kind. He was the leader and had a lot of confidence. When

Trent came in, it was, "Hey! How you doing, Trent?" Always a nice guy. Were they friends? No—Trent was fourteen, Sheldon was seventeen—but just a "hi" to the younger guys meant more than he'd ever know. Trent would keep his head down and find a place at the end of the line. At five foot nine, he wasn't going to outshine anybody. He was just happy to be there.

Graham James was their coach. He focused on speed, puck handling and the power play. As sick as he was as a person, on the ice, he let the creative players be creative. Nobody wanted small defencemen like Darren Kruger or Dan Lambert, but when they got to Swift, they found a home because they moved the puck out. Graham's philosophy was that if you control the puck, you control the game. Unfortunately, hockey has an undercurrent of creepy guys like him in every walk of life. Later it came to light that James headed up the list. I certainly remember a creep in Red Deer. My best friend and I went over to this guy's house. He tried putting his hands on us and we were outta there. Trent was fortunate that Graham never bothered him. He heard rumours and there were a few jokes, but in his entire time with the Broncos he had no idea that Graham was molesting Sheldon Kennedy and Todd Holt.

Lorne Frey was another one of the coaches. Trent loved Lorney. He thought Lorney had one of the best hockey eyes ever. He was the guy who spotted Duncan Keith, Shea Weber and Josh Gorges after all were passed over in the WHL draft. Lorney's crystal ball could see into the future and tell you how a kid was going to develop and where he would end up. He knew Trent was never going to be a goal scorer, but he saw that Trent was faster than most and made a good penalty killer and shot blocker—

and he liked to agitate. Lorney told Trent to keep working hard because there are other roles on the team besides scoring.

It was a couple of days before Christmas—December 20, 1986. The Broncos were on their way to a game against the Pats in Regina. Trent was hanging out at home watching TV, but the radio was on in the background because the family would always listen to the Bronco games when the team was on the road. All of a sudden a story came on saying that the Broncos' team bus had slid off the road just outside Swift Current after hitting black ice. And then the reports started coming in saying players were injured and maybe dead. Trent ran to the radio. "Don't let it be Sheldon or Joe or . . ." The names and faces of all the guys on the team ran through his head like ticker tape. Alarms were going off in his fourteen-year-old brain. "They just came back to town. What's going to happen to the team? Holy smokes! Don't let it be true!"

Scotty Kruger, Brent Ruff, Chris Mantyka and Trent Kresse all died in the accident, and Swift Current was devastated. To this day, no minor or major hockey team in the city has jerseys with the numbers 8, 9, 11 or 22. It's a tremendous tribute to the four young lives lost. And back in 2000, in tribute to the players who died, the city and the team banded together and, despite the loss, the Broncos made a run for the playoffs.

The third year Trent skated with the franchise, 1988–89, the team was so dominant that there was little room for him, so he was called up for only three games. Meanwhile, he continued to play Midget AAA with the Legionnaires while attending more and more practices with the Broncos. The Broncos won the Memorial Cup that year, but Trent didn't want a ring. He was on the roster, but he wasn't really part of the team yet. If he was going to wear a ring, he wanted to earn it.

Finally, at seventeen, going into Grade 12, Trent landed on the Broncos' fourth line. He knew that to be noticed he had to become valuable. He was skinny and light, so he tried every trick in the book to gain weight—protein shakes, hamburgers, you name it. But nothing worked. He had too much energy. He was a chirper, always good with a comeback line, a tough checker and a shit disturber, mixing it up with the opposing team's enforcers and drawing penalties. Thankfully, his buddy Mark McFarlane was a good guy. He saved Trent's hide more than a couple times.

In Trent's second full year with the Broncos, the *Leader-Post* printed a list of stats they called the "Best of the West." The results were voted on by WHL coaches and the media. Trent made the top five in skating and hitting. He had learned to rocket himself at people. He used Newton's Second Law—force equals mass times acceleration. At that time, you weren't called for charging as long as you made sure to glide the last couple of feet. Thanks to his skating style and strong ankles, he'd get going fast and then throw everything he had at guys, turning himself into a 175-pound missile. The two-hundred-pound defencemen he hit would be pissed when helmet and gloves would go flying, and so one of Trent's teammates would jump in. But Trent often fought one Regina player, Derek Eberle, Jordan's older cousin. Those battles got Trent noticed.

One of the assistant coaches, Bruce Sutherland, became a scout for the Ottawa Senators. Trent had just finished his season as a nineteen-year-old when Bruce told him, "We like you.

Keep up what you are doing, play hard, compete." Trent wasn't drafted, but he got a tryout in '92 with the Senators. He wasn't the most talented, but he was a cannonball. Everyone was given brand new Senators gear—white shirt, white socks and black pants. On his first shift, Trent ran an East Coast League player who turned around and popped him in the kisser. Trent's nose exploded. He couldn't see, but he dropped his gloves and started swinging, spraying blood everywhere. Afterward, he cleaned up his face, came back on and continued to finish his checks and get involved. He was easy to spot in his blood-red-and-white jersey.

Brad Marsh was on the ice, but he was wearing a helmet so Trent didn't realize it was him. Because Trent was in a live-or-die situation, he continued flying around hitting guys, and he happened to smoke Brad. When the play came back the other way, Brad zeroed in on Trent. As Brad skated up the ice toward him, Trent could see steam coming out of every pore on his body. Trent glanced around quickly and saw his teammates shaking their heads, planning his funeral. But the buzzer went off and so Brad stopped. He narrowed his eyes at Trent and growled, "You little pissant!" Marshy was a senior man. He had the right to keep coming and clock Trent, but he was too classy for that. Trent's teammates told him, "You are so lucky you're still alive."

Trent did whatever it took, including blocking shots. He wasn't dumb about it—he tried to manage the angles—but he was optimistic. Trent was always convinced things were going to go his way. He'd try to get the puck to bounce forward off his shin pads so that momentum would carry it past the defenceman and create a breakaway. This meant constant swollen and bruised ankles and knees, and the odd charley horse that took him out of a game or two. The puck would bite like a son of a bitch, but for the most part Trent was rarely injured, and stopping a goal was more fun than scoring one. He didn't like doing the flamingo or trying to get out of the way. To him, that meant he was putting himself ahead of the team. Besides, he was getting good at managing contusions with ice and flexing.

Near the end of camp, general manager Mel Bridgman called him into the office and asked, "What are you doing?"

Trent didn't have a clue how to answer. Bridgman continued, "Why are you here? We drafted all these talented guys and all anybody keeps talking about is you."

Trent shrugged. "I don't know what to say."

"Why would you run Kevin Hatcher? You play one game and you run our best defenceman. Why?"

Trent said, "Uh, I have no idea."

Bridgman shook his head. "Okay, we're going to give you a contract. This is it. There's no negotiating. You have the same contract as all these other free agents that we got. And this isn't going to be a good year for us, so go down to New Haven, play in the American League and get better." Trent took the two-way contract—$100,000 guaranteed, $300,000 if he played in the NHL, with a $25,000 signing bonus—and he was over the moon with happiness.

By the next year's training camp, Mel Bridgman had been fired and a whole new management team had come in. This meant there was no room for Trent, not even with the farm team in PEI. So he was sent to the Thunder Bay Senators of the Colonial Hockey League. The experience in Thunder Bay was a lot like the movie *Slap Shot.* I reffed a few of his games and he told me later I didn't give him any reason to chirp, but Trent was the least of my worries.

One of the tough guys was Bryan Wells. When he was with the Regina Pats, he was the first player thrown out of the WHL for a wild stick-swinging joust with Mark Tinordi in Lethbridge and a vicious cross-check on Lyle Odelein, and it was rumoured he bit off somebody's finger in another league. Thunder Bay had eight of the league's top ten heavyweights. One guy, Mel Angelstad— a.k.a. "Mel the Mangler"—became Trent's good buddy. Mel wore number 69. After a couple of weeks, Trent looked around the dressing room and said to himself, "Dorothy, you're not in Kansas anymore."

Trent could see that there was no future for a guy like him in the Colonial Hockey League. He figured if he didn't make the American League the next year, he would quit and go to university. But 1994–95 was the lockout year, so he went right to PEI's training camp, and because it was his last kick at the kitty, he decided to cause trouble.

The team was playing an exhibition game in Cape Breton. Link Gaetz, a.k.a. "The Missing Link," was trying out for the minor-league team there. Link was unpredictable and considered a dangerous player. While on defence, Link was stickhandling out of his zone when Trent flew in and just rocked him. Link went down, slid to the red line, got up and dropped his gloves. Trent looked back and started to run.

Link chased him into PEI's end and tried to hammer him into the boards, but Trent was quick and slipped out of the way. This irritated Link even more. Although Darcy Simon was one of PEI's tough guys, the Western guys stick together. So he jumped on Link's back and put him in a headlock, but that barely slowed him down. Meanwhile, everybody else paired off. It was chaos. Link was going after Trent while trying to shake Darcy off and yelling, "Let me go! I'm gonna kill 'im. Let me go!"

Darcy refused. He knew Link might literally commit homicide. He continued to hang on for a few minutes even after the ref came over and ordered him to let go. Finally, the ref took Link's arm and Darcy let him go. As Link skated off, Cape Breton coach George Burnett told Link to calm down, and Link went berserk tearing up the bench.

PEI's coach, Dave Allison, liked Trent's nerve, and so he made the team. In January, Trent found himself in a game against the Cape Breton Oilers where he almost lost his left eye. He was standing in front of the net and moved to deflect the puck, but at the same time Boris Mironov lifted Trent's stick, which followed through into Trent's eyeball, tearing the retina.

Trent immediately covered up his eye with his glove. The trainer came out and said, "Okay, let go. I gotta see it."

Trent replied, "I can't. It's going to fall out."

Here he was, finally getting a look from Ottawa and with a potential career-ending injury. Trent was in the hospital a week before he regained any sight, and then the team sent him home to Swift Current to recover. Healing an eye is like a concussion. You rest.

Trent's pupil would always be dilated, but two games into the playoffs, he was finally cleared to play. He hadn't skated because of the danger to his eye, so he was eased into the lineup, but he knew his career was inches from being taken away, so he came onto the ice like a man on a mission.

The next year he was called up to Ottawa. Trent was a fourth-line spare part—valuable in the lineup but not a development prospect. He did a bit of penalty killing, but his main function was as the energy guy. When the team needed a spark, they'd wind him up and send him out. He'd get three or four minutes a game, but they were the three or four most interesting minutes.

At the end of the year, when salaries were disclosed, Trent learned he was the second-lowest-paid player in the NHL. Sandy McCarthy was the lowest, at $150,000 Canadian. Trent was making five thousand more. But Trent didn't mind. His lower salary made him affordable.

After the 1995–96 season, he was traded to Boston, where he played a year and then was sent down to the Detroit Vipers of the International Hockey League. There were almost a hundred guys in the lineup and Trent got lost in the shuffle, so he asked to go to the Las Vegas Thunder. Chris McSorley, Marty's brother, was the coach in Vegas until he got fired later that year in favour of assistant Clint Malarchuk. Chris and Clint were different birds, but Trent liked them both.

That summer, Trent was still Boston's property, but general manager Harry Sinden wouldn't return his phone calls. So the first day of training camp in Boston, Trent showed up uninvited. Harry was standing with a whole bunch of reporters when Trent walked up and said, "Hello, Mr. Sinden. My name's Trent McCleary. I played here two years ago. I came here to try out, or get my release."

Sinden said, "Yeah, we'll give you your release."

By this time, Trent had an agent, a lawyer named Ed Ratushny. Ed arranged for Trent to walk on halfway through Montreal's camp. During his first exhibition game, he scored two goals and had three fights, and in another game he kneed Eric Lindros and then fought him. All of a sudden it was "Who the hell is this guy?" And that's how Trent became a Montreal Canadien.

Every year at Super Bowl time, the Habs have back-to-back afternoon games. On January 19, 2000, they were playing Philly and Trent was out on the ice. The puck was scrambling around, so he went down in the zone to help his defence. When the puck bounced off the boards and came straight out to the point man Trent was covering, Chris Therien, Trent went down to block it. But the puck slowed down, so when Chris stepped into it, Trent was already sliding. At first Trent thought, "Okay, it's going to hit me in the pads." And then, "No, it's going to hit me in the stomach," and then all of a sudden, *bang!* It got him right in the throat.

The pain was indescribable. Many times, he'd taken hard shots to his ankles, and in those times he'd thought, "Okay, chop my leg off. This is horrible!" But this pain was so excruciating it raged through his entire body.

It started to subside a little by the time he was hauled up by the team trainer, Gaétan "Gates" Lefebvre. But his perception was a little wonky. He heard Bill McCreary, the referee, tell Gates, "Take your time." And Gates yelling back, "The hell with you. We're not taking our time. Let's go."

And then, all of a sudden, Trent felt like he was breathing through a straw that somebody was slowly pinching shut. He grabbed his throat, thinking, "I can't breathe. Why can't I breathe?" Maybe it was his chinstrap—he flipped his helmet back. He yanked out his mouth guard, but nothing helped. He started to panic as his airway closed. "What's going on?"

In those days, team doctors didn't sit behind the bench like they do now. And so Dr. David Mulder, who attended the Habs' games, was sitting in the doctor's room, which was around the corner from behind the bench. He saw Trent go down on the television and ran around to the area between the benches, where there are two big doors that open up. Trent got to the threshold and saw Dr. Mulder coming toward him. He thought, "Okay, they'll take care of me," and then his eyes rolled back and he collapsed.

Gates and Dr. Mulder carried him the ten steps from the main doors into the clinic, and at that point you couldn't see his neck anymore. The swelling was past his chin and getting bigger. They were met by another team doctor, Victor Lacroix.

Still in his skates, Trent started thrashing around, reaching for his throat. He thought there was a rope around his neck, squeezing the life out of him, and he was desperate to remove it. The room was in chaos. The medical team was trying to intubate him, but he was a young, strong NHLer and they couldn't hold him still enough to get through the fracture and the swelling. The trainers—Gates, assistant trainer Graham Rynbend, and two more—were trying their best. Each had an arm and a leg, and everyone was yelling at Trent—"Calm down! Calm down!" But he was literally lifting them off the ground and flailing, his razor-sharp skates slicing through the air close to their heads.

Dr. Dave Fleiszer was in the stands. He'd seen the choke sign and watched as Trent passed out. A former student of Dr. Mulder's, Dr. Fleiszer was head of trauma at Montreal General. His wife, Ruth, prodded him to go try to help. He rushed down and could see that Trent was coughing up blood and had stopped breathing. In an attempt to get Trent some air, Dr. Mulder grabbed a giant hypodermic so he could perform what's called a needle tracheostomy, or a needle cricothyrotomy. He tried to plunge the syringe into Trent's trachea. But Trent was still struggling too much—he couldn't do it. In fact, Trent almost threw Gates over the table.

Drs. Mulder and Fleiszer had to get some air into Trent or they were going to lose him. Dr. Fleiszer did what's called a "jaw thrust"—he put his hands under the corners of Trent's mandible and lifted towards his head. When you lift the voice box muscles that attach to the base of the tongue and the larynx, it reduces the fracture, so the manoeuvre opened Trent's airway. But his larynx was shattered. That meant they couldn't do a tracheostomy outside of an operating room. Unlike what you see on television, a tracheostomy is a horribly delicate procedure, and to do it in the field is next to impossible.

They started to bag him, pushing in air as much as they could. The problem was that, while oxygen was getting in, no gases were getting out, so his body was filling up with carbon dioxide, nitrogen and helium. He was poisoning himself.

There was an ambulance on standby for every game, so doctors were able to load him immediately. As the ambulance pulled away, sirens wailing, Trent's jersey was left behind on the floor. Graham had cut it off, the scissor trail going around the Canadiens' crest—even in a life-and-death situation, the Habs logo is something you don't mess with.

At Montreal General, the emergency room is on the first floor and the operating room is on the eighth. There was an elevator waiting, and Dr. Michel Germain, an anesthesiologist, started an intravenous drip with a muscle relaxant in the hallway. Trent suddenly coughed and Dr. Germain saw an opening. He jammed a tube down past the fracture, keeping Trent alive for the moment. Drs. Mulder and Fleiszer, who had been taking turns holding Trent's jaw in the right position, could finally let go. It takes a lot of physical strength to hold up a jaw, and so both their hands were almost paralyzed.

In the operating room, when Dr. Mulder started the tracheostomy, his mind was racing. Were his hands steady enough to make their way through all the damage? What if Trent died or came out of this severely brain damaged? When he completed the surgery and Trent could breathe again, Dr. Mulder looked down below the surgical drapes. Trent was still wearing his skates.

A few hours later, Trent's eyes opened just a slit. He couldn't move—he was still under the influence of the paralyzing agent that Dr. Germain had used. Everything was blurry, but he could hear the doctors talking. They were saying they weren't sure about whether he had brain damage. He tried to shift his thoughts into second gear. "Brain damage? What the hell happened?" A nurse came in and shone a light into his eyes. He heard her remark that the pupil wasn't dilating, which was not a good sign.

Trent was screaming in his head, "Hey! I'm here! It's just an old eye injury! It happened five years ago! Don't worry about it!" But his lips were still and so no sound came out. He would have to *show* them he was okay. There was an oxygen monitor clipped to his index finger, and if he flicked it off, they might know he was there with them. It took everything he had to move the finger. He was concentrating so hard that beads of sweat formed on his forehead. Well, sweating's a sign of infection. Trent heard them discussing it and thought, "Oh my God! Stop! I'm here. I'm fine. Why can't I talk?" And then he lost consciousness.

The next time he awoke, Dr. Mulder and Trent's girlfriend, Tammy, were in the room. Tammy had been at the game but had missed the accident. She'd seen the replay in the waiting room on TV but had no idea of the severity of Trent's condition. He could hear Dr. Mulder saying, "It was close, but he's alive."

Tammy responded, "What? What do you mean, 'He's alive'? How badly was he hurt?"

Trent managed to open his eyes, but he still couldn't talk. Dr. Mulder examined him and then made eye contact. He knew Trent well and could see that Trent could understand what was going on. He said, "It's okay, Trent. You're going to be fine. We're going to repair your shattered larynx, so don't worry, you will likely talk again."

Dr. Mulder got Trent paper and a pen, and Trent scrawled a message to the team. When there's a big game, you put money on the board to pay for a team party if you win. Montreal was playing Boston the next day. So Trent wrote, "Here's $500. Go Habs." That way the guys would know he was okay. Afterward, he thought maybe he should have said *fifty* dollars. The guys might think he had brain damage if he was putting in five hundred.

Gates calls Trent's survival "a perfect storm." From the moment he blocked the puck and was helped off the ice, to passing out in the doorway of the tunnel, which enabled them to drag him into the clinic, to the three doctors in attendance, to the quick ride to Montreal General without a blizzard or traffic jam—seventeen minutes. It was a miracle.

The Canadiens flew his family out and paid for everything. Their attitude was, "Whatever you need, you got it."

Trent couldn't swallow, so he was fed through a feeding tube for six weeks. He lost twenty pounds off his already lean frame. In that time, he went from an elite athlete to a guy who could barely shuffle down a hallway. He started back on solids with a pot of overcooked Kraft Dinner, and it was one of the best meals he'd ever had.

He got his voice back. Vocal cords are like two barn doors, when you breathe, they open and get out of your way, when they come together, sound is formed. One of Trent's cords is permanently closed, which means his airway is partially obstructed. It makes him a bit raspy. He sounds like Clint Eastwood.

By the end of the season, Trent had started some light training on the bike, but his fitness level was nowhere near NHL standards. Nevertheless, he was sure he could play again. He considered himself a cat with nine lives.

In training camp the next season, he blocked a few shots without hesitation. But fifteen or twenty seconds into his shift, he was just dying, skating through quicksand. He couldn't take deep breaths to get the volume of air he needed to get rid of the lactic acid in his muscles. Inside, he knew he wasn't able to play up to the level he'd been at before the accident, but he refused to give up.

Dr. Mulder was watching him like a hawk. The Canadiens played Vancouver in an exhibition game, and afterward Dr. Mulder sat him down. "Great try, good effort, but you're impaired, Trent. You can't do what you've done in the past. It makes you a liability out there because you can't get off the ice fast enough. You're too tired. I'm pulling your medical clearance."

It was almost a relief. Trent appreciated not having to make the decision to leave. He just wasn't a quitter—it wasn't in his DNA. Unless you're Jaromír Jágr, who can still produce at forty-three, or Lanny McDonald or Wayne Gretzky, who retired on a high, few people go out on top. Trent gave it everything he could. Nobody predicted he'd have a seven-year pro career, with four in the NHL. It was always, "He's too small. He's not talented enough," but he proved everybody wrong and didn't fade off into the sunset. In the end, he was sad, he was disappointed, but he didn't argue. He knew he couldn't breathe.

Later, he was often asked, "Would you block the shot that almost killed you again?" His answer was always the same, "Of course."

That's just who he is.

Red Deer

ALBERTA

———————

POPULATION:
90,564

Suds

In my office at home, sitting at the computer stuck for ideas or words, I'll glance to my right and stare at one of my favourite landscape paintings. It's called "South of Red Deer." Dirt road, a few poplar trees, some sage bush and rapeseed with plains of full white clouds filling a big sky. It's the wonderful work of Judy Sutter, whose husband, Brian, played and coached in the NHL.

The painting makes me think about how austere beginnings can be. The phrase "out of nowhere" always comes to mind. And I relax, knowing that the writing rut in the road I'm on will smooth out in a mile or two.

I first laid eyes on Brian Sutter in 1972 in my hometown when he skated for the Red Deer Rustlers. Brian, a left winger, and his centre-ice man, Terry Wittchen, were a dominant pair—heroes in my eyes. I remember them winning the Alberta Junior Hockey League crown and then facing the Kelowna Buckaroos on the Centennial Cup trail. I have in my head this image from an overtime game in that series. There was a delay to fix the chicken-wire screen behind the Kelowna net, so the Rustlers gathered at their bench. Sutter sat in one open gate, Wittchen in the other. They were sucking on orange quarters, and the sweat was pooling on the ice at their feet. They looked totally spent. The Rustlers lost the series in five, but Red Deer won that night on a goal engineered by one of Brian's relentless forechecks. Quit was not a word in his vocabulary.

Brian was the captain of the St. Louis Blues in 1984, my first year working in NHL television. On one of my first broadcasts, producer John Shannon arranged for Brian to be an intermission interview. Brian used a simple, thoughtful gesture to help me feel like I belonged and to create that same perception for the viewer. He used my name. "Well, Ron, we felt if we could stay disciplined . . ." and "You know, Ron, the Flames had a game last night in Edmonton, so . . ."

In 1988, the Blues hung his jersey, number 11, in the rafters at Scottrade Center in St. Louis. He's the only Sutter brother to have his number retired. When his playing days were done, Brian launched a great coaching career. In 1991, after he won the Jack Adams Award as the NHL's coach of the year, we all retired to a suite at the Westin Harbour Castle in Toronto where Blues chairman Michael Shanahan was staying. Among the guests that evening were Iron Mike Keenan and the notorious chairman of the NHL board of governors, Chicago's Bill Wirtz. At 5 a.m., Mr. Wirtz called down to the kitchen and ordered hamburgers for everyone. Another beer, another bite and the hockey stories started to flow.

And in 2009, Sutter coached the Bentley Generals to an Allan Cup.

The greatest compliment I've ever seen Brian receive is one he may not even be aware of. When Bob Bourne retired from the NHL in 1988, New York writer/broadcaster Stan Fischler wrote a glowing tribute along with a Q-and-A with Bourne for The Hockey News. Stan brought up Bob's four Stanley Cups and how he'd led the Islanders in scoring in the 1983 playoffs. He mentioned Bob's Bill Masterton Trophy and his having been named Sports Illustrated Sportsman of the Year for his work with children who have disabilities. Then Fischler asked Bourne, "Bob, in your fifteen NHL seasons playing with the very best, and skating against the very best, who is your most valuable player?"

Bourne replied, "Well, I've had the pleasure of playing along-side Bryan Trottier and Denis Potvin, and of course we all know about Wayne Gretzky, but for me the MVP of the NHL is Brian Sutter over in St. Louis. He does more to lift that team over there than any other player on any other team in the league."

And that brings me to my favourite Sutter memory. After Bill Ranford won the Stanley Cup in Edmonton in 1990, Bill, whose parents lived in Red Deer, was in town during the annual summer fair. Bill was asked to be exhibition parade marshal. I was invited to be assistant marshal. So there we were aboard the float, making our way along the route on the big day, smiles wide, waving to the citizens and perhaps feeling our oats, when I glanced to my right and spotted something that pulled me hard back down to earth. There in the crowd was a slender man in a plaid shirt and jeans. Chiselled, tanned and arrow straight, the next year he'd win the 1991 Canada Cup as part of the coaching staff. Like everyone else in the audience, he was gracious, even a little excited to wave and applaud. Brian Sutter, my boyhood hero. Out of nowhere.

---

*B*rian Sutter was really green when he was called up to the St. Louis Blues in December of 1976 for a game against the Boston Bruins, one of the toughest teams in the NHL. Coach Don Cherry had the likes of Terry O'Reilly, Brad Park, Mike Milbury, John Wensink, Stan Jonathan and Gary Doak on his bench. St. Louis, meanwhile, had only one really tough guy—Bobby Gassoff from Quesnel, British Columbia—and he needed some help.

Brian wasn't a big guy—under six feet and just 170 pounds—but he had made a name for himself in junior. In 1975–76, playing for the Lethbridge Broncos, he had ninety-two points and 233 penalty minutes.

The game against Boston was on the road. Brian was flown in. He practised with the team and was all set to go, but that night at the Garden, Blues coach and general manager Emile Francis sat him out. Turns out Francis had brought him in for a front-row view of his future.

But he was back on January 6, 1977, this time in Philadelphia, and it was World War III. Dave "The Hammer" Schultz had been traded, but the Flyers still had guys like Bobby Clarke, Mel Bridgman, Bob Kelly, Orest Kindrachuk, Paul Holmgren and André Dupont. Nineteen fights broke out. Back then, you were allowed three before you were kicked out of the game. Brian says that what the Flyers would do to get rid of guys on the opposing team was to challenge them on their way to the box after their first fight. So when Bobby Gassoff got sent to the dressing room for the night, Brian looked around, and it suddenly hit him—he'd been called up to take care of his teammates. There he was, just twenty years old, taking on the Broad Street Boys.

St. Louis had the oldest players in hockey, and they were struggling. They posted a 17–18–5 season. But there were some great role models for Brian—Red Berenson, Jimmy Roberts, goalie Eddie Johnston, defencemen Barclay and Bob Plager, Claude Larose, Garry Unger and Derek Sanderson. Brian played on the fourth line, getting fourteen points in thirty-five games while spending eighty-two minutes in the penalty box. The next season, he was a first-line player. Just a year earlier, Brian was ready to quit hockey and stick with farming and paving roads in Red Deer.

Emile Francis had been brought in from the New York Rangers in 1976 to turn around a franchise that was in disarray and lucky to attract five thousand fans a night. That June, in the draft, the Blues had taken Bernie Federko in the first round before choosing Brian in the second round, twentieth overall. They offered Brian a three-year contract at $15,000, $20,000 and $25,000.

Brian had also been taken in the World Hockey Association draft—fourth round, thirty-sixth overall—by Edmonton, and the Oilers were offering him $50,000, $60,000 and $65,000. It was also a one-way deal. A two-way contract means you're paid a lower salary if sent down to the minors, so the Oilers' offer was much more appealing. Plus, Edmonton was close to home. Brian thought about it, but not for very long. By '76, WHA franchises were constantly changing hands and moving from city to city. Some had even folded. Going to the WHA meant you weren't sure you were going to get paid. In fact, a lot of the guys didn't, and so they jumped back into the NHL. Brian was confident he'd get paid in St. Louis, but he'd get paid a lot less.

Francis called Brian to hear his decision. Brian said, "Mr. Francis, I am not coming to St. Louis. My wife, Judy, works for the City of Red Deer as a clerk at the courthouse, and I have a good job on the paving crew. We figure that between what Judy makes and what I make, well, it's more money than the contract."

Francis asked, "Well, what do you want?" Brian and his agent negotiated a three-year contract paying $25,000, $30,000 and $35,000. It was still a two-way deal, so if he got sent to the minors, he would only make, $7,000, $9,000 and $11,000. But Brian appreciated that Francis added a $50,000 signing bonus—half when he signed, and the rest after he played forty games. Brian ended that first year with only thirty-five games under his belt, but Francis sent him the second $25,000 anyway.

But Brian wasn't happy when it came time to do his taxes after his first year in the NHL. He owed more than he'd made. So he fired his agent, determined that he would negotiate for himself from then on. He and Francis understood each other—both were from small farming towns. Francis was a North Battleford, Saskatchewan, boy, and Brian's family farmed near Viking, Alberta. Brian's dad told him, "Hockey is a game, and you are a farmer. Never forget that."

Every team had a rookie initiation party. Usually, they shaved guys and stuff like that, but when Brian arrived, that practice stopped because he wouldn't let them do it. But he did go along with St. Louis's really fun tradition, snipe hunting. All the Blues, going back to the early years of Glenn Hall, Red Berenson, Phil Goyette and Doug Harvey, went through it. The team would load thirty guys into four half-ton pickups and drive west to Eureka, Missouri. The entire town was in on it—farmers, fish and wildlife officers, the police. When it got dark, the veterans took the 1977 rookies—Brian and Bernie Federko—down near the river to hunt snipe.

The boys were left sitting at the end of a long, cultivated field, which was all mushy because of the extremely fertile soil. They were given two nets, a flashlight and a case of beer. The vets jumped into the trucks and drove to the other end of the field. They said they were going to make a lot of noise by banging pots and pans in order to drive the snipe down the furrows toward the rookies.

Brian was pissed off and scared. He was in the middle of a field, it was pitch black outside and he was terrified of rats and snakes. As he held up the net, he could feel the cold muck seeping through the knees of his Levi's. Bernie was crouched beside him, shining a flashlight down the furrow. They could hear the vets yelling, "They're coming! Do you see them? A whole herd of them!"

Brian was a farmer—he knew the whole thing was ridiculous. He rolled his eyes and said, "Bernie, this is friggin' bull."

And then, all of a sudden, two big headlights flicked on behind them and a couple of police cars rolled up with their sirens blasting. The police charged Brian and Bernie with illegal snipe hunting. The boys were handcuffed, thrown into the back of the police car and raced into Eureka, where they were locked up.

As the officers tried to push Brian into the cage, he tried to kick one of them, yelling, "You get the eff away from me!"

Bernie was beside himself. "No, Sutter, cut it out! Don't do anything! We'll be deported!"

The officers managed to get the guys into their cells and then they left—turning off all the lights.

Dave Dietrich was a high-ranking, well-respected criminal attorney in St. Louis. About an hour after the boys had been incarcerated, he stormed in and demanded that "his clients" be released. And then he loaded them into his car and drove them to join the team, who were eating pizza, and drinking Busch beer at a local bar.

The Blues seemed always to be run on a shoestring. They trained in Regina to save money, and some years they didn't even have a farm team. Most teams had at least forty players under contract, but Brian remembers one year when St. Louis had only twenty-four under contract. From 1978 to 1981, the years when Alain Vigneault, Alain Lemieux, Mark Reeds and Paul MacLean were drafted, Brian says the team would rent out its hired guns to the Central Hockey League's Montana Magic.

For years, the Blues traded their first-round picks for a couple of young guys. At one point, they had ten ex–Montreal Canadiens, all under the age of twenty-five, including Doug Wickenheiser, Mark Hunter, Rick Wamsley, Ric Nattress and Kent Carlson. The players would shake their heads when they knew the Habs' Al MacNeil was in town because it meant they were going to lose a top young prospect and get a third- or fourth-liner back.

Other teams travelled with two or three trainers. St. Louis travelled with one. As the guys got settled into the hotel, the equipment was driven to the rink, but Brian would throw his suitcase in his room, hop in a cab and head over to help the trainer unpack. Brian took less money to sign with St. Louis, and sometimes he wasn't even paid everything he was owed on time, but he'd wait a couple years until new owners would take over and then he'd receive a cheque for back pay. Didn't matter, he stayed loyal to his team.

In 1979–80, when Brian was twenty-two years old, he was made captain. He was playing more than twenty minutes a night. A lot of his job involved shutting down the other teams' best players. That didn't always sit well with the opposing teams, so he would get ambushed. A guy might dump the puck in, and when Brian went in to forecheck, another opponent might grab him from behind while he'd get sandwiched from in front. One time, he was beaten so badly, he played the rest of the game with one eye, because the other eye was seeing stars.

In 1980–81, the Blues finished first in the Smythe Division and faced the Rangers in the quarter-finals. By now, the Blues were the *youngest* team in the league, with draftees Wayne Babych and Perry Turnbull and college free agent Joey Mullen having developed into valuable players. And they were loaded with talent thanks to the collapse of the WHA. Mike Liut, their goalie, had come from Cincinnati. Including the preseason he won close to fifty games that year and was runner-up behind Wayne Gretzky for the Hart Trophy. In 1982, another ex-WHA player, a big, tough scoring defenceman named Rob Ramage, would arrive from the Birmingham Bulls via the Colorado Rockies for a first-round draft pick.

Brian loved the American national anthem. To him, it was the greatest song ever. He was a Canadian through and through and thought "O Canada" was special, but "The Star-Spangled Banner" in Chicago, Philly, New York or Boston on a Sunday night was like a call to march into war. *Oh say can you see by the dawn's early light . . .* He'd feel the blood burning like pepper through his nostrils. *And the rockets' red glare, the bombs bursting in air . . .* His jaw would clamp tight. *O'er the land of the free and the home of the brave!* And his heart would wrap around his whole body like a suit of armour.

At the start of the series, Brian was thinking about taking on Ed Johnstone, Ron Greschner and Don Maloney. The teams were standing on the blue lines at Madison Square Garden as the anthem started up, when suddenly Brian and the boys could hear loud cracks exploding all around them. They looked at each other. "Gunshots? What in the hell is going on?" The game started and nothing more was said.

The next game at the Garden, the anthem started playing again, and again they were surrounded by what sounded like rifle shots. Brian looked around and noticed his teammates starting to shuffle away from him.

Ramage shouted over to him, "They're throwing frickin' walnuts on the ice from the upper decks . . . at *you*."

In September of 1983, Brian was back home, harvesting. He and Bernie Federko both had contracts up for negotiation, and Bernie was really upset. He had been calling the farm, telling Brian there was no way he was reporting to training camp because Francis wasn't giving him what he needed to play. A seventh-overall pick, Bernie was making $75,000 a year. He was looking for an average of $150,000, which Brian thought was fair. Over an eight-year span, Brian says he thinks the only other tandem that scored as many goals as he and Bernie did was Wayne Gretzky and whoever was on his wing.

In those days, the league had a strict rule—you had to be checked into your hotel by midnight of the first day of training camp. So each year, Brian would leave the day before and drive straight through to St. Louis. It was twenty-eight to thirty hours of easy driving, but he could make it in twenty-six if there were no delays at the border, and he always pushed it. Being a farmer himself, Francis understood when Brian arrived late. He would make a big deal about fining Brian, but when things settled down, he'd mail him his cheque back.

This year, Brian drove twenty-four hours straight, stopping in Columbia, halfway between Kansas City and St. Louis, to get gas. He called Francis and said, "I'll be there in a couple of hours." And Francis said, "I'll be waiting for you, even if it's two in the morning." Brian arrived at the old Checkerdome just before midnight.

Francis's office was on the third floor of a four-storey tower, and there was a little eight-by-eight-foot waiting room off the lobby. In St. Louis, the humidity can make it feel like it's about a hundred degrees Fahrenheit at that time of the year, and nowhere in the building was air-conditioned except for Francis's office. Bernie and his agent were sitting in the waiting room. They'd been negotiating with Francis the entire summer and hadn't gotten anywhere. Training camp started in the morning, and they had reached an impasse, so Francis had given them the boot. Both men were drowning in sweat. Bernie's agent was dressed in a three-piece suit and his tie hung around his neck like the tongue of a thirsty dog in the hot sun.

Brian breezed in, excited to be back in St. Louis. Bernie's agent asked, "Where are you going?"

Brian said, "Up to see Mr. Francis."

Bernie's head was hanging in his hands. He looked up and said, "Suds, I'm not reporting to camp."

Brian hopped into the elevator to go see his boss. Francis wasn't a big man—he stood five foot four—but his presence made him a foot taller. He had a long office with a big, tall desk and a big, tall chair behind it. There was a low couch placed way across the room, and when Brian sat down on it, he felt like he was a child on the floor, staring up at a giant.

Francis talked about harvesting and cattle, and asked how the hell Brian got there so quick, and then he left the room and came back with a couple of Busch beers, Brian's favourite. As they talked, Brian told Francis that he and Judy had used every nickel he made playing hockey to buy farmland. Francis nodded, took a swig and swallowed, and said, "Well, what are we going to do about this contract?"

Brian replied, "Yeah, well, what should we do?" He really had no idea, because it was the first contract he had ever negotiated, but he did have a number in mind. The average in the league a year earlier had gone up from $75,000 to $125,000. Somebody in the league office had told him that other top-scoring left wingers like Clark Gillies, Steve Shutt and Billy Barber were making that. But those boys were a little bit older and they played in New York, Montreal and Philadelphia, the top teams in the league. Brian made $35,000 in St. Louis, but he had scored forty-one goals, so he thought, "Well, jeez, if I get an average of $75,000 for the next three years, I'll be happy!" And of course, there were bonuses too. So he said, "Here is what we will do, Mr. Francis. We will each write on a piece of paper what we think I'm worth for the next three years."

Both men wrote their numbers down, Brian scribbling "50, 75 + 100." Francis stood up, walked out from behind his desk, set his note on the coffee table in front of Brian and then returned to his chair.

Brian reached for the paper, trying to keep his hand steady. He was scared and his heart was beating hard, but at the same time he felt a certain calm because he trusted Francis. He cupped the paper in one hand and opened it up with the other. It said, "100, 125 and 150."

While Francis talked to him, Brian tried not to keep glancing down at the paper. He was having a hard time digesting the big numbers. Finally, Francis said, "Okay, let's see your piece of paper."

Brian shook his head. "No, Mr. Francis, you don't have to see my piece of paper. I'll accept your offer." And then, the talk turned to bonuses. Back then, fifty-goal scorers were really hard to come by—you could count them on one hand—so Francis wanted to offer Brian bonuses for forty, forty-five and fifty goals. Brian said, "Mr. Francis, you don't have to give me personal bonuses. I'd like team bonuses instead." So they worked out a plus/minus quarterly bonus for the whole team.

As well, Brian asked for a loan of $100,000 so that he could pay off his farmland. And so Francis wrote into the contract that it was "a separate loan, an undisclosed amount, that is between the St. Louis Blues and Brian Sutter entirely," and the beauty of it was, Francis made it non-repayable.

Altogether, the two of them worked out the contract in about half an hour. When Brian stepped off the elevator, he was on cloud nine. Bernie and his agent were still in the waiting room. The agent asked, "What happened up there?"

Brian answered, "I just did my contract," and both their mouths dropped open.

Bernie signed a couple of days later, and he and his wife and Brian and Judy all bought houses in a small town nearby called Chesterfield, which was less than twenty miles from the rink. Brian played for four more years, becoming great friends with guys like Doug Gilmour, who scored 105 points in 1986–87.

In 1988, team executive Jack Quinn brought him in and said, "Brian, did you ever think about coaching?" A year earlier, Brian had signed a new contract paying $200,000, $225,000 and $275,000. There were only a few players making the kind of money Brian and Bernie were earning at the time—Wayne

Gretzky, Dave Taylor, Larry Robinson. Brian knew that coaches, even great ones like Al Arbour and Scotty Bowman, made only $100,000 to $150,000, and he didn't want to take the pay cut. But Quinn told him he could coach at the salary his playing contract called for. At thirty-one, he was the youngest coach in the league.

In the middle of the summer of 1988, Brian was on his way back from coaches' meetings in Minnesota. He was at the airport when he called the Blues' general manager, Ron Caron, to check on Dougie Gilmour's contract. Brian saw Dougie, who was among the team's leading scorers, as one of the keys to the team's success.

Some allegations had been made about Dougie off the ice, so Caron had traded him to the Calgary Flames. (The allegations didn't last, with a grand jury declining to indict on any criminal charges, and a civil lawsuit ending shortly afterward.) He listed the guys he got for Gilmour—Mike Bullard, Craig Coxe and Tim Corkery—but Brian didn't hear him. In his mind, it was a typical St. Louis move. Calgary was now doing the same thing to the Blues that the Montreal Canadiens used to do, and the team was using the "allegations" as an excuse. Brian was so mad he started banging the receiver against the phone. Security came running from all directions, but he didn't care. He was in such a fury he grabbed the whole phone unit and ripped it right off the wall.

Doug Gilmour went to Calgary and became one of their top players and an important part of their 1989 Stanley Cup win. The Blues now had a whole group of fourth- and fifth-liners from Calgary. A year earlier, they had traded Rob Ramage and Rick Wamsley for Steve Bozek and another guy that nobody in the league wanted—Terry Crisp was coaching the Flames' farm team, and *he* didn't even want him back there. The guy in question became one of the greatest goal scorers in the history of the NHL—in Brian Sutter's opinion, the greatest right winger ever. His name was Brett Hull.

Brian had played with him for a year, so he had an idea what kind of player "Hully" could become. Having lost Gilmour, he needed a guy who could score. Brian's philosophy was that the two greatest words in life are *trust* and *respect*. So he took a team full of young players and misfits and totally rebuilt it in one year. Between playoffs, exhibition games and the regular season, Brett Hull scored a hundred goals for St. Louis in three different years.

But once again, the team was going through a change of ownership and guys weren't getting paid. Even so, Brian managed to take the Blues to the playoffs in each of his four years behind the bench. In 1992, after a first-round loss to Chicago, the NHL's coach of the year for 1990–91 was fired. To date, the Blues have never won a Stanley Cup.

On March 24, 1977, Brian was playing in Montreal for the first time, and he had a chance to meet Sam Pollock and Jean Béliveau, who told him, "A winner isn't somebody who wins the Stanley Cup, or plays on a winning team." And over the years, Brian learned they were one hundred per cent right.

You Know How to Whistle, Don't You?

At the 2005 Juno Awards in Winnipeg, k.d. lang sang Leonard Cohen's song "Hallelujah." It was transcendent. Kathryn Dawn Lang attended Red Deer College. It was there that she formed a Patsy Cline tribute band called the Reclines.

At the same time k.d. was studying Friday Dance Promenades, I was in the church of Saturday night hockey. Red Deer College hockey coach Allan Ferchuk was on the forefront. He was one of the teachers overhauling the game. The narrow escape we had in the 1972 Summit Series gave rise to a lot of introspection. Red Deer College paid for Ferchuk to visit Russia in 1976 so he could learn about their hockey uprising. He discovered the Russians were using the physiology teachings of a Canadian, Lloyd Percival.

Percival was the director/host of Sports College of the Air on CBC Radio. He later ran the Fitness Institute. When Percival's The Hockey Handbook, the first how-to book of hockey fundamentals, was published in 1951, most professional Canadian coaches thought it was bunk, but Russian and European coaches used it to guide players to international success.

The Russians borrowed from soccer to design a power play, creating a series of two-on-ones. They borrowed from basketball to press on the forecheck and from volleyball to bump back on offence. It was a time when educators from Canadian colleges and universities found a voice in the entrenched old school of the professional game.

That brings me back to Leonard Cohen. When he wrote eighty verses of "Hallelujah," in 1984, he was at a low point in his career. Just as Wayne Gretzky owns sixty-one NHL records, and will tell you that scoring fifty goals in thirty-nine games, as he did in 1981, is "The Record," Cohen has said his version of fifty in thirty-nine is the five verses of "Hallelujah" he recorded.

For me, it's the third verse that takes me back to Red Deer.

Baby I've been here before.
I know this room, I've walked this floor.

*I used to live alone before I knew you
I've seen your flag on the marble arch,
but love is not a victory march
it's a cold and it's a broken Hallelujah!*

What does this mean? Well, when I was a boy in Red Deer, I recall how my mom, Lila, was a person you could not put one over on. Mom explained that the fight was fixed. So Lila and Leonard were in agreement—do your best, even if it isn't much, if you cannot feel, try to touch, tell the truth and don't come to fool the few. And even if it all goes wrong, you'll stand before the lord of song with nothing on your tongue but hallelujah.

———————

*W*hen I was a kid and worked the Alberta Junior Hockey League penalty box at the Red Deer Arena, the St. Albert Saints, coached by Mark Messier's dad, Doug, would come in and play John Chapman's Red Deer Rustlers. Those games were wars. Lance Roberts was one of two referees that could handle them. The other was Bernie Haley out of Innisfail.

One night, Lance was officiating a St. Albert game in Taber. It was dangerous that night. The fans in Taber were starting to come down toward the bench when Lance saw Doug Messier step up on his bench. Lance grabbed Doug, saying, "You're not going anywhere!" Doug didn't argue—he knew Lance was looking after him. If Doug went into the stands, he'd be suspended.

I just loved the way Lance refereed. In those days, there were a lot more nineteen-year-old players in the AJHL, so it was a fairly high-level, tough brand of hockey. Because there was no such thing as a game misconduct for fighting, there were a lot of bench-clearing brawls. I remember one fight where Lance gave two players delay-of-game penalties instead of calling them for roughing or fighting, which was kind of a shock. Lance would let the players play, and if they didn't want to play, then he had the strength to make sure that penalties were called.

It was all about communication and credibility. The players had confidence in him. I remember a big brawl in Red Deer, under coach Wynne Dempster. There were so many penalties to assess that Lance sent everyone off before the end of the period, but Wynne refused to leave the bench. Lance skated over and told him, "Fine, you stay out and watch the Zamboni because we're all going to the dressing room."

When I reffed I never, ever showed up the players. It they blasted a puck right at me from five feet, I would never snap, "Hey, watch where you're shooting—have a look!" Instead, I'd apologize for getting hit. That's what I learned from Lance—to be a "players first" guy. I tried to have that swagger, without ever showing it. Make sure everyone in the house recognizes not the star, but the leader of the event.

I also loved the way Lance signalled his penalties. He put so much coolness into the game. When he called a high stick his left hand was in the air as though holding a torch, leaving the impression this guy was more a player than an administrator. It's like the military—you cannot trump the look of the air force pilots. Or, like with patrol cops and their shades, it's hard to define that look that says, "I welcome the danger here, I've seen it all, and I have it under control." Lance was cooler than the rest.

He was my favourite referee by far. In fact, I would later borrow that high-sticking signal.

When Lance played minor hockey with the Maple Leaf Athletic Club in Rosslyn, which was a suburb in northwest Edmonton, it was tough to get guys to referee. A lot of the games were outdoors, and in Edmonton it averages twenty-four below from December through February. But Lance was looking for a part-time job and a buddy called him to come help ref a game, so Lance thought, "Why not?" One game led to another, and before he knew it, he was officiating AA and rep games all over the city. For the first few years, he never saw indoor ice, but then he was selected to do an all-star game at the old Edmonton Gardens and he couldn't believe the luxury of it.

A year or two later, he decided refereeing might be something he could do for a living, so he headed to Banff to attend Dutchy Van Deelan's referee school. After that, he set his sights on the NHL, but first he'd have to make his way up through the WHL. Lance decided to track down a fellow Edmontonian, Brian Shaw, owner of the Portland Winterhawks. Maybe Brian would hire him? So he drove two thousand miles to Portland, Oregon, walked into the arena and ran into Wayne Myers, a buddy from the Maple Leaf Athletic Club. Lance asked him where Shaw was, and Wayne replied, "He's in Edmonton. You should give him a call." It was a long way to go for a phone number.

Brian told Lance there was an officiating camp that weekend in Calgary, and that's where Lance caught his first break. He was hired to work the lines in Lethbridge in 1979. It was a three-man system, so he had the ability to call the game on his own. Night after night, he'd talk to the coaches, letting them know what kind of game he was going to call. Communication was everything—the players had to feel safe, but also know that they had freedom to play, because if the players didn't believe in you, it was a long night. He worked the finals for four years in a row, including the 1986 and 1987 Memorial Cups, and then he got the call.

His first NHL game was between Hartford and the Red Wings at Joe Louis Arena in Detroit, November 3, 1989. It was also Jimmy Carson's first game in Detroit. He and Kevin McClelland had been traded from Edmonton for Petr Klíma, Joe Murphy, Adam Graves, Jeff Sharples and the Oilers' fifth-round draft choice. Lance awarded Carson a penalty shot at 2:09 of the second period after Dave Babych pulled him down on a breakaway. Unfortunately, Lance was so nervous, he forgot to signal, so no one knew what was happening. When he skated over to the box, the linesman, Bob Hodges, asked, "What did you call?"

Lance said, "I'm calling a penalty shot."

Hodges replied, "Well, you're supposed to point to centre ice."

Carson skated down and tried a deke and then a backhand on Mike Liut, but Liut slid to his right and stopped the puck. There'd been such a big buildup about Carson, a hometown boy, coming to Detroit that you could hear the air leave the Joe Louis Arena after the miss.

Jim Gregory, who was executive director of hockey operations for the NHL at the time, came down after the game and found Lance. He said, "What's the signal for a penalty shot?"

Lance said, "I know it, Mr. Gregory. You point to centre ice."

Gregory nodded. "Well, now you'll be a stronger official from your mistake."

Because he was a great communicator, Lance had good control. In 1992 in Quebec, a fan jumped over the boards onto the Buffalo bench and they threw him back on the ice. But when he came back, Rob Ray got hold of him and began furiously punching him.

Just ahead of that incident, there was a five-on-five brawl going on thanks to a hit by Herb Raglan on Buffalo goaltender Clint Malarchuk. Lance was trying to get the ice under control when he saw the police rushing in to grab the fan, who was being pummelled by Ray, so Lance yelled, "Check out the bench!" And when they saw what was happening, they stopped fighting and skated over to watch.

But there was a game in March 1998—on Friday the 13th between Anaheim and the Stars at Reunion Arena in Dallas— that nearly got away from him. Anaheim was tied for the bottom spot in the Western Conference, with no chance of making the playoffs. One of their stars, Paul Kariya, was out with a concussion from a cross-check to the head by Gary Suter at a game against Chicago. The Ducks had not only lost eight of their last ten games with Kariya gone, but they were taking a lot of heat because nobody on the team had responded to the Suter hit.

With about four and a half minutes to go in a 5–1 game over the Ducks, Craig Ludwig, a big Dallas defenceman, met up with the NHL's top scorer, Teemu Selänne. At the All-Star Game that year, Selänne would become the first European to be named the MVP of the game. Selänne had skated the puck all the way down, beating Ludwig along the boards and into the corner, so Ludwig spun to the middle and charged the boards, leaving his feet as he gave Selänne a big elbow to the head. Selänne went down and Lance called a five-minute major.

Centreman Steve Rucchin and defenceman Jason Marshall took some swats at Ludwig, but Lance got hold of him and skated him over to the net. Ludwig argued, swearing he saw Selänne peeking up at him and insisting he was faking his injury. Lance told Ludwig that he was underestimating. He had rocked Selänne and Teemu was really hurt. Finally, one of the linesmen grabbed hold of Ludwig on either side of his sweater and skated him over to the box while the other linesman tried to corral Jason Marshall, who was waiting for an opportunity to clean Ludwig's clock.

Ducks coach Pierre Pagé was furious. Now his two most talented players might both be out with concussions. One of his tough guys, Dave Karpa, skated to the penalty box and tried to jab Ludwig through a gap in the glass with the butt end of his stick, but Ludwig got hold of it and chucked it up into the stands, which made Karpa even madder. Meanwhile, Dallas right winger Jamie Langenbrunner came over to intervene for Ludwig, so one linesman wrestled Karpa down while another subdued Langenbrunner.

Selänne finally got up and headed to the dressing room, and Ludwig was being escorted to the Dallas room, so everything seemed under control until a kid named Peter Leboutillier from Minnedosa, Manitoba, jumped up and reached over the boards, trying to get at Ludwig with his stick. Now both benches were up and ready to go, so Lance came over to settle the kid down. He sent Leboutillier off after Jason Marshall, who went down the tunnel just ahead of him.

As the teams lined up for the faceoff in Dallas's end, Pagé felt he had to send a message, so he sent out his fourth line. Lance watched Anaheim's tough guys line up, and he knew it was going

In Burnaby, B.C., with Kirk McLean. Kirk's become a legend in Vancouver thanks to an overtime stop on Calgary's Robert Reichel in 1994. But in this photo, he's telling me how his save on Al MacInnis in the third period of the same game was bigger.

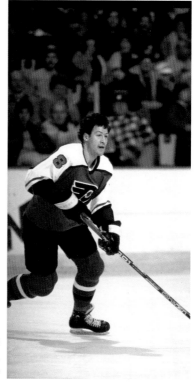

The MacLean-Hunter minor hockey team, formerly the Southwest Bobcats. Brad Marsh (*middle row, centre*), Craig MacTavish (*middle row, far left*), Robin Smith (*front row, third from right*), Doug Berk (*middle row, second from right*) and coach Bruce Stewart (*left*).

Brad Marsh with the Philadelphia Flyers circa 1985.

Ian Jenkins and his best buddy, stepbrother Lester. COURTESY THE JENKINS FAMILY

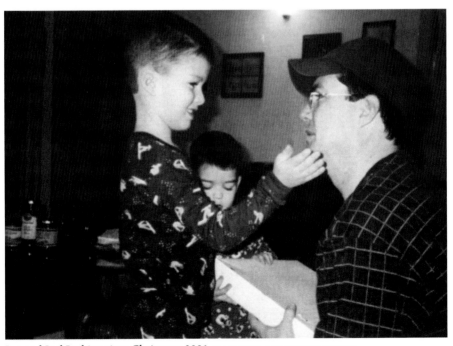

Ian and Joel Jenkins circa Christmas 2001. COURTESY THE JENKINS FAMILY

January 16, 1989: 13-year-old Eric Lindros playing on the backyard rink with brother, Brett. Jeff Goode/Getty Images

If you want to make it in hockey, you don't have to dream it. You have to love it. Eric Lindros with the Philadelphia Flyers. Dave Sandford/Hockey Hall of Fame

Trent McCleary in October 1998, two years before Habs doctors made the greatest save ever, rescuing Trent from almost certain death.
C. Anderson/Getty Images

Trent McCleary in Montreal, January 11, 1999, one year before his accident. Trent is the definition of character, which is to do something outside your comfort zone and to contribute.
Robert Laberge/Getty Images

Rogers Hometown Hockey in Saskatoon with Colby Armstrong and members of the Western Canada Montreal Canadiens Fan Club. Rogers Media

It didn't take Brian Sutter long to figure out why Emile Francis wanted him in St. Louis.
COURTESY BRIAN AND JUDY SUTTER

Brian, next to his wife, Judy, picks up his 1990–91 NHL Broadcasters Association's Jack Adams Award for Best Coach.
COURTESY BRIAN AND JUDY SUTTER

Rogers Hometown Hockey in Lethbridge, Alberta, with (*left to right*) Mark Messier, Cassie Campbell-Pascall, Rich Sutter, Tara Slone and Paul Brandt. ROGERS MEDIA

I loved the way Lance Roberts refereed. Like those of John McCauley, Lance's signals were cool, leaving the impression he was more a player than an administrator. DAVE SANDFORD/GETTY IMAGES

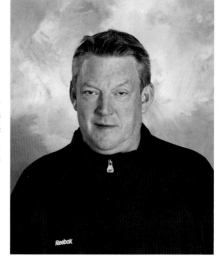

Toronto Maple Leafs' Gary Roberts, Dmitry Yushkevich and Bryan McCabe object to Lance Roberts after having a goal called back during second period NHL action. Edmonton, March 7, 2001. REPRINTED WITH PERMISSION OF SUN MEDIA

Rogers Hometown Hockey in my hometown, Red Deer, Alberta, with guests (*left to right*) Jamie Salé, Grant Fuhr and Darcy Tucker. ROGERS MEDIA

A street photographer snaps Red Berenson, Bill Hicke and Terry Harper, all wearing their incredibly cool jackets, circa 1955.
COURTESY THE HICKE FAMILY

Bill with his arm around his wife, LeeAnne, "The Bride." Back row: Ryan Ostertag and Dylan Ostertag. Middle row: Jim Ostertag, Lisa Hicke-Ostertag, Bill Hicke and LeeAnne Hicke. Front row: Danny Hicke. COURTESY THE HICKE FAMILY

A young Doug Wickenheiser in his backyard rink. COURTESY THE WICKENHEISER FAMILY

Fans called Doug Wickenheiser "Dream Weaver," after the Gary Wright song.
B. BENNETT/GETTY IMAGES

to get ugly. Sure enough, the puck was dropped and all five skaters went at it. Warren Rychel was first to drop the gloves, with Craig Muni. Brent Severyn, who had received a lot of heat for only warning Suter after the Kariya hit, went after Sydor and then let him go, but Sydor came back and jumped on his back, so Severyn lost his temper and whacked him hard. Sydor went down and stayed there. To this day, Severyn regrets losing it on a smaller guy.

The fans were on their feet, joining in with the song playing over the system—the Beastie Boys' "You Gotta Fight for Your Right to Party."

When all was said and done, Dallas's Darryl Sydor and Craig Muni both got five for fighting, Sean Pronger and Greg Adams were assessed double minors for roughing and Guy Carbonneau got two for roughing. For the Ducks, Rychel got two for instigating, five for fighting and a ten-minute misconduct, Severyn got five for fighting and a ten-minute misconduct, Drew Bannister received five for fighting and Pronger got two for roughing.

Once that mess was cleaned up, Lance went over to Pierre Pagé and said, "Okay, are we done? We're done, right?"

Pagé shrugged and turned away, which was a good sign. Next, Lance approached Dallas coach Ken Hitchcock—they'd known each other for years. Ken had coached midget hockey in Sherwood Park. He said, "Ken, we're done?"

Ken said, "We haven't had our turn yet."

Lance said, "Ken, no. Don't tell me that."

"We haven't had our turn," Ken repeated.

Lance shook his head. "Okay." He skated to his linesmen and said, "Get ready because they're going to go again."

Hitchcock put out Grant Marshall, Jason Botterill and Pat Verbeek. The puck was dropped, and things got started when Botterill went after Steve Rucchin. It turned into another line brawl, and Lance tossed some more guys out. Now Anaheim was left with four skaters on the bench—Tomas Sandström, Matt Cullen, Jeremy Stevenson and Pavel Trnka—and there were maybe three on the bench for Dallas. But there was still three minutes left in the hockey game, so Lance was going to have to make sure there were no other incidents. Anaheim had pulled starting goaltender Mikhail Shtalenkov and put in Tom Askey, who was fresh from Ohio State University. Lance skated over and told him to keep moving the puck and not to freeze it, and then he let everything go and the horn sounded.

Lance was taught to make sure to look after the good players and not to protect the fighters—they could handle themselves. One night, during a game in L.A., he was watching big Winnipeg left winger Keith Tkachuk. It was Tkachuk's rookie year, and Lance could see the kid trying to line up Wayne Gretzky, but Gretzky could see him coming down Broadway. Finally, Gretzky dumped the puck in and Tkachuk finished a check on him, hitting hard. Gretzky went down. Tkachuk looked around as if to say, "What happens now?"

He soon found out. Marty McSorley was on the ice, and he came at Tkachuk like a freight train. When Tkachuk turned around, Marty got him with a single punch right in the face and he dropped like a sack of potatoes.

Lance skated over and said, "That'll be two minutes, Marty."

Marty said, "I'll take that," and skated straight to the box. Lance understood that Marty was just doing his job, delivering the message, "This isn't going to happen on our ice." Meanwhile, Tkachuk got up, dabbing at his bleeding lip and looking at Lance. "What about my lip? What about my lip?"

Lance shook his head. "Hit Gretzky again, Stupid, and then see what happens!" And then he skated closer to Tkachuk and pointed to Marty. "He isn't going anywhere, so just think about that."

There were a few times when players lost it on Lance, but he never feared them. Bob Probert came at him one time—he thought he'd been hooked with no call and so he looked pretty intense. Lance started backing up a little and called Probie for unsportsmanlike conduct. But as soon as he got out of the box, Probie skated over and said, "Sorry, man, I shouldn't have acted like that."

Lance said, "No problem." He loved Probie.

Lance worked a lot of playoff games with Bill McCreary. In Lance's book, McCreary was the best NHL official ever. Lance thought Bill knew the game better than anybody.

At the last commercial break in 1999 during the playoff series between Pittsburgh and Philadelphia, the score was 6–2 with two minutes left in the third period. McCreary skated over to Lance and said, "They're gonna go. As soon as we drop the puck, they're definitely gonna go. I just know it." And, as he predicted, there was a five-on-five, but thanks to Bill's prescience, they handled it.

I believe that the coaches set the tone for a team's behaviour unless a strong referee with good presence and communication wins the players' respect, in which case they ignore the coach and follow the zebra. Lance is right about Bill McCreary. Bill was more of an influence than anyone in the building.

Lance spent fourteen years in the NHL and twelve years trying to get there, but in 2001 he was terminated without cause by the league's new director of officiating, Andy Van Hellemond. That was hard for Lance to digest, but he was picked up by the Swiss league and was chosen to referee the Spengler Cup in Davos, Switzerland. Played around Christmas each year, it's the oldest hockey tournament in Europe. It was the first time in the Cup's seventy-five-year history that a Canadian referee officiated the gold medal game with Canada in it, and that's why today his sweater hangs in the Spengler Cup section of the Hockey Hall of Fame.

Regina

SASKATCHEWAN

POPULATION:
193,100

The Life of a Thousand Men

Regina, the capital of Saskatchewan, is the home of the Pats, the oldest junior team in Canada, named for Queen Victoria's granddaughter, Princess Patricia of Connaught. Patricia is also honoured by one of our country's greatest military regiments, Princess Patricia's Canadian Light Infantry.

A boyhood hero of mine has ties to both—Ed Staniowski. Ed was born in Regina and raised in Moose Jaw, after which he embarked on a brilliant goaltending career with the Regina Pats in the WHL. In 1973, '74 and '75 he was named the Pats' most valuable player. In 1974 he backstopped Regina to the Memorial Cup, and the following year he was named the inaugural winner of the Canadian Major Junior Player of the Year award. He is, to date, the only goalie ever to receive that award.

As a child in Red Deer, I was thrilled to listen to Calgary broadcaster Eric Bishop finding new superlatives to describe Staniowski as he befuddled the powerful Calgary Centennials. After his Regina days, Staniowski played pro for a decade, winning the Terry Sawchuk Trophy as top goalie in the Central Hockey League in 1978 and playing parts of ten NHL seasons with St. Louis, Winnipeg and Hartford.

When he retired, Staniowski joined the Canadian Forces Primary Reserves. He quickly rose through the ranks and became a lieutenant colonel. Staniowski was the senior military liaison officer for the 2002 G8 summit in Kananaskis, Alberta, and was chosen *for United Nations peacekeeping and peace enforcement missions in Croatia, Bosnia and the Middle East. In each situation, he served alongside the Princess Patricia's Canadian Light Infantry.*

Once a Pat, always a Pat.

When the winter winds sweep over the prairies, wheat fields give way to hockey rinks, and young men and women pay homage to a game that's been celebrated here since 1917. The Regina Pats folded in 1934 but returned in 1946 when the Regina Abbotts and Regina Commandos merged to create a stronger team.

So many hockey greats hail from the heart of the prairies—eighty-eight NHLers to date. It's a tight town. The population doesn't tend to shift much—Reginans like their regal hockey town. Today, if you ask anyone in the Queen City about the NHL, you'll get a story about Ryan Getzlaf, Chris Kunitz or Jordan Eberle. Yesterday, it was Bob Turner, Lorne Davis, Paul Masnick and, of course, Red Berenson and Bill Hicke.

The Hicke family lived just half a block away from the rink, in the 1400 block of Royal Street, just east of a tougher area. Bill's dad, John, was a barber when it was a dollar a haircut. One night, John came home with a hundred bucks for the day. He was pretty proud of that. He owned a pool room at the back of the two-chair shop. It was called Top Hat Billiards and was located next door to the King's Hotel downtown on Scarth Street.

John was a shark, and he made as much playing pool as he did cutting hair. He was born in Austria in the early 1900s and had a tremendous facility for languages. He could speak Ukrainian, German and Austrian and, thanks to his customers, he picked up Japanese and Chinese along the way. His family settled just south of Moose Jaw. John was old-school and really hard-nosed. His father, also named John, had a temper too. One day while John Sr. was milking the cow, she kicked him. He fetched a sledgehammer and whacked her in the head so hard she fell over and died.

Hockey wasn't really on Bill's dad's radar. He never came to the boys' games. Instead, he was busy playing his prized pearl accordion with his orchestra at weddings around the area on weekends. Bill's mother, Catherine (Kay), was a kind, wonderful woman who took care of the books. She used to sneak Bill and his brothers, John, Eddie and Ernie, money for skates and sticks, whatever they needed.

When John died later in life and the boys, now men, were going through his things, they came upon his straight-razor strap. The one he used in the barbershop to sharpen his tools. It got even more use on the boys. You did not talk back to John Hicke.

Bill had a laid-back personality. He could play a little accordion, but he was totally focused on track and field and hockey. In fact, he loved hockey so much he played on two teams simultaneously. He was a silky stickhandler and really good on skates. Like Pavel Bure, he had remarkable acceleration and could skate from blue line to blue line in less than four seconds. This was in the '50s and '60s, when skates weighed about two pounds each. Today, skates weigh mere ounces.

Bill grew up watching the Regina Pats at the Exhibition Stadium, where the Brandt Centre is now. He was fifteen years old in Grade 10 when he was called up to join the team on

February 2, 1954. Most of his teammates, like Murray Balfour, were older, so the press nicknamed him "Billy the Kid."

Billy the Kid's first game was a 5–1 win over the Moose Jaw Canucks in front of 645 fans. He picked up two assists in the next game, an 11–0 win over the Lethbridge Native Sons. When Billy picked up another four assists his third time out with the Pats, Coach Murray Armstrong decided to keep him.

Because his dad wasn't very involved, Bill would walk to the rink. It would take about half an hour to make it all the way down Dewdney Avenue. In the winter of 1954, Regina got down to minus-34. That meant frostbite in less than ten minutes. So Bill would show up at the rink with his fingertips, toes, nose and earlobes frozen solid. Sometimes he'd stop at Murray Balfour's on the way to warm up, and the two of them would "bumper tag"—grab the bumper of a passing bus or car and ski part of the way. But you couldn't do it all the time, because it wore out the bottom of your boots.

The Regina team was good that year. They had an eighteen-game winning streak between November 8 and January 5 in the five-team Western Canada Junior Hockey League. The Pats played the league semifinal against the Medicine Hat Tigers. In the second game, Billy scored two goals for the overtime win. The Pats went all the way through, winning the Abbott Cup over the Winnipeg Monarchs. Their third win of the series was their forty-fifth of the season, the most wins the Pats had ever had. They lost the Memorial Cup that year and the next, 1955 and 1956, to the Toronto Marlboros.

In 1957–58, Bill and his teammate Red Berenson led the Pats to a first-place position in the Saskatchewan Junior Hockey

League. They lost in the Memorial Cup final once again, but Billy was the league's most outstanding player with ninety-seven points, including fifty-four goals in fifty-four games, two points ahead of Red.

Three appearances in four years. In the thirty-seven years prior, the Pats had made it that far only eight times. Billy gave the team an offensive jump. He was on the specialty teams, a key man on their power play, with a goal-scoring knack.

Billy was the property of the Montreal Canadiens. Habs general manager Frank Selke had signed a sponsorship agreement with the Pats in 1948, after the Canadiens missed the playoffs and needed new talent. In 1958, the Habs sent Billy to their farm team, the Rochester Americans.

The Americans had finished the 1957–58 season in fifth place and were out of the playoffs. With Billy on the team, they climbed to third. He had this great jacket the Americans gave him that his younger brother Ernie, who had just made the Pats, really admired. Billy came home to visit, and as Ernie was going out the door, Bill said, "Score three goals tonight and I'll give you my jacket." That night, Ernie scored a hat trick, and when he rushed home to deliver the good news, the jacket was already on his bed. Billy had so much faith in Ernie, he'd left it there before the game.

Billy was named the AHL's outstanding player and top rookie and led the league with ninety-seven points (forty-one goals and fifty-six assists). Frank Selke sent him a letter in 1959. It read, "Your principal job, you will understand, is to take Maurice Richard's place if and when he retires . . . and that is quite an assignment." Bill felt honoured to get a letter like that, but he didn't quite understand it. He knew the expectation wasn't realistic. Bill had some good qualifications, but he was never going to take over for the Rocket.

Billy signed with the Canadiens for $7,000 plus bonuses. It was a lot of money for a twenty-year-old. You could buy a house in Regina for $13,000. He was called up for Game Three of the 1959 Stanley Cup final against the Maple Leafs. Toe Blake was the coach, Jean Béliveau was in the stands with a spinal injury and the Rocket spent most of the game on the bench with a groin injury. Billy played in front of a sold-out crowd of 13,121 in Toronto. Dickie Duff scored at 10:06 in sudden-death overtime to give the Leafs the win. Montreal went on to win the series. One game was enough for Billy to have his name engraved on the Stanley Cup for the first time.

Ernie was watching the game on TV with their dad, John, who knew very little about hockey. John asked Ernie, "How come he's not getting on the ice so much?" Ernie said, "Well, Dad, he's a rookie playing with Dickie Moore and Ralph Backstrom on the third line, behind the Rocket and Jean Béliveau. Hell, he's lucky to get any ice time at all."

Bill and his high school sweetheart, LeeAnne Rickard, had known each other since Grade 7 at Benson Elementary. They began dating in Grade 11 at Scott Collegiate. When the Rocket found out they were to be married in July 1959, before Bill's first full season with Montreal, he started calling LeeAnne "The Bride." And that became Billy's nickname for her forever.

The next season, after Hicke started out with Rochester again, Montreal coach Toe Blake called him up for good. Billy's jersey hung between the Rocket's and Dickie Moore's. The Rocket couldn't speak English and Dickie Moore grew up in Montreal, so he and the Rocket would speak French and Bill would have no idea what they were saying. Dickie was a jokester, always cutting off ties or skate laces, and if he stood behind you, his lighter would be out and he'd set your pants on fire. He was the team tough guy.

Nobody would say boo to Toe Blake, not even the Rocket. Before a game, the dressing room would be wild with excitement, everybody yapping and yelling and screaming, but as soon as Toe Blake walked in, you could hear a pin drop.

But the Rocket would do some things behind his back. When the team travelled, he'd go to the train steward and slip him a few bucks to pick up a couple cases of beer at the first stop. When Toe went to his cabin on the other side of the train, initiations would start. Back then, if you weren't initiated, you weren't part of the team. When Richard was on the train, rookies would find a top bunk and hide. One of the things Richard and the boys would do is take beer caps and squeeze them until they were as sharp as razor blades, and then someone would hold the rookie down and Richard would flay him, running the caps up and down his legs and back and arms. Every NHL team had a "sheriff," someone who made sure things didn't go too far. For the Canadiens, that was Jean Béliveau. He was the guy who'd step in and say, "That's enough."

Guys would get bored on the trains, so there were some fun things the veterans would think up. They'd make the rookies dress up like women—skirt, wig, lipstick, the whole bit. It was embarrassing as hell, but really funny watching them totter on high heels all the way from the train to the hotel.

You had to be the best of the best to play in the league. This was before the expansion era, so there were only six teams—the Boston Bruins, Chicago Blackhawks, Detroit Red Wings, New York Rangers, Toronto Maple Leafs and Montreal Canadiens—and they were loaded with talent. With Jean Béliveau, Bernie "Boom Boom" Geoffrion, Doug Harvey and Jacques Plante, the Habs roster was a tough one to crack, but the 1950s dynasty was coming to an end. Billy played on the third line, behind Geoffrion and Claude Provost. Montreal swept the Chicago Blackhawks in the semifinals that year. Billy scored the first goal of the third game. He won his second Stanley Cup when the Habs beat the Maple Leafs 4–0 in the final on April 14, 1960.

In 1957, Senator Hartland de Montarville Molson and his brother, Thomas Henry Pentland Molson, bought the Canadiens. The players were loyal to the Molson beer brand, especially because it was free. After the Cup win, fans were lined up downtown to greet the team, but the boys had had so many celebratory pops that Blake arranged for the wives to meet them at an earlier stop.

When the Rocket retired in 1960, Bill's playing time increased, but he was still on the third line, playing with Phil Goyette and Gilles Tremblay. His best season with the Canadiens was 1961–62, when he scored twenty goals to go with thirty-one assists.

But with just six teams in the league, there was always a player standing right behind you, ready to take your job. In 1960–61, right winger Bobby Rousseau was called up. He had played with the 1958 Memorial Cup champions, the Hull-Ottawa Canadiens. A Calder Cup winner in the AHL, Rousseau could play on all units. And then there was the Roadrunner, Yvan Cournoyer, who joined the Habs in 1963. He was used as a power-play specialist, so the team's depth at right wing was growing and Bill found himself riding the pine. He finally had enough, so just before Christmas 1964 he went to general manager Sam Pollock. He said what he later called "the five worst words" he ever uttered, "Play me or trade me."

A day later, he was on a train—sent down to Cleveland for a short stint before being traded to New York to join the Rangers. He, LeeAnne and their two-year-old daughter, Lisa, had only a couple of days to pack up to leave. The building super at their place in Cleveland lived in the basement. He had kids but not enough money to buy a Christmas tree, so Bill lugged his big cut spruce, with all the lights and bulbs, down the stairs and gave it to the guy.

Moving from Montreal to New York was like going from heaven to hell. The city was big and it was hard to get around. They lived out in Long Beach because that's where everybody else on the team lived. It was an hour's drive to practice in the morning, and if they had a game, it'd be another hour there and back in the evening.

Bill liked his teammates—Rod Gilbert, Vic Hadfield, Phil Goyette, Jacques Plante, Billy Taylor, Lou Angotti—and the general manager, Emile Francis, who was from North Battleford, Saskatchewan. But Bill joked that instead of the Rangers' victory song, their theme song should be "Born to Lose."

New York was not for Billy, and the Bride didn't like it either.

While at his first training camp with the Rangers in 1965, Bill played a round of golf at Westchester on a chilly, drizzly, foggy day. When he came home, he wasn't feeling well. He went to lie down and didn't get up for three weeks. After day three, LeeAnne borrowed a neighbour's phone because theirs wasn't hooked up yet and called Emile Francis. A few hours later, a helicopter picked Bill up and flew him to St. Clare's Hospital in Manhattan's Hell's Kitchen area. It was built in the 1930s to serve poor Catholic immigrants. It was still a sketchy neighbourhood at the time, but it was where the team doctor had privileges. LeeAnne rushed to meet him there. She was sitting near the triage desk when she heard the nurses talking. "You know the hockey player who was just brought in? He's in really bad shape. I don't know if he's going to make it through the night. I should be sponging him down, but I just don't have the time."

LeeAnne sat there stunned, and then she jumped up and said, "I'm the wife of that sick hockey player. Tell me what to do!"

Together they gathered ice, alcohol and cotton pads and hustled into Bill's room. His temperature was 106 degrees Fahrenheit—he had developed pneumonia and was barely coherent. LeeAnne worked fast, cooling his wrists, underarms, head and groin. She had to get his fever down. She stayed with him through the night, but by morning he had slipped into a coma.

He opened his eyes a few days later and looked up at her. "I think I've been out of it for a while," he said.

Bill stayed in the hospital for two weeks. Recovery was slow and he was bored. He looked forward to early mornings, when he could look out the window and watch the rats run around the garbage.

He finally came home but was as weak as a kitten. His chest was constricted and he'd have terrible coughing bouts. The doctors told him he had bronchial asthma, and along with that he was itchy everywhere because he'd developed severe allergies.

He eventually started skating and got himself back onto the ice. In 1967, Bill was one of the veterans claimed by the Oakland

Seals in the expansion draft. Alan Eagleson was just getting into player representation, and he negotiated Bill's contract.

Bert Olmstead was his coach in Oakland. "Dirty Bertie" was a tough guy and really hard-nosed. In his book *The Glory Years*, Toronto Maple Leaf right winger Billy Harris tells a story about how, one summer, Bert entered a rifle competition back home in Sceptre, Saskatchewan. He had the lead but lost on the final day. A buddy who had been drinking saw Bert in the men's room and accused him of not trying hard enough, so Bert tried to drown him in the toilet bowl.

As a coach, Bert was uncompromising. One practice, while Olmstead was bag-skating his players, Bill felt so sick he took the bench. This was uncharacteristic of him, but Bert followed him over and told him to get back on the ice. A few minutes later, Bill collapsed on the ice and was rushed to the hospital. The asthma was back.

He scored twenty-one goals despite missing twenty-two games that first season, and by December 1968 he had thirty-four points, tying Dennis Hull as the tenth-highest scorer in the league. Bill thought most Oakland fans didn't know a stick from a broom, but he appreciated the ice time he was getting. He became friends with Peanuts creator Charles Schulz, who was an Oakland season-ticket holder and came to all of the games. Bill was his favourite player. They had a hockey school together up in Santa Rosa. Once, Charlie showed Bill a cartoon of Snoopy playing hockey. "Look what number he's wearing," Schulz said. It was number 9, Bill's number with the Seals.

The 1968–69 season was one of Bill's best in the NHL, with twenty-five goals in sixty-seven games. But during one game, when the Los Angeles Kings' goalie came out of his crease, Bill checked him and got into a stick-swinging incident with six-foot, four-inch, 210-pound defenceman Dale Rolfe. When LeeAnne saw Bill in the middle of a scrum, with the whole team on his back, she didn't want to see him with a broken leg on top of all his other problems with allergies and asthma, so for the first time in ten years as an NHL wife, she suddenly jumped up and yelled, "Bill, you asshole, get out of there!"

The Hickes loved Oakland. Their son, Danny, was born shortly after they moved there. The city is located just across the bridge from San Francisco. There are 260 days of sunshine every year, and it's close to Carmel and Monterey Bay.

Bill's daughter, Lisa, was under school age and would run around the Oakland-Alameda County Coliseum Arena with all the other kids while their dads practised. Afterwards, the players would go to the bar and the kids would hang out at their own table in the back, with non-stop pop and colouring books.

Bill and LeeAnne impressed upon the kids that they were Canadians, and so when Lisa was in Grade 1 in Oakland, she didn't like school—partially because she didn't want to sing the US national anthem and didn't want to pledge allegiance to the United States of America. One morning, she ran away from school and headed home. Bill gave her a hug and told her to hop into the car. He drove her back to school and walked her into her classroom, where he took a seat at the back. Each day for the next four days, he sat in that same little desk, until Lisa finally told him she was okay and that he could go home.

The team had trouble drawing flies. At most games, there were fewer than five thousand fans in the stands. After three seasons, the Seals were sold to Oakland Athletics owner Charlie

Finley, who renamed the team the California Golden Seals and changed the uniform colours to match those of the A's.

At the end of the 1969–70 season, the Seals made a trade with the Canadiens—Bill's younger brother Ernie and Montreal's first-round pick in 1970 for cash, François Lacombe and the Seals' first-round pick in 1971. The Seals ended up in last place in 1971, so Montreal wound up with the first-overall pick, which they used to take Guy Lafleur, after winning the Cup that year.

Bill was thrilled to be playing with Ernie. The brothers were ten years apart, but close. Their families even lived in the same Oakland apartment complex. One night, Bill and LeeAnne went to dinner with Ernie, his wife, Barb, and some of the other players. Ernie and Barb left the restaurant first, and on the way home Ernie was pulled over for speeding. He pulled out his driver's licence, told the cop he was from Saskatchewan and played for the Golden Seals. He was still issued the ticket. Twenty minutes later, Bill and LeeAnne headed for home. Bill was pulled over for speeding by the same cop. When he said his name was Hicke, he was from Saskatchewan and he played for the Golden Seals, the cop held up his hand. "I've heard this story before."

Billy was traded to Detroit before the 1971–72 season but spent most of the year in the minors. He played one last professional season, for the Alberta Oilers in the World Hockey Association in 1972–73, but he just didn't have the lungs anymore.

Billy loved talking about his days in hockey. He'd often say this guy or that guy had "a heart as big as a bathtub." In truth, that's what most thought of him.

Lisa married Jim Ostertag, and they had two boys, Ryan and Dylan. "Papa" became their best friend. He taught them how to swing a golf club, throw a football and, of course, shoot a puck. He'd bring the little boys with him to watch the Pats, and it would take them a whole period just to make it to their seats, because Billy would have to stop and talk to everyone he knew. Dylan looked at him one time and said, "Papa, I can't believe you're famous—not with the way you dress."

In 1998, when Ryan was six years old and Dylan was four, Billy discovered he had prostate cancer. He underwent more than thirty radiation treatments, several surgeries and chemotherapy treatments. He spent most of the summer of 2003 in the hospital but managed to pull through. Two years later, when the Stanley Cup was on tour across Canada, it made a stop at the Hicke residence. Billy showed his grandsons his name engraved on the Cup in three different places. But he was getting sicker.

Near the end, LeeAnne told him how sorry she was that he had cancer because it was taking away his quality of life. He shook his head and squeezed her hand. "Are you kidding?" he said. "I'm one of the luckiest guys ever. I have lived the life of a thousand men."

The Next Wayne Gretzky

He was supposed to be the West's Wayne Gretzky. Just three months older than the Great One, Doug Wickenheiser tied Wayne's bantam scoring record—ninety goals. Wayne's hero was Gordie Howe, and when Doug skated after school on the back-yard rink his dad, Charlie, had made for him, he pretended he was another great stickhandler—Buffalo's Gilbert Perreault. In his mind, Doug was part of the French Connection line along with his invisible wingers, Rick Martin and René Robert. He'd shoot over and over again. As he got older and stronger, he left more puck marks on the fence, and it would have to be repainted in the spring.

Doug played in the Regina Parks League with his friends from Holy Rosary every week after school on Rink #3 at the corner of Elphinstone Street and Victoria Avenue. Winds off the nearby fields blew icy snow onto the rink, swirling around their leather skates and bright pink cheeks. Now and then, the kids would head into the shack just long enough to feel the burn as their toes and ears began to thaw, and then it was right back out.

His peewee coach said he heard parents say, "He skated by my son so fast, he knocked him over." Doug was ten when he and his brother, Kurt, were scouted up the ranks, through the Regina Sportsmen to the Early Birds. The whole family would drive to the Al Ritchie Arena for games. Doug could pick up the puck from behind the net, skate through the entire team and let go a cannon so hard that sometimes the goalie got out of the way. He had a quick wrist shot, could always find the hole in the net and had a knack for reading the play. He'd look up the ice and know just where to feed the puck for the best chance to score. Everybody whispered the same thing. "He's just like Gretzky."

NHL scouts first gave Doug a good look when he was fourteen and playing with the Midget AA Pat Canadians, but his mom, Fran, wanted him to go to school. Doug had a photographic memory and could study or read while watching a hockey game and absorb both. When Charlie asked him what he wanted to do, go to school or play hockey, Doug asked, "Why can't I do both?" So he signed with the Pats, finished high school and signed up for a few classes at the University of Regina. His first year with the Pats, 1977–78, he came away with eighty-eight points—on the third line.

The Pats spent the summer rebuilding. Bob Strumm took over as general manager and brought in Bryan Murray to coach.

In 1979–80 Doug scored 89 goals and 170 points. In his 1977–78 season with the Sault Ste. Marie Greyhounds, Gretzky scored 80 goals and 182 points. Both boys gave a lot of the credit to their teammates. The Pats' first power-play unit featured Doug, Mike Blaisdell and Ron Flockhart, with Darren Veitch and Brian Varga on the points. During the regular season, the Pats scored on 33.6 per cent of their power-play chances. All five players finished the season with over one hundred points. A couple of years earlier, when Gretzky played for the Soo Greyhounds, the team scored on 29.4 per cent of its power-play opportunities.

Pats fans called Doug "Dream Weaver," after the Gary Wright song that was always on the radio. The song played in the rink and on the fan buses for away games. But those who knew Doug simply called him Wick.

Wick was always up to something. If he found a book on the bus, he'd cut the last three pages out and watch the face of his teammate as he came to the end. And he was a big fan of the shoe check—crawling under the table to leave mashed potato or Jell-O on top of a guy's foot. In 1978–79, the Russian Moscow Selects were travelling across Canada to play eight WHL teams. The Selects were out on the ice for a practice skate, so Doug and his linemate Mike Blaisdell decided to watch. Walking by the Russians' dressing room, they looked in through the open door and saw the team's ugly matching nylon sweatpants hanging all over the room. For the next five minutes they tied tight knots in the legs of almost all the pants, and then they went after all the shoelaces. They had a big laugh about it until the Selects beat them that night, 7–5.

One night, Coach Murray was mad at an offside call by linesman Darrell Davis. Doug was the captain, so Murray sent him out to talk to Darrell. Davis was Doug's good buddy, so in a low voice he said to him, "Bryan's really mad and I have to look like I'm really giving you hell. So I'm going to start yelling at you." He pointed his finger and yelled at Darrell, "You guys going out after the game?" Darrell yelled back, "Yeah, we're going to Gino's for pizza!" "Okay, we might see you there!" Then Doug skated back to the bench and Murray patted his helmet for stepping up.

The Pats lost the Memorial Cup that year, partly because of Doug's shaky performance out of the gate. But at six foot one, 195 pounds, Doug had size and talent. He also had skill—three or four speeds, and he used them all effectively when he had the puck. Finally, Doug had an exceptional sense of the game around him. All the greats have it. He was named the league MVP and first team all-star, so his name topped the list of draft picks, along with defenceman Dave Babych, who was six feet, two inches and 200-plus pounds, of the Portland Winterhawks, and Denis Savard, a five-foot-nine, 157-pound forward from Montreal who had played three seasons in the Quebec Major Junior League. Doug hated the attention, but his agent, Bill Watters, wanted him in Montreal at the Forum on draft day.

Doug's childhood fantasy came true when Montreal Canadiens general manager Irving Grundman and scouting director Ron Caron picked him number one overall. He no longer dreamed he was Gilbert Perreault—he *was* Gilbert Perreault. Second pick was Babych, who went to the Jets. Quebec star Savard went number three to the Blackhawks. Montreal fans were outraged, and so were many in the media. How could the team pick a big farmer from Saskatchewan over a local hero?

Doug was overwhelmed by the pressure in Montreal when he arrived that fall. He was supposed to be the next Gretzky. The team gave him Jacques Lemaire's number, 25, and in the dressing room he sat between Guy Lafleur and Steve Shutt. He started out hot, scoring in his first two preseason games. And then, in the team's first regular-season game against the Blackhawks, which was on *Hockey Night in Canada*, Coach Claude Ruel decided not to dress Doug. It was a blow to his confidence, especially when Denis Savard scored a first-period goal to put the Hawks up 3–2. He also assisted on their fourth goal in the third and was named the game's first star.

Coach Ruel was hard on Doug. He dressed him for forty-one out of eighty games. When he went home that summer of 1981, Doug told the Regina *Leader-Post* that a lot of his first year in Montreal was spent in the press box. He had no idea how he was supposed to get better by doing that. What Doug was going through was not all that unusual. When I talked with Guy Lafleur on *Rogers Hometown Hockey* in Dollard-des-Ormeaux, Quebec, in 2015, I asked him about his sudden emergence in year three of his Habs career. He said it was not that he changed—it was that the Canadiens finally gave him the ice time.

Meanwhile, Savard had accomplished his goal—he had seventy-five points versus Doug's fifteen. This was all very hard for Doug's dad, Charlie, to swallow. He thought Doug was in the wrong place at the wrong time. He wished Doug had been drafted by Winnipeg or Chicago, the next two teams to choose. Things might have been different on a team with less talent and in a dimmer spotlight. But Doug told him, "Don't blame Montreal. Blame me. I'm the guy who isn't playing the way I should."

At home, Doug wasn't an NHL player. He was just Doug. He played baseball until Ruel found out and told him he had to stop. He helped his dad and his brothers in construction, but the *Leader-Post* took a picture of him leaning over an eavestrough with a hammer, and when Ruel saw the picture, he told him he had to stay off rooftops. It seemed the team was messing with his head. Montreal's big defensive star, Larry Robinson, is on record as saying that the way Ruel treated Doug might have been a way to protest Montreal's picking him instead of Savard.

Doug's rocky first year was waved off as nerves, and by his third season, under coach Bob Berry in 1982–83, his line with Lafleur and Ryan Walter looked like the emergence of a new French–English Connection. But it didn't come to fruition. By December of 1983, Montreal was sitting right around the .500 mark and the team wanted to shake things up. Ron Caron, who had scouted Doug for the Habs and had always been a fan, was now the general manager of the St. Louis Blues. He'd hired Jacques Demers to coach, and together they were rebuilding the team. The Blues traded Perry Turnbull to the Habs in exchange for Doug, Greg Paslawski and Gilbert Delorme. Doug felt Montreal had done him a favour by trading him.

St. Louis was laid-back and Midwestern. It reminded Doug of home. In St. Louis, he didn't feel fan disapproval, and with his pranks and sharp wit he was popular in the dressing room.

He was an excellent faceoff man and scored a few goals even though he was in a more defensive role, but he still hadn't regained his mojo. He didn't have the confidence he once had as a junior player, except in practice, where he'd often play like a superstar.

Doug was having his best NHL season in 1984–85, with twenty-three goals and twenty assists in sixty-eight games. On March 10, 1985, in a 6–2 win over the Detroit Red Wings, Doug scored three goals, the second hat trick of his career. He was moved to the first line and ready to show what he could do.

The Blues had an annual rookie initiation ritual where they'd go on a "snipe hunt," looking for "a rare Missouri weasel." On March 13, they loaded up the vehicles and drove forty kilometres west to Eureka. Doug kept his face neutral as the vets told rookies Kevin LaVallee and Gil Delorme that they had to come back with a snipe. Then they arranged for the local cops to arrest Kevin and Gil for hunting snipe without a licence. The vets went to a nearby restaurant to eat and have a few pops while the rookies were locked up. Afterward, Doug was hoisting himself into the back of a pickup when he lost his balance.

A passing car tried to swerve and brake but skidded, slamming into Doug's left leg and destroying his knee—ligaments, cartilage and part of his quadriceps. Doug was rushed into the hospital, and Dr. Jerome Gilden, the Blues' team physician, had to rebuild it in a four-hour operation. The chance of him playing again was about 60 per cent. That was good enough for Doug. He gave himself nine months to get back on the ice.

By Christmas, he had returned to full practice. On January 23, ten months after the accident, Doug was back in the lineup against the Los Angeles Kings, but he didn't have the same mobility. His beautiful skating stride was gone.

The Blues finished third in the Norris Division. After beating the Minnesota North Stars and Toronto Maple Leafs, they faced the Calgary Flames in the Campbell Conference final. Down 3–2 in the series and facing elimination as they took the ice at the Barn in St. Louis on May 12, 1986, the Blues trailed 4–1 after two periods. A lot of fans found it too painful to watch and left the building.

Just before the start of the third period, Coach Demers came into the dressing room and looked at the dejected faces of his team. He talked about their assistant coach, Barclay Plager, who was fighting to live despite inoperable brain tumours. Demers loved him like a father and a brother. All Barclay asked was that his players come out every night ready to play.

The message hit home for the players. Six minutes into the third, Doug scored unassisted. Brian Sutter, a player Barclay nurtured, guided and coached from junior to the NHL, scored a few minutes later.

The fans were back and the Barn was shaking. After seven minutes and thirty seconds of overtime, Bernie Federko took the puck from between Paul Reinhart's skates. He and Mark Hunter took off down the ice on a two-on-one. Hunter shot on Flames goaltender Mike Vernon. Vernon blocked the puck, but Doug found the rebound and fired in the winning goal. The Barn exploded. It felt like the building was going to topple over. On the radio, the announcers couldn't hold back their cheers. It was called "The Monday Night Miracle." The Blues lost Game Seven in Calgary, but to this day Wickenheiser's goal is replayed annually on TV in St. Louis.

Doug never again saw the same success on the ice. He loved St. Louis and moved there full time, but his performance was in a slow decline, and after the 1987 training camp he was placed on waivers. He squeezed out a few more decent seasons with the Vancouver Canucks, New York Rangers and Washington Capitals, playing up and down.

Doug wasn't surprised to see his NHL career come to an end. He moved on to Europe and then to the IHL. He'd fallen for a Texan, Dianne Pepple. They were married on August 8, 1992, in St. Louis.

Doug returned to North America that fall with the Peoria Rivermen, followed by a season with the Fort Wayne Komets in Indiana. That fall, after the birth of his twin girls, Rachel and Kaitlin, Doug went in for minor surgery to remove a small growth on his left wrist.

A biopsy showed that the cyst was malignant. Doug had a rare form of cancer called epithelioid sarcoma, a cancer of the body tissue. Only about fifty cases a year are recorded in the United States. The ten-year survival rate is 42 to 55 per cent. The disease usually starts in the hands and forearms, and in about half of patients, it moves to the lungs, lymph nodes and scalp. Doug was treated with radiation, which seemed to destroy any cancer cells. And then Dianne gave birth to Carly, their third baby girl.

In August, Doug was pestered by a small, hacking cough that he couldn't get rid of. He thought it was an allergy and went to a specialist who found nothing wrong. Doug went for an X-ray. Dianne was at her mom and dad's house with the girls when Doug called her from work. She nervously asked how his appointment had been. "Come on home and I'll talk to you," he said. He had a lemon-sized growth on his right lung. It was inoperable because it was positioned around his airway.

Doug began chemotherapy in St. Louis. Every four weeks, he spent two to three days on an IV, but the mass in his lung was still growing. There were no more options. He had an incredibly high pain threshold. Mike Blaisdell says that when he played, Doug was a target, bruised head to toe and always getting chopped and hacked, but he never said a word about it. And even though the cancer was painful, he refused heavy painkillers because he wanted to be present for his kids.

The family went home to Regina, where Doug dropped the puck at the WHL's All-Star competition. As he stood at centre ice, looking up and waving, more than five thousand Pats fans were on their feet, cheering for a man who had so much character, a man who gave them so much hope.

Hot Stick

There's a saying, "Belief lifts talent." You need desire and skill, but beyond that, the single greatest determinant is to simply believe it's possible. When Brian Sutter made the NHL, his five younger brothers felt they could make it too, and they did. Lots of people say the best thing an athlete can do to succeed is to choose his or her parents wisely. DNA goes a long way, but for believers, there's another key factor not found in the blood—it's in the water.

The place where you grow up nourishes you in countless ways. Regina, Saskatchewan, has become a hockey factory because everyone raised there believes the NHL is attainable. Of the twenty-five tour stops on Rogers Hometown Hockey *in 2014–15, more NHL players hailed from Regina than any other city—eighty-eight players.*

After the season, I was golfing with my neighbour in Oakville, ex-NHLer Mark Kirton, who is also from Regina. Mark was adopted, so his athletic bloodlines are unknown, but his adoptive dad, Les, who worked for Sears, was an avid sports fan. Les's favourite players were Billy Hicke and Fran Huck, a high-scoring Regina Pat who sacrificed four years of his professional career to play on the Canadian National Team for Father David Bauer. There were several pro athletes living near Parkwood Avenue, the street Mark grew up on. Ted Urness of the Saskatchewan Roughriders, a Canadian Football Hall of Famer, lived next door. Mark remembers visiting Ted when he broke his leg—Ted was at home in bed with a giant traction apparatus holding his big leg cast up in the air.

In the late '60s, when Mark was eight years old, Les would drop him off at Taylor Field, and he'd run in and join all the other kids in the Riders' section to watch the game.

From the time he was four years old on Campbell Street, he was playing road hockey with guys a few years older. Guys like Billy Bell and Glen Burdon, who would play on the Regina Pats' Memorial Cup–winning team in 1973–74. In Regina it was all sports, all the time. The concept of a career in sports was everywhere in the city, and it fuelled Mark.

Mark was always a smaller guy, so when he was in his early teens, he asked his dad to convert their garage into a gym, and he pumped iron daily after running six to eight miles around the nearest football field. He was drafted by the Toronto Maple Leafs in 1978, and in his second year with Moncton's New Brunswick Hawks, who were co-owned by the Leafs and the Chicago Blackhawks, his team made it to the Calder Cup final, where they lost to Hershey in six games. The Hawks were loaded with future NHL coaches—including Bruce Boudreau, Joel Quenneville, Ron Wilson and Darryl Sutter. Sutter was on Mark's wing, as was longtime Hawks forward Rick Paterson. Mark also played his first NHL game with the Maple Leafs that season, and he went on to enjoy eleven seasons as a pro—six with Toronto, Detroit and Vancouver, playing against other Regina natives, including Doug Wickenheiser. Mark was five foot ten and 172 pounds, but he had watched Riders' quarterback Ron "The Little General" Lancaster star in the CFL, so he knew a smaller player could succeed.

Jordan Eberle is the same way. At a key point in his development, Jordan was mentored by Regina's Dale Derkatch—a five-foot, five-inch, 145-pound player who shredded WHL scoring records.

When Jordan was seventeen, in April 2008, he teamed with another well-known Canadian junior prospect, Taylor Hall of the Windsor Spitfires, to lead Canada to the under-18 world title, smoking Russia 8–0 in the final. Jordan led the way with a pair of goals. It was a precursor to his performance of a lifetime at the 2009 World Junior Championship. Thanks to his two-time performance at the World Juniors (in 2009 and 2010), he's acquired the "clutch" tag.

Eberle and Hall also won gold at the IIHF World Championship in Prague, Czech Republic, in May 2015. Seeing two Edmonton wingers flanking the Penguins' star centre, Sidney Crosby, took me back to the 1987 Canada Cup, when Pittsburgh's Mario Lemieux centred Oilers Wayne Gretzky and Mark Messier. Once something has been done, it's easy to believe it will happen again.

Jordan Eberle's just getting started. He reminds me of Dale Hawerchuk with his vision, strength and hands.

When Cari and I visited Prague in the summer of 2015, I purchased a matryoshka doll at a cheesy gift shop. It was painted in honour of the world champs Team Canada. Crosby's likeness was on the outer doll, and players such as Claude Giroux and Tyler Seguin appeared as you opened the dolls. It was fun to guess who would be the man in the middle. Turns out it was Eberle. I bought the doll to give to his folks, Lisa and Darren.

Mark Kirton? Well, after he retired from pro hockey he became a very successful real estate agent—location, location, location.

All Jordan Eberle ever wanted was to be a Regina Pat. When he was a kid, his dad, Darren, took him and his little brother, Dustin, to every home game. When they walked into the big cement Agridome, Jordan and Dustin would shiver with excitement as soon as they smelled the popcorn and cotton candy. The boys would run up to their seats in Section O and jump up onto the red cushions. They were so small they could barely stop the bottom of the chair from flipping back up. Ice cream melting over their knuckles, they'd wait for the lights to go down and squirm in their seats waiting for their hero, Matt Hubbauer, to appear. Hubbauer, a fan favourite, scored forty-eight goals as a nineteen-year-old in 2002. He was a small guy but a highly skilled, high-speed, high-power player.

When he was in peewee, Jordan won a draw and was chosen to skate with the Pats in the warm-up as the seventh man. That meant that when Darren pulled up to the rink, he and Jordan got to walk in through the players' entrance. Jordan got dressed in the coach's room next to the dressing room, pulling his gear on in record time, and joined the players in the lineup as they revved up for the game. Jordan was asked to pick the player who would walk him through the tunnel and take him onto the ice. He chose Brad Stuart, who had sixty-five points that year and would go on to be drafted in the first round by the San Jose Sharks, third overall. Thirteen years later, on November 5, 2010, when Brad was with Detroit, he and Jordan would play against each other for the first time. It was just incredible for Jordan, looking up to someone like that all his life and then to actually be on the ice with him.

But back in 1998, when the lights went down and Jordan heard his name rolling out of the loudspeaker, his feet moved almost as fast as his heart was beating. He skated around the end zone behind Brad and joined the Pats' starting lineup on the blue line for the singing of "O Canada." As he shuffled his feet and tapped his stick on the ice, he looked up at the flag and knew in his heart that he was standing where he belonged.

Hockey was a huge part of Jordan's childhood. His dad was obsessed with it. He didn't get past Midget AA himself, but he was a huge fan. Darren loved the dynasty-era Oilers—Messier, Gretzky and Kurri. Who didn't? Jordan and Dustin would put on their slippery socks and grab their mini sticks and play hockey on the hardwood in the family room, which was on the main level of their bungalow at Janzen Crescent. It was always Jordan's all-time favourite, Joe Sakic, against Dustin's Matt Hubbauer, playing for a cardboard Stanley Cup.

The boys played hockey all over the house—upstairs on the living room carpet, in the hallways, around the kitchen table. It seemed they didn't go anywhere without a stick and a puck. Darren had a liquor bar up against the wall behind one of the nets in the basement family room, and flying pucks broke countless glasses. As they got older, their shots got harder, especially when the boys would move the furniture out of the way. Darren's man cave started to look like a bomb site with all the holes in the drywall.

Darren was fairly tolerant, but one night when he was down in the basement learning how to use his brand new wall-to-wall, fifty-five-inch Pioneer rear-projection TV that had just been delivered a day earlier, he noticed a hole through the screen. He hung his head and took a deep breath. "Aw geez, what have the boys done now?"

The warehouse had forgotten to apply the plastic screen protector to it, so the salesman had told Darren, "Just keep the kids away from it, and we'll get that out to you in the next couple of days." Darren had warned the kids to be careful around the new TV, so instead of playing hockey that day, they threw butter knives at some half-deflated, leftover-from-a-birthday-party balloons that were hanging from the ceiling. Jordan miscalculated and his knife sliced through the screen. Darren laid down the law—hockey was okay, but knife throwing was definitely out.

The boys would get into huge fights playing hockey. Jordan hated losing, and if Dustin beat him, he'd get furious. One time, Darren had had enough. He brought home boxing gloves and helmets so they wouldn't inflict too much damage, and he said, "Okay, you two knuckleheads, go at it."

The brothers were fiercely competitive and fearless when it came to sports, but Dustin was afraid of the dark, so he'd wait until he thought Jordan was asleep and then sneak out of his own room and crawl in with his big brother for protection. Jordan would give him the gears for it, but he never kicked him out.

Their house had a large pie-shaped lot with a long space between the fence and the side of the house. On it, Darren constructed a pad of pavement about a hundred feet long and fifteen feet wide for ball hockey in the summer. There was still room for a big rink in the backyard in the winter, complete with outdoor halogen flood lamps, so that Jordan, Dustin and their sister Whitney could play late after supper. Whitney, the oldest, was a great hockey player and would go on to play for the University of Calgary Dinos. Another sister, Ashley, was an award-winning gymnast.

Darren coached the boys from novice until Jordan was in his early teens. In Regina, Novice Tier I was really competitive. Jordan would often score five to ten points a game. This angered certain coaches. One time, Darren suspected that a competing coach had ordered his boys to go out and hurt Jordan. The boys hacked and whacked him so much, Jordan was injured. Darren lost it, and after a few back-and-forths across the glass, he had to be held back from delivering his message face to face. Darren was fair but tough, especially on Jordan and Dustin. If they screwed up, they heard about it, and today they really appreciate it.

Jordan's parents, Darren and Lisa, had been together since they met in high school—she was fifteen and he was seventeen. Lisa understood and supported Darren's passion for hockey. Jordan was three years old when Darren signed him up for skating at Murray Balfour Arena.

The moment Jordan's skates hit the ice, it was as if he'd been skating forever. Thanks to sliding around in his socks in the living room, he was flying around faster than kids twice his age.

The next year, the Eberles signed him up for Hockey Regina's Initiation League.

Jordan was a natural—shooting, scoring, passing, it all came easy. At ten years of age, he was moved up an age group and he played for the 1999–2000 Tier I Kings. That year, he was only four foot seven and seventy-nine pounds, and yet he scored 216 goals. The Regina *Leader-Post* wrote a feature on him where he was quoted as saying, "I play baseball, fun football with my friends, fun soccer with my friends, and basketball with my friends, but I'm a hockey guy. I love playing hockey." It was at that point that Darren and Lisa realized Jordan might actually have some professional potential. He was always the best in his age group, but they hadn't seriously entertained the thought that he might play in the NHL.

When Jordan was nine or ten years old and Dustin was seven or eight, they joined a fall conditioning camp with forty or fifty other kids. It was run by Jerry Zrymiak, a retired WHA player who was super-tough. He managed to control all the kids at once and mould them into real hockey players. It helped that he had a loud bark, and so they were petrified of him. But they listened. "Okay, your mom and dad aren't here now, so you carry your own bags and lace up your own skates!" He ran great drills and taught them to work hard and to be disciplined on the ice.

The boys also had lessons with Liane Davis, a Regina power-skating coach who now works with NHLers. Liane's dad, Lorne Davis, was a former Pat and a highly regarded scout for the Edmonton Oilers. He's the guy who spotted Grant Fuhr, Kelly Buchberger and Ryan Smyth.

Jordan loved putting the puck in the net, but instinctually he wanted to be a good teammate. He looked for opportunities to pass. His Hockey Regina team, the Kings, won championships in peewee, Novice Tier II and Novice Tier I. Jordan's only source of disappointment was his size. He was smaller than most, so when bigger players started to hit, he used his speed to avoid them. He wanted to prove that he could play with kids who were inches taller and several pounds heavier.

In 2004, as Jordan was entering his second year of bantam, Darren was transferred to Calgary. A week before the new owners were to take possession of the house, the boys got into a fight and Jordan threw a big, blue exercise ball at Dustin, sending him through the wall. Darren was in the basement, so Jordan ran down, fessed up and then ran back upstairs and out the door.

Jordan was fourteen years old when he made the tough decision to stay in Saskatchewan and play for the Notre Dame Hounds. Athol Murray College of Notre Dame, known for its hockey program, is about a half-hour drive from Regina in the town of Wilcox. Countless hockey pros have gone through the program. Today, there are 19 Hounds playing in the NHL, including Brad Richards.

Jordan's Hounds coach, Dale Derkatch, is a small guy. He was a former Regina Pat (1981–85) who held team records for career goals, assists and points and went on to a thirteen-year pro career in Europe. Jordan thought he could learn a lot from Derkatch, and it turned out he was the right coach for Jordan at that time. NHL. com says that Jordan is five foot eleven, but he's actually about five foot ten. He seems bigger because he plays big. Derkatch taught him how to create space and play with a chip on his shoulder.

After talking to his coaches, Jordan got the impression he wasn't going to make the Hounds' Midget AAA team. That made him mad, so he decided to move to Calgary and make the Midget AAA Calgary Buffaloes. At fifteen, he was one of the youngest kids on the team—most were sixteen or seventeen. A few of the players, including Jordan, attended Bishop O'Byrne High School in south Calgary. Their classmates followed them to games all the way to Lethbridge, and they got so enthusiastic they broke the glass around the rink more than once that year.

The Buffs went all the way to the Telus Cup in Charlottetown, P.E.I., in 2006. Jordan was looking forward to a national championship. He'd never made it that far. The Buffaloes played their way to the final against the Prince Albert Mintos.

The Mintos were leading 4–1 in the second period when Calgary scored one shorthanded. In the third period, Jordan put one top shelf over Mintos goaltender Dustin Tokarski, who now plays for the Habs, and the Buffaloes tied it up with just under four minutes to go.

No score in the first overtime period, so a second overtime was needed. But nothing would go in. They went to a third extra frame. Finally, after 102 minutes and 24 seconds of play, Mintos captain Ron Meyers scored the winning goal. It was a tough, tough loss.

Jordan's bantam draft year was 2005, and the Pats had picked him in the seventh round, 126th overall. Pats head scout Todd Ripplinger felt Jordan had enough skill to overcome his size, which was an issue that had kept other teams away. Jordan thought about playing college hockey—he had received some offers—and so there were a lot of discussions with Darren and Lisa about the right thing to do, but he was leaning toward Junior

A. He thought he'd get more playing time. He went to camp with the Okotoks Oilers in the Alberta Junior Hockey League, worked hard and was offered a place on the team. He also attended the Regina Pats' training camp. He had dreamed of playing for them since the day he stood on the blue line, singing "O Canada" beside Brad Stuart when he was nine years old. The Pats were his favourite team next to the Edmonton Oilers.

Pats general manager Brent Parker, coach Curtis Hunt and scout Todd Ripplinger all wanted him. But Darren was concerned that a sixteen-year-old wasn't going to get much playing time. He looked at Hunt and asked, "If Jordan proves that he could be a top-six, would he be able to earn his ice time and play like any other forward?"

Hunt replied, "Absolutely, we're here to win."

Parker, Hunt and Ripplinger left the dressing room, leaving Darren and Jordan to make a decision. Jordan didn't want to go to school—he wanted to play for Hunt. He liked his approach and how smart he was with systems. But Darren thought Jordan was too small to play in the Dub. Jordan was five foot eight or nine and 150 pounds on a good day. He'd be up against guys who were five inches taller and a hundred pounds heavier. Darren thought his kid definitely needed another year of Junior A. They had a big blowout right then and there. Jordan said he was playing for the Pats and that was it. He could stay with Darren's parents. Darren knew that his mother was one of the nicest human beings on the face of the earth, so she would take care of him, and Darren's dad was feisty like Jordan. If Jordan made a mistake or had a bad game, his grandpa would straight-up tell him he "sucked." That would be good for Jordan too.

Darren relented, but as he made the eight-hour drive back to Calgary, he pounded the steering wheel. "Damn it, did I do the right thing by letting him stay?"

Again, Jordan had the right coach at the right time. Hunt believed in him and gave him ice time earned. It boosted Jordan's confidence, and he became one of the team's top goal scorers in his rookie season. In three seasons, he scored 155 goals and had 155 assists.

Regina Pats fans love a hometown player, and they were closely tied to "Ebs," but the rest of Canada really got to know Jordan Eberle when he played for Team Canada. He was lucky to make the team in 2009. He had a horrendous summer camp. Up until that point, Jordan had never faced any real adversity. But at camp, the more trouble he had, the more he got down on himself and the worse he played. On the last day, he met with Benoît Groulx, the head coach, who told him he was one of the worst players on the ice.

Groulx left to coach in the AHL in August, and when Pat Quinn stepped in, one of the scouts, Al Murray—who had coached Jordan at one point—convinced Quinn to invite Jordan to the follow-up camp in September. Quinn tried him on a line with Cody Hodgson and Zach Boychuk, and the trio found a lot of chemistry. Hodgson was pretty much a lock, but Jordan was unsure he was going to make the team. He barely slept that night.

Early the next morning the phone rang, and Jordan wanted to puke. If you got a call, it meant you'd been cut. He couldn't believe it when he picked up and the team asked for a meeting with Cody. Forty minutes later, Cody returned with good news— he'd been made an alternate captain. The phone didn't ring again that morning. Jordan was playing for Team Canada.

Quinn gave Jordan the tap. He stood at centre ice, playing with the puck. Drifting a bit, looking down the ice at Russian goalie Vadim Zhelobynyuk, trying to breathe. At practice just a little over a week earlier on Christmas Day, they had worked on shootouts and Jordan had scored five out of six times. The television crew said he had a "hot stick." He came straight down the middle, left-right, left-right, left-right, left-right. Zhelobynyuk tried to poke check him about eight feet out, and in less than a wink, Jordan switched to his backhand and put it up over Zhelobynyuk's blocker.

John Tavares scored on his attempt while Canada's goalie, Tokarski, stood firm. The team went on to beat Sweden in the gold medal final.

At the post-tournament celebration with the team's families, Pat Quinn invited a few of the players, including Jordan, Tyler Ennis and Zach Boychuk, to step outside with him. Sixteen-year-old Dustin Eberle, Jordan's brother, tagged along. Pat passed around some big cigars and Dustin lit up for the first time. The three players stood there, smoking and shooting the breeze with one of the greatest coaches ever.

Jordan was back on the team in 2010 for the IIHF World Junior Championship in Saskatoon on Boxing Day. Canada's chances for a record sixth straight win were looking good. Late in the third period of the final against the USA, Jordan scored twice to force an overtime, but the Americans scored on a three-on-one, taking home the gold.

Always hard on himself, Jordan was crushed. Defeat was unacceptable. He hated losing to the Americans like that. He was sure his career was over. His family had never seen him so down over a loss. The Hockey Canada team after-party was more like a funeral. But in 2012, a panel of twenty-five experts voted Jordan the number one player in Team Canada's history at the World Juniors.

Jordan was projected to be a late first-round or early second-round pick in the 2008 NHL Entry Draft. He didn't really believe it and was joking around with Dustin about it. But behind the scenes, his old power-skating coach's dad, Lorne Davis, and his son Brad, also an Oilers scout, had been watching Jordan closely for years.

On draft day in June 2008, there was a chair left empty at the Oilers' table in honour of Lorne Davis, who had died of cancer and cardiac arrest six months earlier. Former Oiler Glenn Anderson came to the podium and announced that the team's next pick was Lorne's last recommendation. Jordan waited, but the cameras had already swung around and were pointed at him, so he knew, and so did his family. Lisa started to jump up, and Darren laughingly hauled her back down until it was official.

When Jordan was nine years old, he was on the Saskatchewan Wheatlanders, a summer program Darren was running with his friend Claude Wickenheiser (Doug's brother) as one of the organizers. Jeff Schenn (father of Luke and Brayden of the Philadelphia Flyers) was running the provincial team, the Saskatchewan Hustlin' Huskies, up in Saskatoon. Their kids came from Saskatoon North because Regina had the Wheatlanders. But the Huskies had an in for the Brick Super Novice Hockey

Tournament, the biggest novice tournament in Canada, which is held in the West Edmonton Mall.

The Wheatlanders were in a mini-tournament in Regina, where Jordan scored seven goals and had two assists. The coach of the Vancouver Vipers was at the rink and invited him to come play at the Brick Tournament with Travis Hamonic (now with the New York Islanders), goalie Martin Jones (San Jose Sharks), Tyler Johnson (Tampa Bay Lightning) and Derek Lee (a University of Wisconsin alum who has played pro in Europe).

The Vipers ended up in the final against the Toronto Red Wings, whose lineup included Steve Stamkos (now with the Tampa Bay Lightning), Michael Del Zotto (Philadelphia Flyers), Cody Hodgson (Nashville Predators) and Alex Pietrangelo (St. Louis Blues). The Vipers won on Jordan's overtime goal. He made the first all-star team, was top scorer of the tournament, and was named tournament MVP.

Oilers president Kevin Lowe presented him with his trophies. Nine years later, he was presenting Jordan with his Oilers jersey.

In 2010 Jordan was called up to the Oilers. His first game was against the Calgary Flames, and he scored his first NHL goal, beating Miikka Kiprusoff. It was one of his best so far—a short-handed toe-drag, forward-to-backhand move. It made the high-light reels, but he was just happy to score. Despite all his success, Jordan's not a cocky guy. He and Dustin still chirp back and forth.

Dustin made it to the Junior A Melville Millionaires of the Saskatchewan Junior Hockey League but was sidelined by a big injury—a sliced Achilles tendon. But when he first moved away, Jordan was there for his brother on the phone, giving him advice, helping him out.

Jordan loves rubbing it in that he was on Sidney Crosby's wing at the IIHF World Championships in May 2015. And Dustin has a good time teasing Jordan about his okay guitar playing and awful singing. Jordan picked up the guitar, inspired by Darren, who is the lead guitarist for a classic rock band in Calgary called When Pigs Fly.

On December 5, 2012, when Jordan was just twenty-two years old, the Pats retired his jersey, number 7. Most players are retired from hockey before their jersey is, so it was a shocker for him. He'd been playing with the Oklahoma City Barons during the NHL lockout, and so he flew home for the ceremony at the Brandt Centre. The sold-out crowd cheered him with a forty-five-second standing ovation as Jordan hugged his family, who joined him on the ice.

When he was working his way up, a lot of people thought Jordan would never get there because of his size. So he was always bent on proving people wrong. He doesn't have to do that anymore.

Péribonka

QUEBEC

———————

POPULATION:
464

Gou! Gou!

I ran into Michel Goulet at an airport a few years ago, and I was impressed, both by his career and his down-to-earth attitude. And then, while shooting Hometown Hockey *in the spring of 2015, I spent some time with him again. We hit the bar with Olympic diver Alexandre Despatie and former NHL players Enrico Ciccone and Jason York, and Michel kept us laughing with his stories. But one of his most appealing qualities was his refusal to take credit.*

In 1986, that quality got him in trouble. Montreal Canadiens hero Guy Lafleur had just retired for the first time, and the Quebec Nordiques had high hopes that Michel would be the new French-Canadian golden boy. A year earlier, Nordiques fans had been crying, "Gou! Gou! Gou! Gou!" every time the three-time fifty-goal scorer hit the ice. He ended the season with 104 points and was headed toward similar success in 1985–86, but his low-key style was rubbing Nordiques fans the wrong way. They were looking for some dash and dazzle, and the most Michel could muster after a big goal was to lift his arm.

The Nordiques brass begged him to celebrate his goals more— jump up in the air, hit the glass, hell, they'd settle for a fist pump. Michel scratched his head. He felt the idea was to score goals and win the hockey game. He told them, "I'm very happy on the ice. Obviously, if I have to crash the window every time I score a goal, I might hurt myself." But he agreed to try to "spice up" his style.

He felt a little silly about it, but when he put the puck in, he'd jump a little bit and try to remember to smile. At first, it didn't come naturally, but he scored so many goals that he got a lot of practice.

And then there was a game on March 17, 1986, against Montreal, who would go on to win the Cup that year. The Nordiques were losing 3–0 after ten minutes, and the Montreal fans were already singing. Coach Michel Bergeron called a timeout to put his team back on track. The Nordiques turned it around, winning 8–6. Goulet scored four goals and had two assists against Patrick Roy. After he put the last one in, Michel jumped in the air and allowed himself a little dance.

I wish I could speak French. Not much extends past "Voilà, Monsieur Thibault." But it would be a shame if any part of Michel's story got lost in translation, so with his blessing and help, it is best to let him tell it to you like he told it to me.

My hometown is Péribonka, Quebec. It is about three hours north of Quebec City. We had a rink outside, and when I start getting ready to play hockey, it was always with my brothers. I have seven brothers. I am number five, so it was easy to pick up a game somewhere.

My dad was a very nice man—until he had enough. With eight boys he had a good grip on all of us. His name is Jean-Noël. He was born on the twenty-third of December and baptized on the twenty-fifth. That is why his parents call him "Young Christmas," but sometimes we laugh that he was no gift, that is for sure. I think maybe my mom, Alphonsine, was a bit more in control. She had a way to get things done. Overall, they were very good parents. They turn ninety in the summer, so we are going to have a nice little party for them.

That is where it all started—on our farm. We had cattle and potatoes for a long time, maybe twenty years. I didn't work as much as some of the brothers because I would play peewee and bantam in a city about twenty miles away—Mistassini. It is a beautiful place. What happened there, the bigger-city scouts came over and they see a few games, and they ask me to join them. So I would play in two places, Mistassini—the big city— and with my little hometown team.

I just loved the game. One night, February 11, 1971, I was eleven years old. Everyone was watching *Hockey Night in Canada*. We were waiting for Jean Béliveau to score his five-hundredth goal, and then he score against the North Stars that night. My mother was imagining how many goals I want to score in the NHL. And I said, "I am going to score as many as Mr. Béliveau!"

In Mistassini, that is where they start a new league when I was fifteen years old. At that time, it was Midget C. They open a new arena in there, which gave us a chance to play inside. Every kid was so joyful. It was an unbelievable difference. But even better was to have the chance to play hockey outside and inside. That was really, really a great year.

That's where one of the part-time scouts from the Quebec Remparts saw me play. His name was Jean-Paul Gimael. The guy sold me all year to the team. I think he thought I could do a lot of things on the ice, especially scoring goals, and I could make the play.

They followed me all winter to the junior draft, but no one knew at what round I'd get picked up—maybe second round, third round, maybe fourth round, I don't know. So I went there and all of a sudden, number five! I got picked up first round. So I didn't wait too long, that is for sure.

Our coach was Mr. Ron Racette. Mr. Racette was officially a tough man. That was the old-time hockey there. He was amazing. I learned so much under his wing. I only play a year and a half, but that's where it all started. Before I went to training camp, I called the Quebec Remparts because my skates were not the best, and so I ask for a new pair. They said, "Well, come to training camp and we can go from there. We will take it slow." So I show up with my skates maybe two sizes too big for my feet. I'm a size 9 and my skates were about size 11. I play with those skates for about two years. We were growing up all the time, and my dad bought us bigger sizes so we don't have to buy another pair. At training camp, everyone is looking at my feet, and a couple of days later the coach said, "Hey, get him a new pair of skates!" And you know what? I improved my skating 30 per cent with the new skates.

I was a big shot going from Midget C to the major junior. But then I didn't make my team at first! So I went back down to play Junior AAA in Beauport. At Christmas, one of the players of the Quebec Remparts said the coach was too hard on him, and he just left. Mr. Racette called me and said, "Come and play." And that first game against Sorel, a big, tough team, we were losing 8–2 after two periods, but we won the game 9–8. I had three goals and three assists, so that is where Mr. Racette said, "You are not going to go down again, okay?"

The second year, everything came to me a lot easier. And that is where I had seventy-three goals, sixty-two assists and we made the playoffs. I had just a great year there. It was awesome. After the year, Mr. Gilles Leger, the general manager of the Birmingham Bulls of the World Hockey Association, came over to talk to me. The Bulls at the time, they signed Ricky Vaive, Rob Ramage, Craig Hartsburg, Gaston Gingras, Louis Sleigher, Pat Riggin the goaltender—a bunch of young guys, and he want me to be a part of it. I said, "You know what? I feel ready." So I was eighteen when I move to Birmingham, Alabama.

It was a big, nice city down south. For me, the game is still the same. It doesn't matter where you go, but I don't speak English so it was interesting, for sure. The first day I was in a restaurant, it was an eye-opener. Sometime I would just point to things on the menu. Obviously, a steak is a steak, but to order it cook the way I like was very challenging. On the other side, it was fun. I was just laughing and enjoying the experience I was having.

Mr. Brophy, "Broph," was the coach. He was a big teacher for all of us because we were all so young. First, he wasn't playing me a lot—I was on the fourth line. Then one day we were practising. He did a drill and the first line go, and the second line go and the third line go, and he move to the middle to start the next drill, but he forget there is a fourth line. Our left winger is cutting to the middle, and I go for a little breakaway and I just friggin' hit Brophy so hard, it was unbelievable. All I see is white hair flying in the air. He land on his elbow. I don't know how many stitches he need, but ah, my God, I am so worried. He turn around and he look at me and he said, "Oh . . . you're a strong boy!" He was such a hockey man. So at the end of the day, he move me up with Rick Adduono and Rick Vaive. At the end of the season, I had the most goals for the team and I can see myself progressing, getting better.

November 26, 1978, my first game for Birmingham against New England, we play against the Howe family, Gordie and his son, Marty. Well, Marty, he cross-check a player a couple of times, and so I was like, "Hey, hey, what are you doing?"

And he said, "Hey, you want to go?"

I'm like, "Okay." If you knock at the door, I will open it up, you know? So I have a pretty good fight against Marty. I pumped him two good punches in the face and he goes down.

The next shift on the ice after my five-minute major, Gordie got kicked out of the draw and he stand on the right side of me. I'm like, "Hmm," and I'm thinking about all the stories I have heard, so I move a couple of steps away from him. And I'm watching the puck when all of a sudden I get this stick in my rib and I'm on the ice. I'm thinking, "Oh my God, what happened?" And Gordie lean down to me and he says, "Don't touch my son." You should have seen the eyes on him. My God, that man had a dangerous air. What was he? Fifty years old at the time? I mean, I am eighteen years old, so wow, what do you do? I don't slash him, I don't spear him, I respect him. Look at what he did, what he accomplished and how long he play. He was a natural, he was big, and he was strong as a horse.

But he made me pay for two years until he retire. Two punches I had given to his son, and he fed me his elbows, knees and sticks. Twenty years later, when I got inducted into the Hall of Fame, my son Vincent was thirteen years old. He shake hands with Gordie and he says, "Mr. Howe, why did you spear my dad?"

And like it was yesterday for Gordie, he says, "Well, my son didn't really know how to fight."

The WHA had their young guys like us and Gretzky and Messier. They tried to force the NHL to merge with their teams in 1979. Four teams did that—Hartford, Quebec, Edmonton and Winnipeg. But Birmingham folded, and so that was interesting, that's for sure. It mean the 1979 NHL draft was a big year. There was Rob Ramage, Mike Foligno, Ricky Vaive, Keith Brown, Craig Hartsburg, Perry Turnbull, Brian Propp, Laurie Boschman—everybody played that year.

Rob Ramage went first round. It's always harder to find a good defenceman than a good forward. That is something that everyone knows in hockey. Rob Ramage had a great, great first year. He was built like a man already. He was nineteen years old and he was strong and he play a solid game.

I went number twenty, which is awesome. I mean, at the end of the day, it's just nice to have the chance to be recognized by a team that wants you, you know? And so it happens that was the Quebec Nordiques.

I had an agent at the time who really wanted me to play for the Nordiques, and listen, I think he gambled a little bit. He said that I am not going to report unless I play there. But in my mind, I would be happy to report anywhere. If the Chicago Blackhawks draft me, sorry, I am going! But it was on his agenda a little bit and so after the draft I let him go. It was just politics and I didn't want to be involved with that kind of stuff. So it looked like I was the bad guy. But at the end of the day, I had ten beautiful years in Quebec.

Jacques Demers was the coach the first year, and I learn a lot. He was an amazing man, a guy passionate about hockey and about life. I thought I had a pretty decent first year. He put me with the checking line all year, and I finish the season with twenty-two goals. He help me focus on offence and defence at the same time. In 1981–82, I tied with Wayne Gretzky for short-handed goals. So me and Wayne, we're practising our defence!

My second year, I play under Maurice Filion. He was the team manager and decide to coach a little bit. He didn't last long. He was looking for a coach. Michel Bergeron came maybe a month later. He was my coach for six years after that.

Michel Bergeron had a totally different philosophy about hockey than Jacques Demers. Michel let the skill talk a little bit. We make the playoffs, and that was big news in Quebec. It was fun because of the storied rivalry between Quebec and Montreal. It got bigger and bigger and bigger every game. The Montreal Forum was always something really special, with the big history and the glamour that they have over there. In those ten years I was with Quebec, I thought those games were the best. They were the most intense.

In 1982–83 I have my career high, fifty-seven goals. The year after, I break the record for left wingers with 121 points. I was getting older, getting better and knowing more about players and what's very important—about the goaltender.

I love to practise more than everybody. When I was nineteen, Marc Tardif, who was the leading goal scorer in the history of the WHA, he says, "What you're going to do is you're going to put sixty to sixty-eight pucks between the red line and the blue line, and then you're going to go down the wing and shoot the puck, every single one of them before every practice." And I did that for fifteen years.

I had some injury in January 1985 when there was a fight with Kevin Dineen, who was with Hartford. I could see my thumb was broken on my top hand, and I missed like, three weeks, but I was trying to find a way to come back as quick as possible. So I take my stick with me to the doctor and we set the cast around it. Now, I can play. I have a pretty decent year—around fifty-five goals, I think.

Dale Hunter, he was my centre for seven seasons. What an amazing passer and playmaker. He was a little bit the fuel of our team. Everybody knows he's got three thousand minutes of penalties, but not a lot of people talk about his one thousand points. He played for a long time, and it was one of the saddest days of my life when they trade him in '87. Me and Peter Šťastný at the time were on a line with Dale, and all of a sudden they trade those guys. And you realize that you're getting older, but you don't have much help coming down. The younger core was not there yet. So you see the Nordiques were having some bad years coming up. When they trade Dale to Washington, I was really doubting what they were trying to do. It was sad. He had given the team so much. I feel if they had hung on for a little longer, they would have won the Stanley Cup.

But you know, it's funny, we made the deal and nobody expect a whole lot, and all of a sudden the next season we grab Joe Sakic. He come in to training camp and I look at him and I go, "Whoa! That's a player!"

The whole time I am playing, maybe I have a little secret not too many are knowing about. My second year in Quebec City, the first game of the season, all of a sudden during the national anthem my heart started racing. I went back to the bench and it didn't slow down. So I go back to the training room and I called to the doctor. He said to relax a little bit, maybe you are just nervous, you know? I calm down and go back to play. It's not a heart attack, it's just my heart. It keeps racing like once or twice a month.

The doctor, he was trying to figure out what was wrong, so I went through tests on the treadmill and with oxygen and the electrode stickers for the electrocardiogram, and they tell me I have atrial tachyarrhythmia. What it is, your heart starts racing for nothing. At the time, there was absolutely no cure for that besides taking medication. And that medication would put you to sleep pretty much, which is no good for a hockey player.

I learn that while I was playing, if all of a sudden my heart was racing, I would sit on the bench and press the jugular vein on the side of my throat for a minute or two and then press my fingers on my eyes, and that would make me calm down. The heartbeat for a professional hockey player might be forty-nine to fifty-four beats a minute, but there were times where I was on the bench trying to stop my heart from going all of a sudden over two hundred.

Sometimes, I would be on the bench and I would say to my coach, "Well, you know, I'm going to skip my turn." And I'd go in the trainer's room and relax a little bit, and when it would go back to normal, I'd come back and finish the game. But you don't know when it is going to start, you know? Most of the time, it happen when the body got a hit, like if I fell down on the ice, or a big elbow or a bodycheck. It was a little bit of a problem, and each year it was harder and harder to get my heart to slow down. And at the time, not a whole lot of people knew what to do until ten years later, when I was traded to Chicago.

My second year in Chicago in 1991 at training camp, I just start the scrimmage and then all of a sudden I got hit, and I fell to my knee, and the pounding started—the heart. I go back on the bench and try to squeeze my throat and press my eye with the fingers and it won't stop. So after five, six, seven minutes, I told my trainer, Mike Gapski, "It won't slow down." I went back to the room and tried to relax. He took my pulse and said, "Wow, you are at 220!' After forty minutes, everybody start panicking, including myself. I am thinking, "Maybe it won't stop!"

So they take me to the hospital, and this doctor in Oklahoma City, Dr. Warren Jackman, had a cure. To him, it is an electrical problem with the heart and he is a pioneer in fixing this, what they call atrial fibrillation. So he does what is called a catheter ablation procedure on me. It is a line through your groin and up to the heart to destroy a small area of the heart tissue that is causing my heart to go so fast. Personally, I was watching what was happening on a TV as they play with my heart for about four hours, and then after that, I said, "You know what? I'm tired," and I go to sleep. They tell me when I wake up that the surgery took sixteen hours to finish.

I was back on the ice almost a week later. I didn't miss any games, and I never had a problem with it since.

Mike Keenan was my coach in Chicago. I had played for him at the 1987 Canada Cup. In 1984 at the Canada Cup, Glen Sather was my coach. With Sather was the best time of my career because I play with Wayne Gretzky and Rick Middleton on a production line.

Mike Keenan in 1987 had a totally different approach. I was more like a checker than anything else, but it was great to have the chance to play with Mario Lemieux. He was my roommate for six weeks. That was an amazing time and filled with the pressure and the beauty of representing your country. For me, it was my Olympics, basically, because in those days professionals in hockey weren't allowed to play in the Olympics.

The line in Chicago in 1991–92 was Jeremy Roenick, Steve Larmer and Michel Goulet. For me, it was probably one of the best lines in the NHL. I had some good lines in Quebec, but with this line I score my five hundredth goal on February 16, 1992. I score 499 on the road in San Jose, but we are back home and we are playing at Chicago Stadium against the Calgary Flames. It was such an amazing night. There was a breakaway, which is always special. And it was a dream because it was a little bit like the five hundredth goal scored by Jean Béliveau. I come down on the goalie's glove side and it go in on the backhand. My mother remembered I told her I was going to do that when I was eleven.

We end up in the Stanley Cup finals against Pittsburgh that year. Jeremy Roenick was a young guy, just second or third year in the league, and he score fifty goals two seasons in a row. And Steve Larmer was like Hunter, a very, very underrated player. Never missed a game. There was no nickname for the line. I am thinking Roenick would call it "Roenick's line."

We had a very good team—Joe Murphy, Chris Chelios, Ed Belfour. Our problem we had was no Lemieux or Jaromír Jágr or Ron Francis. In the end, it was Mario who beat us. Mario was the key guy. He was just unstoppable. And Jágr was just a young guy coming in who was pretty unbelievable too. But it's just nice to have a chance to win the Cup, you know? And that's what we tried to do.

After five years in Chicago, I am thinking I have maybe three or four more years, but then there is an accident. I didn't remember it until I saw it on TV three or four months later, but it was the toughest time of my career, no question.

I remember in the old Forum that the board was cement at the bottom. I was just going wide with the puck, looking for Roenick. He was going to the net, and I go to turn in, bringing my leg across my body. I'm five feet out from the board, and I am not sure what happen, but I lost balance and after that I woke up in the hospital. My eyes, they opened, but I don't remember absolutely anything. That was a challenge. I was four weeks in the hospital there.

To show you the impact of how hard my head hit, the doctor, he says to me, "You hit the left side of your head and it was bleeding on the right side of your brain." He said, "You know, a football helmet would probably help you a lot." No question, but that is not going to happen.

He tells me, "The level of concussion you have, it is the worst. The next level you wouldn't be able to breathe. But you're alive." So at the end of the day, I know I was lucky. But the brain it takes time to fix, and you need to refocus, recharge and obviously, not give up on yourself, because that's the toughest part.

I was going back home to Chicago and struggling with my coordination and my memory and everything else. Three months later, I couldn't even catch a baseball, I couldn't bench-press thirty pounds. I was weak. I was walking and hitting the corner of the house. So I have to relearn how to live and move, and it mean you go slower. It's not much fun, three or four months later, and you're driving and you know you're going to downtown Chicago, but you're not sure to where. You forgot.

Physically, it was always easy for me, and now to go golfing and you miss the ball, but the worst was to get on the ice and fall down. That is a thing that will break your heart. What help me the most is the doctor saying to me what was going to happen, so I am not surprised. But I still get mad at myself. I learn to just sit down and try to refocus a little bit and try to stay as positive as I can. When I was in rehabilitation, there was a young boxer with me at the same time. One morning, he didn't show up. He had taken his own life. And the doctor, she said, "Michel, that's the thing that scares me the most, when I get that phone call. Sometimes you just have that two or three minutes of weakness, and what you do to yourself could be forever."

I don't know if you can have a worse way to hit a board, but at the end of the day I'm sure you can have a worse injury. But the fact is, I'm alive and have function and am working as a scout for the Calgary Flames. That, for me, is a blessing. For sure, I can have tough days. When I think about a lot of things that happen in hockey and the head injuries that's going on now, you need to be strong. I know I'm going to make mistakes, but it's not going to kill me, you know?

Montreal

QUEBEC

_____

POPULATION:
1,649,519

One Hundred Per Cent

During the 1987 Stanley Cup playoffs, the Montreal Canadiens and Philadelphia Flyers were involved in a battle royal. By the time Game Six rolled around, we on the telecast were aware that the Flyers had grown weary of the Habs' Claude Lemieux and his pre-game ritual. Lemieux would remain on the ice until the end of the warm-up, wait for all the Flyers to clear the ice, and then rifle a puck into the Philadelphia net.

For Game Six in Montreal, the Flyers had a plan. Two of their players (goalie Glenn Resch and defenceman Ed Hospodar) would linger in the hallway just a few feet from the ice, and when Lemieux collected his lucky puck to begin the routine, they'd storm back out and intercept the shot. In fact, they did even more. They attacked Lemieux, and a full twenty-minute brawl erupted.

It was a memorable broadcast. After we signed off, a woman suddenly appeared in our CBC studio. I was in my rookie season, so it wasn't unusual for me not to know this person. Don Cherry bellowed, "Well, Ma, that was right up there with the Nordiques' Easter riot!"

The woman replied, "Donald, how many times have I told you there's no place for that stuff?"

Don chortled, "Remember Dick and I did that Quebec game three years ago and Dick was so disgusted, he took off his headset and refused to talk?"

After a couple of minutes, with no introductions coming my way, I felt a bit like a loose wheel standing there. So I blurted out to the woman, "I'm Ron MacLean, and you must be Don's mother."

Ever seen two people bowled over by something you've said? Don actually sat down, but he didn't say a word. The woman, in a miracle of grace through a kick in the gut, replied, "Ha, that's right, I am Don's mother . . . I'm Wilma Irvin—Dick's wife." And she walked out.

When I heard "Well, Ma," I figured Kingston was a little over two hours to the west and I knew Don's mom lived there. And, well, no matter how I pieced it together, the fact is that in order for Wilma to have been Don Cherry's mom in 1987, she would have to have been close to eighty years old. She was fifty. And she was beautiful.

On the taxi ride back to the hotel, Don wouldn't let up. It got to the point where Bob Cole actually got protective of me and my blunder and told Grapes to lay off.

At my home in Oakville, after my wife, Cari, has gone upstairs to watch Kerry Washington in Scandal *on our bedroom television, I stay with hockey on the bigger screen downstairs. It takes about fifteen minutes before I get the munchies. I make popcorn and grab a pop. And always, I think of Wilma Irvin.*

In the years after the "big blurt," Wilma told me she enjoyed quiet evenings home alone, watching or listening to Dick's broadcasts with a bowl of popcorn and a diet cola. Wilma was a great sounding board as I embarked on my career, helping me understand Cari's life and my own in broadcasting. And Dick was my coach on where a story sets out and when hubris sets in.

Wilma is gone now. Dick is our statesman. He slides into every situation with an uncanny way of making the biggest or smallest

Jordan Eberle (*right*) with his brother, Dustin, and his dad, Darren, at the 2010 World Juniors, where Canada would take gold and Jordan was named MVP.

December 5, 2012. Jordan Eberle with his mom, Lisa, grandfather, Al, grandmother, Lynn, and dad, Darren, at his Regina Pats jersey retirement.

The Edmonton Oilers versus Ottawa Senators on March 4, 2014. Jordan Eberle has big stage pedigree.

With Tara Slone hosting Rogers Hometown Hockey in Regina. Our guests are (*left to right*) Wendel Clark, Mike Sillinger and Marty McSorley. ROGERS MEDIA

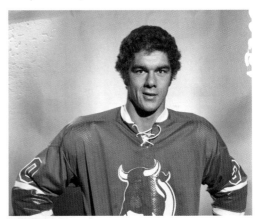

Michel Goulet promised his parents he would score 500 goals just like his hero, Jean Béliveau. His 57 goals in 1982–83 became the most goals scored by a left winger in NHL history.
HOCKEY HALL OF FAME

Out of the unlikeliest roots, Péribonka and Birmingham, sprouted a legend. Michel Goulet could score from anywhere inside 100 feet. Lumberjack power with a surgeon's precision.
PAUL BERESWILL/HOCKEY HALL OF FAME

That's Dickinson (not Richard) Irvin, Jr., an incredible mentor. I'll always be grateful to him for his kindness and wisdom. DAVE SANDFORD/GETTY IMAGES

Dick Irvin, Sr., with the Chicago Black Hawks, circa 1927.
HOCKEY HALL OF FAME

Brad Dalgarno singing "Friends
in Low Places" with Garth
Brooks on stage in 1993 at the
Nassau Coliseum. The pained
look on his face is from
borrowed cowboy boots that
are several sizes too small.
COURTESY BRAD DALGARNO

Brad Dalgarno after re-inventing
himself, with the New York Islanders
in 2000.
B. BENNETT/GETTY IMAGES

Cari, me, Brad and Lesley Dalgarno
at my induction into the Oakville
Hall of Fame in 2015.
COURTESY MCLELLAN DAY
AND MACLEAN

Diane and Charlie Lennox with their children Susan (*left*), Paul (*centre*) and Michael (*top*). Michael was sick, but he was such a big, healthy, cheerful boy that the doctors could not figure out what was wrong.
COURTESY THE LENNOX FAMILY

Away from the money and the bright lights, folks like OHA referee assignor Charlie Lennox are the game's backbone.
COURTESY OF THE LENNOX FAMILY

Lacing up for one of Charlie's assignments.
COURTESY OF THE LENNOX FAMILY

I _Wayne Gretzky_ allow _Rob Gordon_
to write a book about myself, and agree
not to press charges of any kind on him
if this book comes out. Any one else "cannot"
write the book.
Signed _Rob Gordon_
Wayne Gretzky

witness _Scott Forbes_
Don Elliott

Wayne Gretzky had already signed his first seven-figure deal to play hockey, but it didn't go to his head, because he agreed to let a school friend write his first book.
COURTESY ROB GORDON

Boyhood buddies Steve Bodnar and Wayne Gretzky in the Soo, 1978. Wayne billeted with Steve's family there. COURTESY STEVE BODNAR

Shinny in Sault Ste. Marie. Hockey's a great game to play. A better game to win. And the best game to love. ROGERS MEDIA

A young Charlie Bourgeois with his father, Aurèle Bourgeois. Charlie's dignity and dependability have kept the spirit of his father alive.
COURTESY THE BOURGEOIS FAMILY

Aurèle Bourgeois, a Moncton policeman. He was faithful even in small things, and a model of inner and outer strength.
COURTESY THE BOURGEOIS FAMILY

Charlie Bourgeois with the Calgary Flames, circa 1985—in every corner on the lookout for others, just like his father. GRAIG ABEL/GETTY IMAGES

The birthplace of Confederation and Anne of Green Gables, Charlottetown is as idyllic as its legacies would have you imagine. ROGERS MEDIA

shows seem like a trip to the fridge for a pop, and then to the hot stove. Something to be shared or enjoyed alone.

The first year the Chicago Blackhawks went into business, 1926–27, Dick Irvin Sr. was the captain of the team. By 1930–31, he was coaching the Hawks, and they made it to the finals but lost to Montreal. So the summer came and went, and he was packing for training camp when he got a telegram from the owner, Frederic McLaughlin, who was the heir to a coffee business. It said that the board of directors had decided his services were no longer required.

The Toronto Maple Leafs hired Irvin that fall, and in 1932 he won his first of four Stanley Cups as a coach. The Blackhawks, meanwhile, went through three coaches over the next two seasons, before settling on one of the founding members of the NHL, Tommy Gorman. Tommy won the Cup for Chicago in 1934, but he was fired anyway. McLaughlin owned the team for eighteen years and went through eighteen coaches.

Because coaching jobs were so volatile, Dick Sr. didn't move his family around. Instead, he made Regina his home. In late September, when he boarded the train, it was always a sad day. Bertha and their two kids, Dick Jr. and his younger sister, Fay, wouldn't see him again until the end of March or April. Because he was a celebrity, people would ask his son, "What's it like growing up with a dad who's a coach in the NHL?" and Dick Jr. would reply, "I don't know."

Dick Sr. kept in touch whenever he could. He'd call home when the Leafs were on the road in Chicago, where long-distance rates to Saskatchewan were the cheapest, and he wrote a lot of letters, most of them about hockey. His chicken scratch was pretty bad, so Dick Jr. would get his mother to decipher it.

When her husband was away, Bertha raised the kids by herself. Her father-in-law lived with the family in Regina until he died in 1944, but he sat in the corner and smoked his pipe all day.

Dick Sr. coached in Toronto for nine years altogether and made it to the Stanley Cup finals six more times. During the 1939–40 season, Leaf owner Conn Smythe spoke to him about coaching the Montreal Canadiens. The city's other NHL team, the Montreal Maroons, had gone out of business in 1938. Now, the Canadiens' owner, Senator Donat Raymond, was seriously considering folding too. The Canadiens had won only ten of forty-eight games that season and fans had lost interest. Raymond couldn't keep the team alive with only 1,500 people buying seats at the Forum.

Early in the season, the league had a meeting and decided it couldn't afford to lose the Montreal franchise. It was the birthplace of hockey in Canada. But what to do? The problem with the Canadiens, besides their lack of talent, was that they had no discipline on the team. Conn Smythe told them, "I have just the guy to send in there. I got Irvin. Let me talk to him."

In January of his last year with the Leafs, Dick Sr. had brought the whole family to Toronto to live with him for the rest of the season. Dick Jr. was in Grade 3. The team made it to the finals against the Rangers but lost in six games. Bryan Hextall Sr., whose grandson Ron is now the general manager of the Philadelphia Flyers, scored the winning goal right in front of Box 4, where Dick Jr. was sitting, and the little fella started to cry.

On the way home in the car, his dad surprised him by saying, "Think you could cheer for the Montreal Canadiens?"

Dick Sr. coached in Montreal for fifteen years, where he had players like Rocket Richard, Doug Harvey and Jean Béliveau, and together they won the Stanley Cup three times, in 1944, '46 and '53.

Bert Olmstead once told Dick Jr. that whenever he had a problem, he'd think about something Dick Sr. had taught him. He said that back when he played for him, if he was in a slump, Dick would have him go one on one against Doug Harvey, one of the great defencemen of his era. But beforehand, Dick would quietly tell Harvey to let Olmstead beat him. Olmstead said Dick Irvin Sr. was better than a sports psychologist. "He was father, brother, coach, you name it." In April of 1950, Montreal was in the semi-finals with the Rangers. The Rangers were ahead in the series 3–0 when Montreal's goalie, Bill Durnan, a six-time Vézina Trophy winner—the best goalie in the league at the time—came to Dick Sr. on the train and asked him to pull him. Durnan told his coach his nerves were on edge "and I don't want to crack up all at once." Dick called for his backup goalie, Gerry McNeil, to join them. Gerry had been playing with the Montreal Royals in the QSHL and the Cincinnati Mohawks in the AHL. He'd only been called up for a few games with the Canadiens here and there when Bill was injured. When Gerry entered the compartment, Bill was crying and Dick was crying, and then Gerry started crying. Durnan never played another game. With Gerry in goal, the Canadiens won the next game against the Rangers but lost in Game Five.

Dick Jr., who graduated from McGill University in 1953, played for the varsity team, the Redmen. Their home rink was the Forum, and they practised each day at noon, which meant his dad's team would skate off and his team would skate on.

He got to watch all the Canadiens games for free because he worked in the press box, keeping statistics for his dad. Dick Sr. was one of the first coaches to use them. He'd have his son watch for different things on different nights—from faceoffs to body checks to hits—and Dick Jr. would always keep track of who was on the ice when the goals were scored.

On April 16, 1953, the Canadiens beat the Boston Bruins to win the Stanley Cup. Elmer Lach, who died at the age of ninety-seven in April 2015, scored the overtime winner in Game Five. The only tears Dick Jr. shed this time were tears of joy.

The next year, 1954, Montreal played Detroit in the finals, and the Red Wings won Game Seven in overtime. This time, the winning goal was scored on goaltender Gerry McNeil by Doug Harvey—he punched at the puck in the air to try to knock it down, and it deflected into the net. Years later, when Dick Jr. was writing his book *The Habs*, Gerry told him, "You guys [the media] call it the Leswick goal, after Tony Leswick, the Wings forward who got credit for it. I call it the Harvey goal."

The next year was Dick Sr.'s last in Montreal. It was the year of the Richard Riot. Maurice Richard was hockey's top goal scorer. Dick Sr. told his son that Richard not only scored his way to the top, but he fought his way to the top too. So it rocked the hockey world when NHL president Clarence Campbell suspended the Rocket for the last three games of the season in addition to the entire playoffs for hitting linesman Cliff Thompson. The official story was that Hal Laycoe, a Boston defenceman, hit the Rocket with a hard check late in the third period, cutting him in the face with a high stick. So Rocket went after Laycoe, cross-checking him in the mouth. And when Thompson tried to pull Richard away from the fracas, Richard threw a left hook and got him in the jaw.

Richard, Dick Sr. and Canadiens executive Ken Reardon—who would be inducted into the Hall of Fame ten years later—went to the hearing together. In his book *The Habs*, Dick Jr. says Reardon defended the Rocket, and when he came out of the meeting his shirt and suit coat were soaking wet with sweat. Richard didn't lie and say it was a mistake, that he'd lost his balance or anything like that. He admitted that he had gone after Laycoe, but said he was mad because Thompson kept grabbing him from behind and jumping on him while Laycoe delivered some retaliatory punches. Dick Sr. stuck up for the Rocket too, but Campbell sided with the official. Laycoe later told Dick Jr. that there were no hard feelings between him and the Rocket. "Hell," he said, "we used to play tennis in the summertime."

The Canadiens played the Detroit Red Wings at the Montreal Forum four nights later, and Richard was in the stands. Clarence Campbell sat in a box seat a few feet from him. Campbell had been advised not to go to the game that night, but he said there was no way he was going to be bulldozed or intimidated into staying away. Between periods, there was a lot of unrest. Fans pelted Campbell with tomatoes, eggs and programs. A guy ran up to Campbell, pretending he was going to shake hands, and instead he threw a sucker punch. Jimmy Orlando, a tough guy who had played for the Red Wings, had followed the guy up the stairs. Dick Jr. says that as soon as he saw Mr. Campbell slapped, Jimmy grabbed the attacker "and just drilled him. There were teeth flying in all directions."

At the end of the first period, with Detroit up 4–1, someone threw a tear gas canister into the crowd and it landed right in front of Dick Jr. His eyes wouldn't stop tearing and his lungs were on fire, so he joined 15,000 other fans who made their way outside for fresh air. After a few minutes, Dick Jr. stopped choking and his eyes started to clear. The fans were upset, but aside from shouting and protesting with signs, everything seemed under control. And then the taverns and bars began to empty onto the street and the real trouble started. Rioters picked up bottles and huge chunks of ice and started breaking windows. They overturned cars and started looting shops. Eight policemen and twenty-five fans were injured and sixteen people were arrested. The game was forfeited to Detroit. Dick Jr. says that Kenny Reardon always insisted that the bomb had been set by the police to clear the building.

Losing to Detroit meant Dick Sr. had a tough job ahead of him. But as much as he was a terrible loser, he kept calm that night, before and after the loss. The Canadiens wound up in the finals against Detroit, who took the series, but even without Richard the series went all the way to Game Seven.

Dick Sr. had had a tough season. Some days he didn't feel so hot, and he took it out on the players. At the end of the year, he was offered a chance to stay with the Canadiens, but not as coach. He had just accepted an offer from Jim Norris with the Blackhawks, who were in last place, when he was diagnosed with bone cancer. He took some pills—he called them his "blockbusters"—which enabled him to live a pretty normal life for another year as coach of the 1955–56 Chicago Blackhawks. The only thing that was different for Dick Sr. was that he couldn't skate. His legs were too weak.

The Hawks improved a bit, but they ended the season in last place again. About a week into training camp the following September, he called the players together. Years later, in 2012, Forbes Kennedy—a small, tough checker who was in the dressing room at the time—met up with Dick Jr. and me in Charlottetown when we were shooting *Hockey Day in Canada*. He told us what Dick Sr. said to the team that day. "I've always asked you guys to give me 100 per cent, and now I can't give you 100 per cent, so I am going to have to leave." Forbes said players in the room were crying. It was a scene he'll never forget. Dick Sr. died at home in the spring of 1957. He was sixty-four years old.

Dick Sr.'s death wasn't the end of hockey for the Irvin family. In 1961, Dick Jr. quit his job at Shell Oil and got into the broadcasting business. He was always fascinated when he watched his dad interviewed. Dick Sr. had been involved in a couple of broadcasting milestones. He played in the first hockey game ever broadcast on radio—March 15, 1923, when he was a centre for the Regina Capitals of the Western Canada Hockey League. They were up against the Edmonton Eskimos that night. And on October 11, 1952, he coached and won in the first game ever televised in Canada, a 2–1 win for Montreal against Detroit.

After he left Shell, Dick Jr. says Frank Selke Sr., the Canadiens' general manager, made him the official scorer at the games at the Forum. But the job wasn't quite panning out, so Dick had lined up a job as a teacher in the Montreal school system.

The owners of CFCF radio in Montreal had just been granted the city's first private television licence, and they'd hired a broadcaster named Brian McFarlane to become the station's sports director. But Brian was by himself and feeling overwhelmed.

During one Saturday night broadcast, Dick was invited on as part of a hockey panel. The station was looking for on-air talent, and they were impressed with what he said on the show, so they asked him to come back for an audition, but later changed their minds and let him know they wanted somebody with experience instead. Thinking he was going to have a crack at going into the business had convinced Dick he wanted to be a broadcaster. Now, all he needed was a chance to audition.

Doug Smith, a successful broadcaster from Calgary, was Danny Gallivan's predecessor in Montreal. In the early '40s, Doug had written Dick Sr., whom he'd never met, wondering if he, as a fellow westerner, could help Doug land an audition with the Montreal Canadiens broadcasting team. Dick Sr. did that, and Smith got the job.

So now Dick Jr. went to see Doug, who told him that Brian McFarlane owed him a favour. "He's really struggling in this market right now and you are just the guy they need. You leave it with me."

By the time Dick walked through his front door that night, the phone was ringing. It was Brian who said, "You know, Dick, we've been discussing this, and maybe we'll give you the audition after all."

Dick wrote out a sportscast in longhand, bought a humongous tape recorder, and sat in his basement and practised. When he arrived at the studio and they started recording, he noticed a guy holding up three fingers. Dick wasn't sure what was going on, so he just kept reading. Soon after, the guy held up two fingers, and Dick still didn't have a clue what the fellow was up to. A minute later, the guy held up one finger, and suddenly Dick realized it was about timing! So he wrapped up. Brian came in, gave him a quick interview, slapped his knees and said, "You're just the guy I want." Dick was offered the job at $75 per week.

Dick consulted with a family friend, Lyman Potts, who was an experienced executive at CJAD radio in Montreal. Dick said, "I'm not sure I should get into the business. My voice is too squeaky." And Lyman replied, "You can whistle sports and nobody will care."

Dick was supposed to observe at CFCF for six weeks, but they were short-staffed, so he was put on the air after nine days. On his way to work on August 8, the day of his three-month review, he was convinced he was going to be told, "Thanks, but no thanks. It's not working out." But that didn't happen. In fact, nobody said a word. He started to breathe a bit easier when his next paycheque reflected a $7.50 per week raise.

The CTV network, of which CFCF was part, carried *Hockey Night in Canada*'s Wednesday games. Dan Kelly, a CBC employee in Ottawa, was Danny Gallivan's colour man in Montreal, but the CBC wouldn't let Kelly appear on CTV, so there was an opening. Dick got the job. He started on as a part-timer in the fall of 1965. The next year, Dick did play-by-play on a Montreal Junior Canadiens game. Scotty Bowman was the coach and Jacques Lemaire scored a hat trick.

Today, announcers may be assigned to work a game anywhere—Toronto tonight, Montreal tomorrow, New York the next day. But in those days, Montreal and Toronto had their own distinct broadcast teams. So Danny Gallivan and Dick were never allowed to do a game from Maple Leaf Gardens, while Leaf broadcasters Brian McFarlane and Bill Hewitt never covered games from the Montreal Forum. That was the way it went. The people in Toronto had to suffer through Dick and Danny, and the people in Montreal had to listen to what they perceived as Bill and Brian's home team–loving broadcast.

Dick eventually got to work the Saturday games carried by CBC, making him the only guy who ever worked full time for CTV and CBC at the same time, and it was because his boss in Montreal, a fellow named Bud Hayward, saw the value of having one of his on-air personalities on a national show. So Dick would provide colour for Danny Gallivan at the games, jump into a taxicab and go back up the hill to the north end of town to appear on the CFCF late news that same night.

In 1970, Dick and Danny were on the air for Game Four of the Stanley Cup final between the Boston Bruins and St. Louis Blues, which ended with Bobby Orr's overtime goal. The broadcast booth in Boston Garden was the only one in the league where they risked being hit by a puck. Dick remembers that, as soon as Bobby's goal went in, somebody from above threw a beer and both he and Danny were covered in spray. Orr had won the scoring championship that year, so Dick called out, "It's now officially the year of Bobby Orr in the NHL!"

Today, all the videotape clips of that goal feature Dan Kelly's call for the CBS network in the States. Dick loved the way Danny Gallivan called that goal, so he asked his producers, "How come whenever I hear that Bobby Orr goal on our show, it's Dan Kelly and not Danny Gallivan?" He was told that the CBC, lacking storage space on the shelves for videotape, erased their tape. All that's left is Dick's memory of Danny's call.

Dick travelled for thirty-three years with the Montreal Canadiens, doing radio and television, and never had a battle with anybody. To this day, he credits his dad for helping him sound like he knew hockey better than he did. "Some of the smarter things I said, it wasn't me at all—I was remembering things that he taught me." Dick was the original media renaissance man. He could do it all—hosting, play-by-play and colour commentary. Today, he says he has trouble with iPhones and iPads, but he doesn't need one. He's a living hockey library.

When he retired from CFCF in 1991, they threw a little dinner for him. He got up and thanked everyone, and then said, "You know, no one ever officially told me I got the job here. So for the past thirty years, I've been working here on probation."

Oakville

ONTARIO

———

POPULATION:
182,520

Night Train

I play in a Tuesday night beer league, and my right winger is for-
mer NHLer Brad Dalgarno. When Bob Probert was traded to the
Soo, he fought Brad Dalgarno, the kid who took over for him as the
team tough guy on the Hamilton Steelhawks. Brad did a good job
of holding his own in the fight, which took him from a projected
second- or third-round draft pick to a first-rounder—sixth overall.

But he was never that guy. He really struggled with a lot of
aspects of NHL life, so at twenty-two years of age, he retired. It
was an unprecedented move. He stepped away, but after a year of
independence, he got the itch to go back. In 1993, he wound up
playing with Glenn Healy on a team that upset Mario Lemieux's
Pittsburgh Penguins. Mario's two-time Stanley Cup champions had
won seventeen straight games to end the regular season. They rolled
through the first round and then they ran into Brad's Islanders,
coached by Al Arbour. Winning against the Penguins was Brad's
crowning achievement before playing beer-league hockey with me
on Tuesday nights. But he's a dear friend, and a good musician and
a really interesting guy.

---

*B*rad Dalgarno's family moved around when he was
young. To get ahead in the printing business, his dad
accepted opportunities in different cities—Vancouver

and, when Brad was five, London, Ontario. His parents wanted Brad to make friends, so they took him down to the Oakridge Arena and signed him up for hockey. He was big for his age but a terrible skater, so he fell on the other kids a lot. In order to stop him from inflicting pain on his new friends, his parents put him in skating school.

He got bigger and more skilled, making better and better teams, but he never had professional hockey in his sights, even when he was a teenager and drafted thirteenth overall by the Brantford Alexanders, the team that moved to Hamilton and became the Steelhawks in 1984.

The Hamilton Steelhawks were full of tough, well-known guys like Bob Probert, Shayne Corson and Jeff Jackson, and Brad was their first-round pick. That meant he got special treatment, which is not a good thing for a rookie.

He was sent to an August camp in Hamilton and was staying at the Royal Connaught Hotel with a veteran roommate. The first afternoon, guys started dropping in. Brad didn't think anything of it until, after a few pops, one of the guys turned to him said, "All right, time to strip down, Big Guy." It was time for his rookie initiation.

This took Brad by surprise. "What? No." But when a few of them grabbed his legs and started hauling off his pants, he said, "Whoa! Whoa! I'll do it myself." He was ordered to sit in a little wood-frame chair where his feet and hands were bound and a skate lace was tied around his neck with his room key on one end—the other end was looped around his penis. It took a few guys to pick him up and carry him down the hallway and into the elevator. Someone threw a bucket of ice in his lap and then they ran away after pushing every button, so he stopped at every floor.

Thankfully, the hotel was relatively empty, but each time the door opened, Brad could hear the guys laughing in the stairwell, and when the door would start to close he could hear their feet storming down the cement fire stairs to the next floor.

On one of the last floors, a businessman, all decked out in a suit and tie and holding a briefcase, was ready to get in, but when he saw Brad he stepped back and looked at him, expressionless. As the door slid shut, Brad lifted his head and asked sheepishly whether the guy needed any ice.

Brad continued to travel down to the lobby, where the door slowly opened and there stood a young family. The parents grabbed their kids in a panic and tried to cover their eyes. Brad felt bad for them, and as they ran toward the front desk, he called out, "I'm really sorry about this!" The door began to close when a hand reached in and pushed another button. He was on his way back up. It opened on the mezzanine level, where a female security guard was waiting, arms akimbo. She shook her head and said, "What the hell do you think you're doing?"

She rode with him to Coach Dave Draper's floor, where he untied Brad, gave him a towel and escorted him back to his room.

The rookie party was a couple of weeks later, in the preseason. It was held in a big barn in Brantford, between the Massey-Ferguson plants just off the highway. Probert hadn't been traded yet, and so he was the ringleader. The rookies were instructed to line up at a folding table full of booze, and each guy took turns drinking a tall-boy beer, one of those big red plastic beer cups full of tequila and then just a regular beer. Brad was supposed to shoot the tall boy, chug the tequila and then chug the regular beer. *Bang. Bang. Bang.* He somehow managed to get through it and pumped his fist in victory! And then he was told to line up again. Later that night, he passed out in a farmer's field and woke up on his landlady's doorstep in Hamilton. Half his hair was gone and his eyebrows were shaved off.

Barb, his billet, was a lovely lady. She got him into the house and rustled up some food and looked after him. Finally, he stumbled into the bathroom to take a shower, looked in the mirror and thought, "Oh no." On his forehead, written in marker, was "Barb sucks."

Coach Dave Draper and Bob Probert didn't mesh. Dave had a different way of communicating, and it didn't work with all of the guys. Instead of saying, "Come on, boys, let's see some guts out there," Draper might say, "Come on, fellas, we need some intestinal fortitude today." He couldn't handle Probert, who was mercurial. Probie could go from being the sweetest guy in the world to someone in a very dark place. In any case, as Probert says in his book, *Tough Guy*, Dave Draper had enough and sent him packing.

Probert landed with the Sault Ste. Marie Greyhounds. During a televised game in March 1985 between the Hounds and the Hawks, he and Brad ended up squaring off. Brad hung in there for a minute and a half, which impressed the hell out of every general manager in the league. Suddenly, his stock began to rise. He had been rated in the middle of the second round of the NHL draft, but the fight rocketed him to the first round.

Come draft day, Brad went sixth overall to the New York Islanders. Like everybody else, the Islanders thought he was a combination of Clark Gillies and Bobby Nystrom, but Brad was neither. He'd grown up with a sister who was a year and a half older, so he didn't fight a lot. Boys who grow up with two older brothers who are in fighting range grow up a lot tougher. Brad played a physical game, but unless someone else chose to drop the gloves, he didn't consider fighting to be an option. Being a first-round pick was great, but ultimately he knew he could only disappoint.

The NHL smells like, looks like and feels like men. Some of the Islanders had been playing hockey for a long time—since near the time Brad was born. The hits sounded bigger, the crowds louder—at that time, the Islanders were still drawing big crowds to their games. In 1985, walking through the tunnel for his first NHL preseason game, Brad's adrenaline was spiking as he neared the ice. "Holy crap!" he thought. "I'm literally going to jump on the ice and black out from stress." He skated on, and during his first shift he got bumped. He fell, got back up, managed to shake off the stars and finished the fight.

Brad scored a goal against Boston a few games later. It was a beautiful goal, over the glove top shelf—*bing bong*. He got to the bench and sat down beside Mike Bossy, the legend. The guy had scored consecutive Stanley Cup–winning goals just a couple of years earlier, in '82 and '83. Mike Bossy didn't tap Brad on the leg. There was no "Good job, kid." He just stared straight ahead at the game and said, "Oh, you're not going to score many like that."

Brad said, "Say what?"

Bossy said, "Yeah, don't think you are going to score many like that."

Brad said, "Okay." Turns out Bossy was right.

Brad found out in a hurry that the difference between the minors and the NHL is substantial. In junior, he was a point-a-game player, and close to it in the AHL. In 1987–88, his first full season in the NHL, he felt lucky to get ten points.

Bryan Trottier had roomed for years with Mike Bossy. They'd done everything together—sat side by side on the bus and on planes, played cards, hung out. They were so much like an old married couple, Garry Howatt nicknamed them "Bread and Butter." But Bossy was dealing with a bad back, so he started playing less and less, and then he retired in 1987. All of a sudden, Brad was injected into Trottier's rooming situation.

Trottier treated Brad like gold. He was one of the best guys Brad ever met in hockey, and still is to this day. Trottier loved the game and was helpful in calming Brad down before games and making him feel like part of the team. On February 13, 1990, Bryan Trottier scored his five hundredth career goal for the Islanders, after fifteen years with the team. A few months later, he drove Brad from Nassau Coliseum to a practice rink, and the whole way he talked about team loyalty. He told Brad, "If you just give your heart to this organization, they'll pay you back in spades." And then he was gone. The Islanders released him. When Brad heard the news, he realized that if one of his favourite guys who had given the team so much could be unceremoniously dumped, then no one was special. And since he was way down the pecking order, he'd better not get too comfortable.

For his first few years as a pro, Brad was up for a bit and then he'd get sent down to the farm team—Springfield at first, and then Capital District in Troy, New York, just across the river from Albany. Over his entire career he moved twenty-two times.

After their dynasty run, during which they won nineteen consecutive playoff series between 1980 and 1984, Brad says the

Islanders stopped developing players. He felt he really had no personal connection with Al Arbour. Miscast in the role of tough guy, Brad didn't think he was a project for Al.

The coach who worked on developing him was his minor-league coach, Butch Goring. The trainer would come out and say, "Hey, Brad, Butchy wants to see you in the office." Butchy would kick his feet up on his desk. "How you feeling? How you doing? What are you thinking? What do you think? I know you want to get back there, but how do you feel? Here's what you're going to do. I'm going to put you in all these situations. You're going to get a lot of chances to work on this or that." It was awesome.

In the NHL, Brad found the attitude was "Figure it out or you're gone."

On February 21, 1989, against Detroit at the Nassau Coliseum, Brad took a boarding penalty for a cross-check on Gilbert Delorme. He was in the box when Joey Kocur came out on the power play. Kocur yelled at him through the glass, "I'm going to effing get you!"

Brad thought, "Aw crap. Okay, I've got a date with Joey Kocur that I don't want to have."

He served the penalty and Arbour kept putting him out, and every time he did, Joey Kocur would come out too. Joey was spoiling for a fight, bumping him and slashing him, but Brad was running scared. There was no way he wanted to mix it up with Joey. This went on for a couple shifts when, at a faceoff, the linesman turned to Brad and said, "Are you going to get this over with?"

Brad had no choice. His coach wanted him to fight, the Detroit Red Wings wanted it to happen, and now the officials were telling him to get it done. Brad knew half his team was thinking, "Geez, Dalgarno, get it over with. What are you doing? It's embarrassing," while the other half probably understood— "Oh man, if I were him, I would be running too."

The puck got dumped into the Islanders' end and Brad thought, "All right, we're here, let's go." He dropped the gloves and did pretty well with a flurry of punches, and then he and Joey got tied up. When that happened, the ref would usually come in and break it up, but this time, he was on his own.

Brad could feel Kocur working his right arm out of his sweater, and then, suddenly, Kocur popped him in the temple with a right that came from New Jersey. Brad felt an egg break in his cheek. The warmth spread like runny yolk down to his jaw. He went down with Joey on top. The linesmen, Bob Hodges and Pat Dapuzzo—who would have his nose severed by a skate during a game in 2008—came in and broke it up. Joey got up, commenting, "How's your face, dickhead?"

Brad was immediately in a lot of pain, so he knew something was seriously wrong and skated right off the ice. But he had to wait until the end of the game for one of the team doctors to drop him off at Huntington Hospital to get looked at.

Brad was admitted overnight, and in the morning a doctor came in and told him he had multiple facial fractures. The structure that held his eye in place was gone. He ended up having reconstructive facial surgery weeks later at Manhattan Eye, Ear and Throat Hospital. They needed two entry points to fix the damage, so they sliced through his temple and cut his bottom eyelash away. The doctors were so skilled, they didn't add any hardware to the orbital bone. Just like a piece of Lego, they snapped it back into place and it was held there with tension. The surgery was more like engineering carpentry with crowbars than delicate work. It was remarkable what they were able to do.

The highlight for Brad that summer was his wedding to Lesley, his longtime sweetheart. He's got a black eye in the photos.

All summer, he dealt with anxiety and a lack of confidence about fighting. He understood outlaw justice in the NHL—"We'll beat the crap out of you if you take liberties with our stars." He'd seen situations where the tough-guy approach worked to protect people, but he felt that the NHL regulating itself was a flawed mechanism. And having his ass handed to him by Kocur made him feel he had a huge target on his back. He showed up at camp wearing a visor. He'd developed ulcers, but he naively convinced himself that if he wore a face shield, everything would magically work out. During training camp and through the exhibition games, the team kept calling his agent, Rick Curran, and asking, "When's Brad going to take the visor off? Because until he takes his visor off, we're not going to bring him back."

But Brad didn't want to take his visor off. Not wearing one had almost cost him his eye six months earlier. He found the whole business of hockey despicable. The process, the decision making, the posturing, the bullcrap. He knew he was making a lot of money—$95,000 per year. Mind you, it wasn't money he could retire on, although he wasn't complaining. But for him at that time, hockey was the least productive place he could be.

Some of the players bound for the minors were called to line up outside the secondary dressing room at the Nassau Coliseum. They were supposed to meet one on one with general manager Bill Torrey before getting sent down. Brad had always liked Bill.

From the time he was drafted, Bill had been good to him, but this was a tough day. Brad thought the big, empty blue dressing room looked like a studio. There were two folding chairs facing each other in the middle. Torrey had been pumping guys up—"Go down there, work hard. Someday you'll be back!"

He said to Brad, "We got to talk."

Brad said, "Bill, yeah, we do."

Bill paused. "All right. You first."

"So, here's the deal. I am going to hang 'em up. I just think there's a lot more to do with my life than trying to prove something here that I'm just not ever going to be able to do for you."

Bill's eyes widened. He got up, shot out the door and returned with a group of guys, from the old scouts that hadn't given him the time of day, to the trainers, to other management. Suddenly, everyone was treating him like a long-lost son. Brad knew the team had made an investment in him, but he wouldn't budge. On his way out, Brad said goodbye to the guys lined up in the hallway, and at least three of them said, "I wish I could go with you today. I just can't."

As he walked across the cement walkway back to the Marriott hotel, he felt light as air. It was the first real decision Brad had ever made about his life. Up until then, all his decisions had been motivated by external forces—pats on the back from coaches or praise from family and friends. He was always part of someone else's plan. But that day, he made a decision he believed in. It wasn't popular, but it was life-altering.

Lesley became their main means of support. She was a teacher and brought in enough to give Brad a chance to get his fitness-equipment sales business going. Brad learned a ton about himself that year as he sat in his in-laws' basement office, trying to make some sales. Whether he had a good day or a bad day, there was no one other than himself to measure it. He was 100 per cent in control. He took a weekend course taught by Bob Proctor, who presented some interesting ideas. Some he didn't buy into and some he did. What Brad took away from it was that your subconscious often overrides what your consciousness tells you, and so you make decisions that are actually detrimental. If he had listened to his gut and not fought Joey Kocur, despite all the external pressure, he would have been safer. And in the long run, he would have been mentally tougher for making his own call.

In March, the Islanders came to Toronto. Brad still had some good friends on the team, so he bought a scalped ticket up in the rafters and after the game he made his way down to the dressing room. Bill Torrey walked by and said, "Hi, Brad, nice to see ya." Al Arbour did the same. The next day, Brad got a call from his agent, saying, "Bill Torrey thought you looked great. He said if you were interested in coming back to try out in September, he'd certainly be willing to have you. What's going on? What do you want to do?"

Brad hadn't really been working out, but he carried himself differently. He had learned a lot about himself that year, and so he looked confident. He thought about it for a week and then decided to try to come back, but to do it differently. He wanted to play on the second or third line, in a very physical role, not as a top scorer but as a presence, but not fighting all the time. He also determined that if he was relegated to sitting on the bench the whole game, waiting to fight, he was going to hang 'em up for good.

His first shift back was an intrasquad practice game, a scrimmage. The other dressing room had a couple of guys going, "Eff Dalgarno coming back. Eff that. He quit on us. He's a quitter. Let's go get him!" But big defenceman Dean Chynoweth was the voice of reason. "Come on, guys, give him a break. Let him do his thing."

Brad was on the ice in front of the other net when the puck dropped and bounced by his feet. He looked down to go get it and Chynoweth came up with a two-handed cross-check that hit him in the jaw. Five teeth popped out, and the top half of his jaw was broken. He'd been on the ice less than a minute and he was picking up teeth and on his way to the orthodontist.

He had the teeth wired back in, and the dentist replaced the broken bone with synthetic bone. He was back on the ice three days later, wearing a football helmet. Brad began to settle into a third-line checking role, and he found he really liked it. Every once in a while, he'd even get a shot on the second line or filling in on the power play, or penalty killing. He reinvented himself. The team was receptive, and everything began falling into place, but you can't control what management wants to do, whether it fits with your plans or not, and so over the next couple of years Brad was toiling away, but a little frustrated about the amount of ice time he was getting. The Islanders played a game in Quebec City, and Brad sat on the bench for most of the game.

After the game, on the bus with Ray Ferraro, lamenting his situation, Brad talked about a few of the great players, including Bob Probert, who would continually do something wild and detrimental and still get these great opportunities to come back and start again—and people loved them for it. Brad said, "Ray, I'm not sure what I've got to do, buddy. Here are these guys who keep getting shot after shot and I'm hitting a wall here."

Ray thought about it and said, "Look, Brad, we've got to give you a makeover. You're too nice a guy. You're a misfit. We've got to make you one of the boys. We've got to create a character for you. That's what we've got to do."

Brad had been rooming with Pierre Turgeon. After games, he and Pierre would go back to the hotel, go for walks together, order ice cream or watch a movie. He'd hear guys talk about going out the night before and getting silly and some funny, goofy thing that had happened. But he was worried about staying out, because he wanted to be ready for the game the next day.

Ray started riffing on a new persona for Brad. He created a whole fake backstory—Brad had a bunch of DUIs, he and his wife were kind of sketchy in terms of their relationship and he had a secret nickname, Night Train. It was all pretty funny considering the type of guy Brad was, but he embraced the humour.

A couple of days later, after a game, some of the guys came by and asked, "So is Night Train coming out?"

And Brad replied, "Oh, Night Train's rolling tonight." And he started going out frequently. He left an awful lot of full beers in bathrooms, but he stayed out late and talked and hung out. He found he could be tired and still perform. His place on the team changed in terms of respect and in terms of people sharing and opening up. He'd never fully understood the value of what it meant to be part of a team. He learned it wasn't enough to show up, head down, do the drills and go home. You had to invest time in people. At one point, he decided, "I'm going to be the last guy to leave. I'm not going to be drunk, but I'm going to be the last guy at the table." Night Train became a huge part of his resurrection. His reputation on the team changed his standing. It transcended the joke and became something very valuable.

Night Train hung out a lot with Travis Green and Marty McInnis. The three of them had been shuttled back and forth between the parent club and the Capital District farm team so much that they began to bond in the iron lung. Every NHL team uses different-coloured jerseys that represent whether you're on the first, second, third or fourth line or an extra. The guys who aren't on a set line pretend not to pay attention to the fact that, on any given day, they may get a promotion or a demotion, but secretly they are elated or depressed depending on the colour of the jersey they're given.

Al Arbour decided to put Brad, Travis and Marty together as a third line, and for the next year and a half Brad didn't show up in the morning wondering, "Am I on the fourth line? Am I on the extra squad?" The green jersey was delivered into the room, and *boom*, he'd take it and not think twice. After a while he thought, "Oh, this is what Pierre Turgeon feels like every day. No fear."

Brad was twenty-five and Marty and Travis were twenty-three, but Al called them "The Kid Line." They had a nice run together. In December of 1993, three defencemen were out with injuries, so the Islanders were looking at their forward lines, and the Kid Line was considered the best. They had nine goals and nine assists during a five-game unbeaten streak.

His first year in the NHL, Brad had been staying in Springfield, Massachusetts, in a Holiday Inn. He went to a music store one night and picked up a three-hundred-dollar guitar and started learning to play. He has a nice voice, although he considers it only passable, and started with country songs because they were easier.

In November of 1993, the team had to work out at their practice rink because Garth Brooks was doing two shows at the Coliseum. After practice, Brad grabbed his guitar and asked the trainer for the key to the Islanders' dressing room, where he planned to camp out during Garth's sound check in hopes Garth would come by and sign the guitar. When Brad heard the sound check end, he stood in the dressing room doorway, holding the guitar. Garth whizzed by and stopped cold. He said, "Oh hey."

Brad said, "Garth, sorry. I'm with the Islanders—would you mind signing my guitar for me?"

"Absolutely." Garth came into the dressing room, sat down and started asking Brad all about the guitar. "What do you do here? Do you play?"

Brad told him the song he worked on all through the minors was Garth's big hit, "Friends in Low Places."

After about ten minutes, Garth said, "Listen, could you do me a favour?"

Brad said, "Sure, what's that?"

"I'd love you to bring this guitar up on stage and help me sing 'Friends in Low Places.'"

Brad laughed, "No. As cool as that is, there's not a friggin' chance."

Garth said, "I'm not taking no for an answer. What are you doing right now?"

Brad said, "I'm just going to wait upstairs for the show."

"No, no, come with me." So Brad went up and hung out with Garth for an hour before his concert. They ate and talked, and Brad thought Garth was just awesome. But the whole time, Garth kept coming back to the subject of bringing him up on stage, and Brad kept saying, "No, but this is the most flattering thing in the world. I can't believe it. Thank you very much."

After a while, one of the security guards poked his head in the door and said, "Garth, we've got a bunch of New York Rangers out there who want to come meet you." Garth smiled. He knew they were Brad's archenemies.

Brad said, "Which guys are out there?" And the guard named three guys, including Joey Kocur. Garth looked at Brad, who shook his head no, and Garth said, "Sorry, I'm a bit busy."

The show was about to start, so Brad stood to say goodbye. Garth said, "Okay, Brad, I know you said no, but if you change your mind, go find Mickey. He'll be at the side of the stage, and I'll be looking for you."

Brad went upstairs and ran into Dennis Vaske and Tom Kurvers. He told them his Garth Brooks story and they couldn't believe he had refused to join the King of Country on stage, but Brad told them he was too embarrassed to do it. "Look, I'm wearing loafers, for God's sake."

Dennis ripped the cowboy boots off his feet and said, "Here you go," and the boys broke out a few pops to help him summon up a little liquid courage. Fuelled by their support, Brad decided he was going to give it a try. The boots were so small that his toes were folded over, but he did his best to get to the stage in a hurry. The security guards who knew him from hockey were holding his guitar for him, and when he told them he was heading to the stage, they ran behind him like a bunch of excited schoolkids. "Brad's doing it!"

It was dark, but as Brad waited backstage, he was feeling sick to his stomach. What the hell had he gotten himself into? He felt like a kid in the stands with a baseball glove, hoping that maybe a fly ball was going to come his way. And sure enough, "Friends in Low Places" started and nothing happened. Then, about halfway through the song, someone put his guitar in his hands and pushed him towards the stage.

By this time, his toes were totally numb, so he stepped gingerly through the side curtain and saw Garth, wearing an Islanders jersey. He was all the way down at the other side of the stage, which was the width of the ice. So Brad started strumming and singing and tiptoeing to meet him. As he passed one of the guitarists, Brad turned to him and said, "I think I play it differently than you guys."

The guy shook his head and said, "Don't worry. We're not plugging you in, for Christ's sake."

There was no light on Brad, but he could see people in the first few rows looking at him as if to say, "What is this? Who are you? What is going on?"

He thought, "Oh crap. I made a mistake. I'm out of here," and he started to turn back. The guitarist ran up beside him, tucked him under his arm and pushed him down front. Suddenly, Garth came running across the stage and put his arm around Brad, and together they finished off the song. The reception wasn't the same as if Mike Bossy had come on stage, but the crowd appreciated an Islander playing with Garth.

By September 1994, the run was over. Brad had developed a connection with coach Al Arbour and appreciated and loved playing for him, but now Lorne Henning was the coach, and as nice as he was, there was less opportunity for Brad with so many new faces like Brett Lindros and Zigmund Palffy working their way into the lineup.

Brad was back in the position of wondering what colour jersey he'd be getting at practice. He was disappointed, but he understood that teams start peeling and rebuilding every year. And it seemed like he was constantly getting injured.

In 1995–96, both Brad and Pat Flatley were in the press box for a bunch of games, and they started talking about the Great American Bagel in Chicago. Pat's brother had started the company, and every time the team was in Chicago, Pat would bring these incredible bagels down to the dressing room. He had sold the master franchise rights for the Great *Canadian* Bagel, but Pat told Brad the Oakville, Ontario, location was available if he wanted it. Brad had no intention of retiring, but he bought the Oakville franchise and decided to hire staff to run it. He broke his wrist a little while later and used the downtime to get the business rolling. Later that year, the doctors told him he was going to have to retire due to the wrist injury, and so he dove into the bagel business with both feet and got himself a seat-of-his-pants street MBA.

His store became one of the top five earners in the country. Brad eventually sold the bagel franchise and founded Starshot, a digital and event marketing agency. Part of the reason the company became really successful, aside from partnering with his buddy Brad Friesen, was thanks to what he learned about creating teams from his experiences as Night Train.

When Brad shared with me the story of how and why Night Train needed to exist for him to fit in, my first thought was he should have just quit and never come back, which would have made a statement. What good was it rejoining the team and then pretending to be somebody else? But Brad disagreed. He saw it as more of a testament to a broader understanding of team and a broader understanding of how to fit in. He thought it was a really great lesson that tied his whole journey together, and as the years passed I came to look at his story in a different light. One night, the whole point of it struck me— the idea that life really is about collecting people you like to be around, and when you come across them, you don't take them for granted. If you want them to remain in your life, you've got to make an effort to keep them in your life. As goofy as Night Train is as a character, it opened up a world to Brad that he didn't understand before.

Inspired, I sat down one night and wrote lyrics to a song I asked him to record for me—called "Night Train," of course. It ends with, *The Night Train's tremor I feel no more, but I'm on track . . . I'm me. . . feeling fine . . . feeling free.*

The Assigner

What do you do with someone who has been through the worst experience you can imagine? How do you get involved in someone's misery? Is it gauche or unacceptable even to ask them about it, knowing you are causing more pain, stepping on an arm that is healing?

My only answer is respect. And there is no one I respect more than Charlie Lennox. He is a quiet man, humble. Almost all athletes are like-minded in that they are reticent to put themselves forward.

Charlie and his wife, Diane, have managed incredible pain with love, forgiveness and yes, even humour. When I started refereeing in Oakville, Charlie Lennox was my assigner. He would send me over to the old Oakville arena to do the Blades games, and there was a fan named Schultzy who would really give it to me. "Hey, MacLean! You're missing a good game!" I'd yell back, "Yeah, I know, but this is the one they sent me to!" Charlie taught me that one.

————————————

*L*ike every ref I know, Charlie Lennox played hockey all his life—peewee hockey in the Toronto Hockey League, three years of Junior B with the Leaside Rangers and Woodbridge Dodgers. He played for forty-five years until his knees got so bad, he couldn't skate anymore.

Charlie remembers officiating with Tom Brown, the referee who did the World Hockey Association's Canada–Russia series in 1974. Tom took Charlie on the lines with him, and together they were at two Allan Cups, both in Calgary. Charlie was on the lines for two Memorial Cups too. His first was in 1968, and the second, in 1972, was the first year that three Tier I Junior A (now called major junior) leagues competed—the Quebec Major Junior Hockey League, the Western Canada Hockey League and the OHA. So the competition was between the Edmonton Oil Kings, Cornwall Royals and Peterborough Petes.

The Petes were Roger Neilson's team. It was always interesting to ref his games. Neilson was a passionate coach. Six years later, he would become the coach of the Toronto Maple Leafs, the first of his six head-coaching jobs in the NHL. He died of cancer in 2003.

According to the *Ottawa Citizen*, in the 1973 OHA final, when the Petes lost to the Toronto Marlboros on a penalty shot, Roger sat in the empty stands and wept. In his obituary, the Canadian Press said of Roger's time coaching the Petes, "When he pulled a goalie in the last minute of a game, he'd have him lay his stick across the goal line and leave it there. Once, after an opposing team was awarded a penalty shot, he replaced his goalie with a defenceman and told him to rush the shooter. When he had two players in the penalty box late in a game, he'd sneak on a fourth skater because it didn't matter how many penalties his team took at that stage since the rules said it couldn't have fewer than three skaters on the ice. The loopholes were all closed eventually, but Neilson never stopped trying to find others."

In 1968, after Charlie worked his first Memorial Cup, the NHL offered him a job, starting in the Central Hockey League in Dallas, but the pay was five thousand dollars per year. It wasn't enough. Charlie and Diane had three kids and a mortgage, and at the time he was working for Air Canada, making eight thousand. He would have loved to accept the offer but just couldn't afford to take the financial hit.

Michael was born in 1964, Paul in '66 and Susan in '68. Michael and Paul were born on the same day two years apart—September 16. Paul was the spitting image of Diane's father, very Irish-looking with thick, black curly hair and bright green eyes. Michael was dark-haired as well, but he had dark brown eyes, more like Charlie's.

Michael got sick when he was three and a half. Diane saw that there was something wrong. He would be sitting with the kids on the front porch, and when they'd all take off running, he'd start to run with them but immediately slow down and come back and sit on the step. She knew this wasn't normal for a child that age, and at night, when they'd get ready to say prayers, he'd say, "Mom, is it okay if I sit on the bed? I can't kneel."

She and Charlie kept taking their boy from one doctor to another, and every one had a different opinion. He was a big, healthy-looking, sweet little boy who never complained, so none of them thought it was serious. One of the doctors suggested it might be his tonsils, so he was admitted to hospital and had some blood work done. Charlie and Diane didn't hear back until two months later, when Michael had just started kindergarten. She and Charlie were called in to speak with a doctor at Toronto's Sick Kids Hospital who sat them down and told them Michael had a rare muscle disease called juvenile dermatomyositis. And in Michael's case the outcome was fatal. There was nothing they could do. Charlie said, "Tell me, is there any place in the world where they've done some work with this disease where I can take him?" He was told there was a team at the UCLA Medical Center doing some research on the disease. So Charlie flew with Michael to California. They had so little money, there was just enough for airfare and a rental car. So while Michael was under care, Charlie slept in the car in the hospital parking lot. Every morning, he'd get up and head to the public washroom, where he'd clean up and shave. With the money he saved, he was able to take Michael to Disneyland.

Watching Michael spinning on the teacup ride, with his head back laughing, was worth every minute in his rental car bed.

But the diagnosis was the same.

Michael was constantly in and out of Toronto's Sick Kids Hospital. The doctors there knew so little about the disease that they were always taking him for tests and bringing other doctors in to examine him. Finally, Charlie stepped in. He said, "Look, leave the little guy alone. I know you have to do these things, but give him some peace."

Refereeing was good for Charlie, because for those three hours on the ice, he didn't have to think about Michael's swollen hands and feet and how much he was suffering. It was a tough time, and even worse when Michael died five years later, in 1974.

Thank God Charlie had his daughter, Susan, and surviving son, Paul. Paul was a good little hockey centre. Charlie loved going to his games and picking out sticks and gloves and other equipment with him. Paul played rep hockey and rep soccer for years, so the family spent a lot of time at the rink and travelling with the rep teams. Any time the family drove to games, Paul would call the backseat. He liked to sit behind Charlie. One year, they made a trip all the way to Florida.

In the spring, Paul played AA baseball as well. He was a happy, positive kid and a good student who always had a job, like a paper route, or he'd offer to paint people's fences. He liked doing things to help out.

Charlie and Paul were best buddies. Charlie coached his hockey teams, and they started reffing ball hockey together. Paul had set his sights on reffing ice hockey in the future. It was Charlie's dream to work an OHA game with Paul one day.

One of Paul's buddies had a dad who worked at Ford, and the teen was permitted to test-drive new cars. It was a cool thing to be able to do, and he often took his buddies out for rides. Paul would come home and tell Charlie all about the neat new contraptions and upgrades.

Charlie was in Cambridge, Ontario, in October 1982, working a Junior B game, when Paul's buddy and two friends picked Paul up in a brand new test car. Their school was playing a football game at another high school in Oakville, so the four boys decided to grab a bite at McDonald's between quarters. On their way back to the field, the driver took a curve on a residential street a little too fast. The kid went to hit the brake but hit the gas instead, and the car collided with a telephone pole that fell down on the car, crushing the roof over the backseat on the driver's side—where Paul was sitting.

Diane had gone to bed early with a bad cold, but the doorbell wouldn't quit ringing, so she came downstairs to answer it. Susan was right behind her. A police officer and Paul's friend's father were standing there. As soon as she saw them, before they said a word, she said, "Oh no, not Paul," and turned and ran upstairs to his room. She was sure he was in bed sleeping, but of course he wasn't.

Charlie was on the ice refereeing, so he couldn't be reached, but he came home shortly after. He was always after Diane to lock the front door, and when he saw all the cars, he thought, "Oh boy, now she's done it. She's left the front door open and we've had a break-in."

When he walked in and heard the horrible news, he was devastated. He had to quit reffing in the OHA. He couldn't watch the boys coming into the arena with their bags and sticks and laughter and not think of Paul. And the guilt. It didn't really make sense, but he couldn't help thinking that if he hadn't been refereeing that afternoon, Paul might have been driving *his* car instead of driving around with his friends.

The teenage driver was injured in the accident and spent some time in the hospital—nothing too serious, but he was having trouble because it was his mistake that killed Paul. When he got out, Charlie called him and said, "Come on, let's go out for a skate." So they went out on the ice and skated and talked. It went a long way toward helping the boy recover.

A couple of years later, in 1984, Sue had just started university in Toronto, and when Air Canada moved its computer centre to Montreal, he and Diane didn't really want to leave her by herself. So Charlie took an early severance package and decided to try selling real estate up north near the family cottage, but the market had dipped and sales weren't exactly booming.

John McCauley, whose son Wes is a top NHL referee, was the NHL assigner. At the age of just forty-four, John passed away after emergency gall bladder surgery. It was a devastating loss for hockey, and it created a big hole in refereeing. His assistant, Bryan Lewis, who was assigning for the AHL, moved up to his position, and Willy Norris, a retired NHL linesman who had been assigning for the OHA, took over for Bryan, which meant the OHA needed someone to replace him.

Charlie was offered the job. At first, he was hesitant. Paul had been gone only two years, so his death was still with Charlie every other breath and it wasn't getting easier. But refereeing had been a good distraction after Michael died, so maybe this job would help.

It was a long commute to Cambridge, where the job was headquartered, but Charlie took it. He became an assigner and stayed there for twenty-two years. No one has done it longer. When he started, the system was primitive. There were no computers or anything like that.

Assigning was a lot of responsibility. He had to make sure there were officials at every game, and lots of times there were snowstorms or some personal emergency would come up, so he'd have to find a way to get an official on the ice. For one game, they needed a local to fill in, and Charlie found a female. It was the first time a woman ever reffed a junior game.

Assigning was an intense job, but it did help Charlie feel better. He'd meet young referees just out of school and watch them get their first jobs, get married, have kids and go through personal tragedies and triumphs. Coaches would be screaming about this referee and that referee and accusing Charlie of being biased, and he would simply answer, "You're a coach, you have your players for three or four years. I've been with these guys four or five times that long." Because he worked with them so closely and stepped up for them so much, many of the refs he assigned became like sons. Four of the eight officials tapped to work the Stanley Cup finals in 2015 came through Charlie in the OHA— referees Kevin Pollock, Wes McCauley and Dan O'Halloran and linesman Derek Amell.

I was with Charlie for thirteen years. Truth is, he was always after me to be tougher on the players. He would say, "Ron, you like to let 'em rock and roll a bit more than we like to see." Charlie used honey and vinegar to send the message, but he allowed for my version of communication and gave me big games. He and his boss, Brent Ladds, the president of the OHA at the time, were gentle, caring bosses. The kind you would do anything for—except call more penalties.

Sault Ste. Marie

ONTARIO

—————

POPULATION:
75,141

The Soo

Wayne Gretzky played with Steve Bodnar in Brantford, Ontario, in 1971, when they were both ten years old. That was the year Wayne scored 378 goals. The boys met up again at the international peewee tournament in Quebec City after Steve's family moved to the Soo. Sixteen thousand people filled the Colisée to watch ten-year-old Wayne Gretzky play as a peewee.

Wayne was drafted by the Greyhounds in 1977. He called Steve and said he had no idea where Sault Ste. Marie was, but he wasn't happy about it. He said he wasn't sure he wanted to move so close to the North Pole. But the Bodnars offered to have him stay with them, and so he relented. They fixed up a nice room in the basement with a desk and wood panelling, and Steve's mom made him butter tarts and cooked special meals for him before every game.

It was a lot of fun for Steve, living in the same house and playing road hockey and hanging out. Wayne seemed happy except for the flying. The Soo players would travel in an old DC-3, and there always seemed to be turbulence. Wayne was so terrified that he would often get violently ill just thinking about going on a road trip.

Of course, he was a rookie. Craig Hartsburg and Ted Nolan and Greg Millen, all those guys were the veterans on the team. One time, they made the rookies streak through Bellevue, a little park in town, but they set Wayne up. Once he got his clothes off, the police were waiting around the corner. So Wayne got out of the car and started running, when all of a sudden he was caught up in flashing lights and a siren. The police pulled him into their car, and because he had nothing on, he was totally embarrassed. He was also worried that his career was over before it had begun. Meanwhile, the officers were trying to keep a straight face. Part of his initiation also included a complete body shave—every hair. Steve's mother used to paint eyebrows on him so he could go out.

Wayne's nickname in the Soo was "Pretzel," because he was tall and kind of lanky. Later in Wayne's career, Steve dropped into a game in Detroit. Wayne was quite a distance away, surrounded by fans, so Steve couldn't get his attention. He took a chance and yelled, "Pretzel!" Wayne turned around and headed over to say hi.

Rob Gordon's a beer-league hockey player from Oakville, Ontario, where I now reside. He grew up in the Soo. In 1978 he was in Grade 11 when a Greyhounds billet showed up at Sir James Dunn Collegiate. The seating plan was alphabetical, and the new kid's name was Wayne Gretzky, so he was either sitting behind, beside or in front of Rob in seven different classes. Wayne didn't seem to be much different from anybody else, maybe a bit more solid, but he was a lanky guy and fairly normal looking. All the guys wore Levi's jean jackets, brown Levi's corduroys, snap-button checked shirts, and three-striped Adidas sneakers or plat-form shoes. Wayne had a dirty-blond mullet that he tried to tame with a blow dryer, and he struggled with his teenage skin, but the girls liked him, just as they liked all the boys on the Greyhounds.

Rob and Wayne were classroom buddies. They'd chat before the teachers got going and then walk to their lockers together. Rob's dad was a research scientist for the Ontario government. He studied spruce genetics at a big lab in the Soo. Rob had the same sort of curiosity. He had big ideas and was always day-dreaming about things he could invent. He did a lot of ski racing and starting fooling around with the concept of miniature skis. He found an old pair of wooden skis in the basement and spent the whole afternoon cutting them down and then making a ski jump behind the local gas station. Of course, they snapped in half on the first run, but it was fun.

Wayne was gone from school for a couple of days in early June when Rob read in the *Star* that he was off with Nelson Skalbania, a real estate mogul who eventually landed in jail, but at the time he was wheeling and dealing in hockey franchises. Skalbania signed Wayne to his first big professional contract, with the Indianapolis Racers, for $1.75 million.

On Wednesday that week, Wayne rolled in driving a big 1977 Ford LTD. It had a two-tone paint job, a navy blue with kind of a light brown undercarriage. He'd driven the car all the way from the Brantford area. He walked into geography class and found his way over to his seat next to Rob at one of the big wooden tables to the left of the blackboard.

Rob greeted him enthusiastically. "Holy! I read the paper. You are going to be rich one day!" And then he corrected himself. "Actually, you're rich today! Surely I can get a piece of the action somehow?" Wayne kind of smiled. They both sat quietly and thought about it for a moment. Rob said, "How about I write a book about you?"

Wayne said, "Yeah, that would be a great idea. My dad's got a couple shoe boxes full of old pictures."

Rob said, "Yeah, I can put something together and I can write the first book about you." They started to talk about what it would entail when Rob said, "Well, wait a minute. Hold that thought," and pulled out a piece of foolscap from his three-ring binder. He wrote, "I, [blank], allow [blank] to write a book about myself and agree not to press charges of any kind on him if the book comes out. Anyone else cannot write the book. Signed [blank], witnessed [blank]." He handed it to Wayne and said, "Quick, sign this!" And without a thought, Wayne filled in all the blank spots. They both signed it, and then Rob turned to his two buddies, Scott Forbes and Don Elliot, and said, "Here, witness this."

And then Mrs. Morrow came in. She didn't tolerate too much goofing around. So Rob folded the piece of paper and put it in his binder. At the end of the year, he found it while cleaning out his books, so he put it in an envelope marked "DO NOT THROW AWAY" and stuck it at the back of his folks' filing cabinet, in a folder with his little art projects from public school.

Years later, Rob was in university, a poor student eating Kraft Dinner while watching Wayne win Stanley Cups. And then he remembered the envelope. He thought it might be a neat piece of memorabilia. He might even sell it. He went home and rummaged around and found it, but decided not to part with it.

Later, while working near a mine site in the middle of the Arctic and then travelling here and there, he decided to write some of his stories, including the story about Wayne. He called the book *I, Wayne Gretzky* and put Wayne's "contract" on the cover. Wayne, great guy that he is, went along with it and wrote the foreword for his old school buddy. That's not ordinary. It's extraordinary. Anyplace else, I guarantee, they'd Soo.

Moncton

NEW BRUNSWICK

POPULATION:
69,074

The Incredible Charlie Bourgeois

I owe Bouctouche, New Brunswick, writer and playwright Antonine Maillet, Montreal author Noah Richler and Canadian philosopher and writer John Ralston Saul for my understanding of the Acadian people.

In 1755, all Acadians were deported to the thirteen colonies of the future United States of America, with Colonel Robert Monckton carrying out the orders. Moncton, often known as the capital of Acadia, bears the name of the man who exiled them. Many of the Acadians eventually returned near their home without bitterness.

As Antonine Maillet explains, "It was a page of history we carried with us, and the only way to get out of that situation and triumph was to use the tool of humour. It was then that we became human beings and not just survivors."

When I started my NHL broadcasting career thirty-one years ago, I was based in Calgary, hosting Flames games. One of my favourite players to interview was a defenceman from Moncton, Charlie Bourgeois.

In about mid-December, while preparing a story for Christmas, I went to each of the Flames players and asked them for a childhood holiday memory. When I got to Bourgeois, normally my go-to guy for a quip or fun anecdote, his response was lukewarm.

"Ron, nothing really special for me. The Christmas tree and tourtière meat pie on Christmas Eve, I suppose."

I was flustered. Another player, Colin Patterson, was watching the exchange, and when I was done with Charlie, he pulled me aside and explained. "I'm sorry that had to happen," said Patterson. "You didn't know, but the reason Charlie had no answer and went somewhat cold on you is that his father, Aurèle, was a city policeman who was murdered at Christmastime in Moncton in 1974, when Charlie was fifteen. It just caught him off guard and he couldn't fake a better response."

I apologized to Charlie and he, for no good reason, apologized to me. Charlie won a university hockey crown with Moncton, enjoyed a decade in the NHL and was a great coach after his playing days. We've remained great friends. I attended the Flames' training camp in Moncton in 1985 and Charlie took us to dinner at Fisherman's Paradise in nearby Shediac, New Brunswick. I attended his golf tournament in the early '90s and we hit Ziggy's bar next to the Beausejour Hotel together. I walked into my room at two thirty in the morning, assuming we all had our own rooms, but it turned out we all had roommates. Mine was already in his bed—legendary CFL star Russ Jackson! I straightened up pretty quick.

A few years ago, I was in town to help Charlie with a university fundraiser, and I recall a great dinner at Little Louis Oyster Bar. Following my speech, we enjoyed a few beers at the Old Triangle Irish Alehouse and the St. James's Gate, and my most recent trip after Hometown Hockey was an incredible amount of fun, at a bar called Plan B.

I was working on our Stanley Cup final coverage in Los Angeles on June 4, 2014, when I got word that the city of Moncton was in lockdown with a manhunt underway after five Mounties had been shot and three killed. Well, you can imagine my thoughts. I knew that nothing could change 1974 for a kid who would honour his dad's legacy with every breath and every deed for the rest of

his days. And I knew five other families were now thrust into that
reality. The only thread of solace came from the work of Antonine
Maillet and the example of Jean Béliveau.

The Acadians. There is such dignity here.

---

*C*onstable Michael O'Leary was a good family man. The
thirty-three-year-old had a beautiful young wife, Carol
Anne, and two great little boys. In Moncton in the early
'70s, all the guys on the force were pretty close. Mike and another
constable, Nick LeBlanc, lived in the same apartment building until
they built their houses, and Nick was part of a group that ran the junior hockey team. Nick was trainer, equipment manager, everything.

Corporal Aurèle Bourgeois was always at the games. Aurèle
was forty-seven years old. He'd been with the Moncton city
police eighteen years and had four kids, Joanne, Patricia, Charlie
and Guy. Fifteen-year-old Charlie was a defenceman for the
Moncton Junior Beavers.

Aurèle was passionate about hockey. His mother died when
he was two years old, and he was one of eight children, so his
father placed him and some of the younger siblings with different relatives. Aurèle longed to play hockey, but he was too poor.
So when his own kids came along, he made sure his little girls
had nice dresses and that Charlie and Guy had the very best
skates, sticks and hockey gear. They lived on a policeman's salary,
so that meant denying himself new things.

Every Saturday night Aurèle and Charlie would sit down in
front of the television and watch the Canadiens on *Hockey Night*

in Canada. They were big fans of Guy Lafleur, Steve Shutt, Ken Dryden and Charlie's favourite, Larry Robinson.

When Charlie played, Aurèle would use his lunch hour to go to the J. Louis Lévesque Arena. He wasn't Charlie's coach, he was just his dad, and he never missed a game in Moncton or nearby Dieppe. Charlie would always watch for him out of the corner of his eye.

December 11, 1974, was a Wednesday. Charlie broke his stick in the game that night. Aurèle found Nick LeBlanc and said, "Nick, you wouldn't happen to have an extra hockey stick for Boo-Boo?" Boo-Boo was the family's nickname for Charlie. Aurèle always called him that, and as a result, everyone else did too.

Nick said, "Sure," and grabbed a brand new stick for the boy.

Aurèle said, "Oh, geez. He'll love this. He'll just love it, Nick. Thanks a lot."

A very bad guy named James Hutchison had moved to Moncton from Picton, Ontario. He was a forty-three-year-old drifter-type, cocky and balding, with a greasy comb-over. He'd brag to his brother-in-law, James Mulligan, about how he could make a bundle by kidnapping local restaurant owner Simon "Cy" Stein or his girlfriend. Cy had a very successful restaurant. Forty years ago, there weren't many high-end restaurants in Moncton, and his was the place most went for special occasions, anniversaries and such. The specialty was lobster.

Mulligan laughed it off. He thought it was just the beer talking. But when Hutchison met up with a like-minded kid, twenty-two-year-old troublemaker Ricky Ambrose, Hutchison's plan became a reality.

At about 10:30 p.m. on Thursday, December 12, 1974—the night after Aurèle gave Charlie his new stick—Cy's mother, Sara, and his fourteen-year-old son, Ray, arrived home after having dinner at the restaurant. When they stepped into the house, Hutchison and Ambrose were there. Both were wearing ski masks and holding guns.

They tied Sara to the stairway railing and grabbed the boy. They covered his head and face with a toque and shoved him onto the backseat floor of Ambrose's dad's Cadillac, with its light beige body and dark top.

Within twenty minutes, Sara Stein had worked herself free. She called her son and told him Ray had been kidnapped. Cy rushed home just in time to receive a call from Hutchison, who demanded a ransom. After Cy talked to Ray to make sure he was all right, he agreed to go back to his restaurant to see how much money he could quickly pull together, and then he called the Moncton police.

When the kidnappers called Cy back, Cy said he could only come up with $15,000. Hutchison said he'd take it. The Moncton police traced the call to a telephone booth on Shediac Road near the Trans-Canada Highway. But what the police didn't realize was that the phone on Shediac Road had been disconnected and that the number had been transferred to a booth at the Riverview Mall, which was south of Moncton, across the river. Because the Moncton police didn't have enough cars back then, the dispatcher, Chuck Kenny told Aurèle Bourgeois and Mike O'Leary to use his blue Plymouth and a portable radio. They, along with three other cars, set up surveillance on the wrong phone booth.

Hutchison and Ambrose took Ray to an apartment to wait while Cy called Milton Palmer, manager of the Bank of Nova

Scotia, and arranged to pick up $15,000 in ten-dollar bills. The kidnappers were hungry but had no cash. Ray had won them over a little bit and given them ten dollars, which Ambrose used to run to the store for a cooked chicken and some Coca-Cola.

At about 3:30 a.m., Hutchison called Cy again. Cy said he had the money all ready in a canvas bag. Hutchison told him to drop it off in a ditch just west of the Riverview Mall.

Meanwhile, a Moncton police officer was at the New Brunswick Telephone Company building, monitoring the call to pinpoint the location, but they were unable to trace it.

Hutchison and Ambrose loaded Ray into Ambrose's dad's Cadillac and waited by the side of the road near the Riverview Mall. Cy drove up in his big Thunderbird and, as instructed, dropped the canvas bag full of ransom money into a ditch about half a block ahead of the Cadillac. He drove forward about a hundred yards and stopped. The Cadillac drove up to the bag, someone got out and grabbed it, and Ray was released. Cy saw his son stumbling down the road toward him, pulling off the black toque they had used to cover his eyes.

The three police cars that were set up at the wrong location finally got word about the drop at Riverview Mall, and so they sped over, passing Cy and Ray, who were on their way back to the safety of the restaurant.

This was the RCMP's jurisdiction. One of the officers suggested that they notify the Mounties so they could block the city off. That way nobody could get in or out. But a couple of the guys in charge said, "Never mind the RCMP. We'll steal this one from right under their nose."

Detectives Archie Cudmore, Ralph Cassidy and Orly Cairns parked in a private driveway just east of the mall. Aurèle Bourgeois and Mike O'Leary, in Chuck Kenny's Plymouth, were told to wait even further east, and a third police car with officers Crandall and Galbraith set up a roadblock at the west side of the mall.

"The Three Cs"—Cudmore, Cassidy and Cairns—watched as the Cadillac and a blue Dodge drove past. The Cadillac turned south on Wentworth Drive, turned off its headlights, and then pulled a U-turn and turned east on Coverdale Road.

Officers Crandall and Galbraith decided to follow the Dodge, with the Three Cs as backup. But when the five men stopped the blue Dodge, they discovered Police Chief C.M. (Moody) Weldon and two others in the car. Unbeknownst to the team, Chief Weldon had decided to join the surveillance.

At 4:10 a.m., Aurèle and Mike O'Leary were radioed and told to check the Cadillac. Aurèle responded, "Okay," and that was the last their colleagues heard from them.

At 5:30 a.m., the Moncton police called the RCMP and asked for help.

Aurèle and Mike found the Cadillac parked near the school on Coverdale Road. Nick LeBlanc's theory is that, following protocol, one of them, probably Mike, approached the driver's side while Aurèle stayed back. Due to the trajectory of the bullet later found in Mike's shoulder, it appeared that at that point the Cadillac's driver pulled a gun and shot Mike just under the clavicle, in the fleshy part. Then the other guy would have gotten out and said something like, "Drop your gun or we're going to finish off this cop."

Both officers were tied up and forced into the trunk of the Cadillac, and then transported to a wooded area on the outskirts of Moncton. They were taken from the trunk and handcuffed to a spruce tree on top of a hill near a covered bridge. There, they watched their captors try to dig into the frozen December ground with a snow shovel. Nick LeBlanc is sure they'd have never put a shovel in Mike O'Leary's hands. With that Irish temper of his, he'd have killed them right then and there.

Digging with a snow shovel was not working. All they managed to do was scrape through the top layer of the ground. Leaving the officers tied up, Hutchison and Ambrose drove into Moncton and, at about 8 a.m., as soon as Lockhart's Hardware at Mountain Road and MacBeath opened, they went in and bought picks and spades. The clerk found that odd. In December, why would you want to dig?

What Hutchison and Ambrose didn't realize was that a hunter and his brother-in-law had rabbit snares located all around the trees where Aurèle and Mike were tied up. Every day that week, they'd been out checking them but had had no luck. Friday morning, the hunter looked out at the frost-covered trees and decided to wait until Monday before checking them again. It was too cold for rabbits.

Aurèle and Mike were tied up less than a kilometre from a small community of about seven to ten homes. Around seven thirty that morning, some of the children were standing on the side of the road near their houses, waiting for the school bus. They heard somebody yelling for help. After several hollers, one of them went inside to get his mother. She came out and listened, but there was only silence. And so she thought it was just kids playing.

Meanwhile, someone was pounding on Nick LeBlanc's door. It was one of his co-workers, another policeman. "Nick! You'd better come in!"

Nick was grumpy. He'd been planning to sleep in and then get up and have a leisurely breakfast. "This is my goddamn day off," he said.

The officer shook his head. "Cy Stein's young fellow was kidnapped, and Mike and Aurèle booked off and are missing!"

"Holy jeez, give me one minute." He got dressed and headed over to join some other police to look for them by the school on Coverdale Road. They searched both sides of the road but came up empty. Back at the station, Nick and another guy came up with a plan. "Let's get on the radio. Dave Lockhart has a talk show at nine o'clock. We'll ask him to put on the air if anybody's seen a dark blue Plymouth parked in an unusual place to please call the police station. We don't have to say why."

Around 9:10, a listener called in, saying there was a dark blue Plymouth parked at the old railway station in Salisbury, about twenty kilometres west of Moncton. Nick and John Miller and Dale Swansburg, two RCMP officers, went together to investigate. Nick thought a lot of John and Dale. Dale was quiet but deep, and John was a drug man, very intelligent. They reached the car and waited for a private helicopter sent by a local company to land with the keys.

Mike O'Leary's brother Blake, another good policeman, waited with them. As they went to open the trunk, Nick said, "Blake, you'd better move back and I'll let you know."

Blake said okay and walked back about fifty feet. Miller opened the trunk and found pieces of yellow fisherman's rope, all cut up. They studied it a moment and then put the trunk down. Nick looked at John and Dale and said, "Listen, I don't know about you guys, but I haven't got a goddamn clue about what we do here now."

Dale sucked on his pipe for a moment and then said, "I've got an idea." They all agreed to meet at the station to discuss it. Dale and John got into their RCMP vehicle and drove back toward Moncton up the Old Fredericton Road and then turned onto the Trans-Canada Highway.

Just past a trailer park on their way in to Moncton, driving in the other direction, was Ricky Ambrose in the Cadillac. Neither officer had been told a Cadillac was involved in the kidnapping. All they knew was it was a big car, but John Miller recognized Ambrose—he was a scumbag.

He said, "Let's pull him over."

Dale said, "No, no, we haven't got time to fool around with Ambrose."

But John had a feeling in his gut, and good police will go with a gut feeling over a computer any day. "He might know something." Dale nodded and turned the car around.

They pulled Ambrose over and got him out of the car. A quick search pulled up Chuck Kenny's car keys, $5,500 of the marked ransom money and a pair of blood-stained gloves.

They took him back to the station, where he was questioned. At first, he refused to talk, but they sent for his dad, Ernie, who was a local bootlegger. Ernie was a pretty hard man himself. He went upstairs to talk to his son, and when he came back down, Ernie had tears running down his cheeks. He looked at the policemen there and said, "Those no-good sons of whores killed them."

Later, when they questioned Richard Ambrose further about the whereabouts of Aurèle and Mike, he said, "Don't worry about them, they're gone."

Geneviève Bourgeois had been married to her husband Aurèle for twenty-four years, since she was eighteen. He proposed by writing her father a letter because her family didn't have a phone. Aurèle was living in Ontario at the time and had come to Memramcook, where she lived, to see a friend. Like many New Brunswickers, they both spoke Chiac, a mixture of English and French.

They met on a double date—Aurèle's friend came to take her out, and he was with another girl. The next day, Aurèle dropped by and asked her out, and that's how their romance started.

When they were newlyweds, Geneviève moved with Aurèle to Toronto, where he worked in construction. His brother was a policeman in Montreal, and that's what he wanted to do too, but he and Genevieve planned to have a family, and Aurèle thought that to be on a big-city police force was too dangerous a job. So they moved home to Moncton. With only about 40,000 people, it was a nice-sized place to live in, quiet and safe.

Eighteen years later, Aurèle was working the night shift. At about 11:30 p.m Genevieve gave him a kiss and said goodnight, and when the kids got up the next morning she fed them and sent them off to school. She was cleaning up when two officers came to the door and told her Aurèle and Mike O'Leary were missing.

Her first thought was to protect her kids from hearing about it from their friends, but she didn't drive. Guy was only eleven, so the officers went to get him and Charlie from class. Geneviève called their priest, and he went to fetch Patricia from business college. Joanne was twenty-two and married to police officer Paul Deroche. They had a twenty-month-old baby named Chantal. The kids came over and so did Geneviève's sisters, brothers and in-laws.

They had the radio and TV turned on so they could monitor the news. Joanne's husband, Paul, was with the search party, so he reported in every couple of hours. Everyone was hopeful. Surely the kidnappers would not kill police. Aurèle and Mike must be locked up somewhere.

Genevieve's friends arrived and took over the kitchen, and the children's friends came over too. Aurèle had bought a house next door to a public skating rink and he'd built a smaller rink in their backyard. Charlie and his friends would go out and skate for a while and then come in for updates, but the youngest, Guy, stayed close to his mother.

All day Friday, they searched for the officers, concentrating on the Riverview side of the river, where the money had been dropped off. The whole city got involved. Mayor Wheeler met with the chief, along with the Local 490 of the Moncton Police Association. They posted a five-thousand-dollar reward for information on the whereabouts of Aurèle and Mike. The Moncton paper reported, "Raiding parties staged lightening [sic] swoops at several points at dusk and this city of 58,000 looked more like Montreal during the 1970 kidnap crisis. Police cruisers blocked off all areas where raids were staged. Officers were tired, tense and determined."

Geneviève got the kids to bed and sat with her sisters. They were staying the night. They talked for a little while and then they sent Geneviève to bed. They knew how tired she was. She had been so strong all day. Determined not to show the kids how worried she was, she hadn't shed a tear. But alone in bed, when she ran her hand over the cold, empty sheet beside her, she wept.

On Saturday, as soon as it was light out, the search parties picked up where they left off. Midafternoon, a guy named Buzz Casey who owned a small convenience store on Pacific Avenue walked into the police station and slammed $20 onto the front desk. "That's for the policemen's kids," he said.

Geneviève awoke with hope. She was sure that Aurèle would soon be found. Their parish priest had returned to the house and he led intermittent prayers, beseeching God for Aurèle and Michael's speedy and safe return.

As Paul joined the search again, Joanne brought little Chantal over. Everyone doted on the baby. She was adorable, and they all adored her. For Geneviève, the little girl was a godsend. Without Chantal there to distract her, she thought she might go mad.

Later that evening, at about 5:10 as it was getting dark, an old hermit named Mr. Fontaine called in. He'd been cutting Christmas trees when he came across a bit of paper. It was a piece of Aurèle Bourgeois's driver's licence. Mr. Fontaine said he found it about thirty-five kilometres from Moncton, beside a covered bridge over the Shediac River. It was an area across the river from where they had been searching. So the search party moved to the site and found a pick and shovel, but it got too dark, so they cordoned off the entire area and postponed the search until Sunday morning.

Later, it was discovered that both Aurèle and Mike O'Leary had been leaving bread crumbs. Aurèle ripped up his licence and dropped pieces along the ground as they were led into the woods. A year later to the day, Don Larson, one of the policemen and the trial's exhibit man, walked down the trail and noticed something shiny. He scooped it up and saw that it was Mike O'Leary's wedding band. It had "Mike and Carol Anne" engraved on the inside.

At about nine o'clock on Sunday morning, they found the officers' revolvers and a radio downstream in the river. And under the covered bridge they found the two points where ground had been disturbed when Ambrose and Hutchison tried to dig with snow shovels. Around noon, two freshly dug shallow graves covered in light snow were found near some spruce trees. They were about ten feet apart. The men carefully uncovered Aurèle and Mike. Both were face down with a handcuff dangling from one wrist.

At the trial, the pathologist testified that there was dirt in Aurèle's lungs, which indicates that he must have still been breathing when he was buried. Each had been shot in the back of the head with the other's revolver, which told the police that Ambrose had shot one officer and Hutchison the other.

Charlie and his three best friends were playing shinny in the backyard when the police cars pulled up. He saw his brother-in-law get out and walk toward him. He could see Paul's face and knew it was not good news. He followed Paul into the house, where his mother and the others were sitting at the table, eating lunch. Paul told them as gently as he could that they had found the bodies of both Aurèle and Mike. They all fell into each other's arms. Charlie closed his eyes and began tumbling down a long, dark, deep tunnel. He had lost not only his father but also his best friend.

Hutchison gave himself up at eleven fifteen that night, and in March 1975 the New Brunswick Supreme Court found both men guilty of first-degree murder. On June 13, 1975, they were sentenced to hang. Both men appealed, but in July 1976, the Supreme Court of Canada upheld their convictions. Two days later, Canada abolished the death penalty and their sentences were commuted to life.

For a while, Charlie couldn't bring himself to skate on the backyard rink without Aurèle there. He was a quiet kid, but his heart was filled with anger, bitterness and fear. It was a difficult time. Geneviève could see him suffering, but he would not open up to her. Charlie was planning to play hockey for the Aigles Bleus (Blue Eagles) at the University of Moncton. Geneviève called up their head coach, Jean Perron, who would later go on to coach the Canadiens. She said, "Mr. Perron, would you talk to Charlie? His world has been destroyed." Coach Perron showed up, but when he began speaking, Charlie left the room. He walked up to his bedroom and quietly closed the door.

Geneviève continued to encourage Charlie to return to the ice. She thought it would be good for him to rediscover the joy of playing hockey. In his own way, Charlie listened, and one day he found himself back on the outdoor rink his dad had built. He felt Aurèle watching him again and his father's love lifted him up.

Charlie went to university in Moncton, and at the 1981 Canadian university hockey championships in Calgary, where the rugged defenceman helped lead his team to victory, he was scouted by the Calgary Flames. He called Geneviève, and outwardly she shared in his happiness, but in secret, the idea of losing him to somewhere out West broke her heart. She cried for two days.

On a Sunday afternoon a couple of weeks after the Flames lost against Vancouver in the 1981–82 Clarence Campbell Conference final, Nick LeBlanc's oldest daughter, Louane, called to him, "Hey Dad, there's a red Corvette in our driveway."

Nick said, "Oh, it's probably just somebody turning around."

She looked out the window and said, "Oh no. God! It's Boo-Boo." Charlie had bought a new car. Nick walked out to meet him. Charlie reached into the car, pulled out a stick and handed it to him. Written on the blade was, "To Nick. A guy that works so hard in the background so guys like us can have fun playing a game." It was signed by Charlie, Lanny McDonald and the entire Calgary team.

Acknowledgements

Ron and Kirstie would like to thank two writers who worked with us, Kaitlyn Kanygin for her tireless research and writing assistance and Julie Folk Woldu for her files and writing on the Bill Hicke, Doug Wickenheiser and Jordan Eberle stories.

A special thank you to Cari MacLean for her unwavering support and guidance.

Thanks to our hard-working researchers, transcribers and facilitators from www.pyramidproductions.tv, headed up by production manager Steve McLellan—Conor Samphire, Alex Sinclair, Cory Jones and Evan Adlington.

Thank you Lloyd Davis and Patricia MacDonald for a remarkable job of copyediting and proofreading.

Thank you to HarperCollins Canada—Jim Gifford for spearheading the book, Kelly Hope (production editor), Lisa Bettencourt (cover design) and our publisher, Iris Tupholme. Many others at HarperCollins rolled up their sleeves to make this book happen—Leo MacDonald, Michael Guy-Haddock, Sandra Leef, Norma Cody, Cory Beatty and Julia Barrett (publicity).

Kirstie would like to thank her sister, Julie Sinclair, for her wisdom and direction, and she expresses her love and thanks to her family for their ongoing support—her husband, Larry; parents, Joan and Bud McLellan; kids and grandkids, Charlie, Lundy, Paul, Geordie, Buddy, Kristin, Téa, Jaxon and Griffin; sister, Jan Folk and brothers, Hugh and Paul McLellan.

Ron and Kirstie appreciate everyone who shared their stories and lent a hand:

"It's God Calling, He Wants Us to Win Tonight"—Trevor Keeper, Trevor Ellerman, Dave Adolph, Doug MacLeod, James Moller, Jarret Zukiwsky, Parry Shockey

"Me Blue, You Blue"—Gerry and Marg James, *Kid Dynamite: The Gerry James Story* by Ron Smith

"Great Sadness"—Kelly McCrimmon, Maureen, Carlin and Liam McCrimmon, Stephen Brunt, Brantt Myhres, Cherilyn Myhres

"Cheesy"—Gerry Cheevers, Betty Cheevers, *Unmasked* by Gerry Cheevers as told by Marc Zappulla, Murray Scott, Jack Martin, Steve Cardillo, www.cardillousa.com, Todd Anderson, *Chariots and Horses* by Jason Dorland

"Little Zee"—Brian Kilrea, Zenon Konopka, Arlene Konopka, Cynthia Konopka, Elizabeth Zabek

"The Role Player"—Steve Bozek, Greg Adams, Mike Bullard, Rick Comley, Brian Verigin, Marcel Dionne

"The Curse of the Leafs"—Terry O'Malley, Barry MacKenzie, Russ Courtnall

"Tea for Two"—Brad Marsh, Doug Berk, Robin Smith, Roy MacGregor, Rob Ramage, Joseph O'Neil, Rich Bain

"One Great Keeper in the Hands of Another"—Joel Jenkins, Garrett Jenkins, Lester Lancaster, Stan Matwijiw, www.bigefoundation.org

"The Big Red Turtleneck"—Eric Lindros, Carl Lindros, Bonnie Lindros, *My Life in Hockey* by Jean Béliveau, *Fire on Ice* by Eric Lindros with Randy Starkman

"Reckless Abandon"—Trent and Tammy McCleary,

Don Cherry, Gaetan Lefebvre, Dr. David S. Mulder, Jeff Odgers

"Suds"—Brian and Judy Sutter

"You Know How to Whistle, Don't You?"—Lance Roberts, Leonard Cohen, Liv Albert and Nicholas Garrison at Penguin Random House Canada, Robert Kory at RK Management

"The Life of a Thousand Men"—Rob Vanstone, LeeAnne Hicke, Lisa Hicke-Ostertag, Ryan Ostertag, Dylan Ostertag, Kale Dolinski, Greg Powers, Terry Harper, Ernie Hicke

"The Next Wayne Gretzky"—Dianne Wickenheiser, Kelly Chase, Mike Blaisdell, Claude Wickenheiser, Charlie Wickenheiser, Marcia Wickenheiser, Kurt Wickenheiser, Ernie Wickenheiser, Rob Vanstone, Darrell Davis

"Hot Stick"—Jordan Eberle, Dustin Eberle, Darrell Davis, Darren and Lisa Eberle, Lynn Eberle, Rob Vanstone, Mark Kirton

"Gou! Gou!"—Michel Goulet, Mathieu Schneider, Lyle Odelein

"One Hundred Per Cent"—Dick Irvin, *The Habs: An Oral History of the Montreal Canadiens, 1940-1980* by Dick Irvin

"Night Train"—Brad and Lesley Dalgarno, *Tough Guy* by Bob Probert

"The Assigner"—Charlie and Diane Lennox

"The Soo"—Steve Bodnar, Rob Gordon, www.iwaynegretzky.com

"The Incredible Charlie Bourgeois"—Charlie and Colleen Bourgeois, Geneviève Bourgeois, Nick LeBlanc

Other friends who helped us include Jamie Macoun, Wendy McCreary, Wayne Groulx, Patrick J. Lahey, Terry and Sheila Crisp, Gerry Iuliano, Michel Bergeron, David Haldane, Red Berenson, Tamara Pringsheim, Shelly Spaner, Troy Schreck, Liv Albert, Jay Sinclair and Doug Folk.

Thank you to all who helped with photos: Craig Campbell at Hockey Hall of Fame; Sue Lennox, Jennifer Cram and Sebastian Gatica at Rogers Media; Dawn Froats at Athol Murray College of Notre Dame; Tony Hansen, Jean-Paul Hebert, Ron Smith, Randal Macnair, Michael Perry at University of Lethbridge Archives, Northern Michigan University; Wendy Sawatzky at *Winnipeg Free Press*; Jeff Krieg at Adanac Antiques; Julie Kirsh at Sun Media; AP Images; Getty Images; Marc Bastarache, Danielle Robichaud at The PostMan Post-Production Studio; Frank Savoie at Connections Productions, www.cptv.ca.